Irma

Irma

A Chicago Woman's Story, 1871–1966

Ellen FitzSimmons Steinberg

Ψ

University
of Iowa Press

IOWA CITY

University of Iowa Press,
Iowa City 52242
Copyright © 2004 by
the University of Iowa Press
Printed in the United States
of America
http://www.uiowa.edu/uiowapress

The publication of this book
was generously supported by the
University of Iowa Foundation.

Printed on acid-free paper

04 05 06 07 08 C 5 4 3 2 1
04 05 06 07 08 P 5 4 3 2 1

Library of Congress
Cataloging-in-Publication Data
Frankenstein, Irma Rosenthal,
1871–1966.
Irma: a Chicago woman's
story, 1871–1966 / [edited] by
Ellen FitzSimmons Steinberg.
    p.   cm.
Includes bibliographical
references (p.) and index.
ISBN 0-87745-896-0 (cloth),
ISBN 0-87745-894-4 (pbk.)
1. Frankenstein, Irma Rosenthal,
1871–1966.   2. Frankenstein,
Irma Rosenthal, 1871–1966—
Archives.   3. Jewish women—
Illinois—Chicago—Biography.
4. Jewish women—Illinois—
Chicago—Archives.   5. Jews—
Illinois—Chicago—Biography.
6. Jews—Illinois—Chicago—
Social life and customs.
7. Chicago (Ill.)—Biography.
8. Frankenstein family.
9. Rosenthal family.
I. Steinberg, Ellen FitzSimmons,
1948– .   II. Title.
F548.9.J5F73 2004
977.3′11004924′0092—dc22
2003063418
[B]

I Dedicate My Book
To
My Beloved Husband And To Young Lieutenant Victor
Who
Will Live As Long As My Memory Lasts
And To My
Parents, Sisters, Brothers And Cousins
To My Friends And To Those Who Urged Me To Write It
And
Most Especially To My Children
And
Grandchildren And My Great-Grandchildren
And Last But Not Least
To Chicago
They Helped Me To Live It
I Only Wrote It

Irma, 1958

I dedicate this book
to Irma.
"May her memory be a blessing to those who treasure it."

Ellen, 2004

Contents

Preface

Irma Rosenthal Frankenstein's journals and diaries were private accounts of the rhythm of her days and the shape of her life. In them, she also recorded her thoughts and short quotations from her readings, jotted down her own poems and short stories, mapped out dinner-party menus, and penned biographical sketches of her family. Interspersed among the records of what she did when and with whom are a number of lengthy reflections on Chicago history, her early life, religious beliefs, education, aspirations, disappointments, sorrows, and successes.

Late in life, Irma noted that she intended to organize her papers and to use them as the foundation of the book she had long promised her family and friends. She mused that were she actually to write an autobiography, she would begin with the history of her beloved Chicago, then move to a discussion of her family members, each in turn, and finally chronicle her own life. She thought she might spice the chapters with love, the laughter of little children, and the smell of roasting turkeys. But her autobiography, like the cookbook she wanted to write, was never finished. She composed only the dedication that appears at the beginning of this book.

The present volume is constructed from the more than half a million words Irma wrote during her adult life. It is, however, more than an edited transcription of her writings. Even though the pre-1891 diaries to which she once refers were not included in the papers I have, I was able to piece together those early times from a number of sources. These include material Irma wrote primarily during the 1950s and family histories she had sent to her daughter Ruth and cousin Dick, which they shared with me.

I spent more than twelve months transcribing Irma's diaries, journals, letters, and other papers, and then researched the historical events she mentioned and the people to whom she referred. Finally, I have placed Irma's writings within a temporal-social-religious framework to explain what might otherwise be unfamiliar to a reader.

The introduction reveals how the diaries surfaced and includes a mélange of comments Irma made about herself and her aspirations at various times throughout her life.

The book actually begins where Irma's autobiography would have begun: with her birth in 1871 right before the Chicago fire. Amazingly, the Great Conflagration did no harm to anyone in Irma's family. Like all who lived through it, they told and retold stories about the disaster. "Remembrances of Chicago, 1871" contains Irma's family lore about the catastrophe that destroyed Chicago's heart.

In "Recollections of Childhood, 1871–1888," Irma discusses Chicago's immediate response to the almost overwhelming devastation caused by the fire, sharing what it was like to be a child growing up during the city's enthusiastic, exuberant postfire reconstruction period.

"Reflections on Education, 1875–1891" outlines early public education and curricula in Chicago. Irma's analysis of these years includes details about her siblings, Emil (1869–1890), Kurt (1873–1957), Esther (Essie) (1870–1964), and Meta (1878–1976), and their schooling, as well as about her eighth-grade teacher, Ella Flagg Young. This remarkable educator, whom she clearly admired, had a profound effect on Irma's first career choice and writing style.

The chapter "Grandpa and Emerson, 1876–1898" is compiled from journal entries and remembrances, and a single newspaper clipping. In retrospect, Irma credits both her grandfather's religious beliefs and examples, as well as Ralph Waldo Emerson's writings, with helping to shape the person she ultimately became. The news article about Irma's charity work in the Jewish ghetto reveals how, even as a young woman, she felt obligated to perform service for others.

"Young Love, 1891" treats Irma's two-week trip to Atlantic City during the summer of that year. The actual entries for that period stand in marked contrast to a possibly fictional essay about the same vacation that Irma wrote much later in her life. This chapter and accompanying notes serve as a segue to the rest of the book. It is here the reader learns about Irma's aspirations to become a writer, and how she met her future husband, Victor.

"Marriage and Children, 1898–1906" is composed of recollections about the first years of Irma's marriage and the birth of her first two children, Emily and Ruth. Her comments about Hyde Park–Kenwood's growth, her studies at the University of Chicago, and what was expected of a doctor's wife add to the scarce first-person material about this period in the city's history.

In 1910, Irma began to outline a book whose working title was "Nursery Ethics." In the draft she quoted famous authors, many of whom were Transcendentalists, and set out behavior codes for parents and children, supported by maxims and aphorisms. During that same year, Irma also jotted down "nature notes," because she had decided to supplement her children's formal education, which at that time incorporated John Burroughs's nature philosophy.

Included in the box of Irma's diaries was one that Emily, her oldest child, kept between 1909 and 1912. Like her mother's journals, Emily's contains personal codes of conduct and author quotes, as well as nature observations. Together, these entries provide an almost unprecedented opportunity to compare what a parent thought she was teaching to what a child thought she was learning. These writings appear in the chapter "Children and Learning, 1910–1912."

Irma apparently wrote very little during the 1920s. The material that does exist touches upon her first voting experience, the Chicago Woman's City Club, and Clarence Darrow, and she mentions her involvement with the Isaiah Woman's Club ("the Sisterhood") and the Chicago Jewish Woman's Aid, large social and philanthropic organizations, and the 1924 Women's International League for Peace and Freedom Congress. Although neither numerous nor lengthy, these accounts, in "Politics, Nature, and Travel, the 1920s," illustrate Irma's views on some of the decade's more important events.

During the Great Depression, Irma chronicled her difficulties managing the household budget. The diary entries, in "Staying Afloat during the 1930s," are poignant and valuable documentation as to when the depression began to affect the self-employed middle class. They also show some of the creative corner-cutting steps Irma took to ward off financial disaster and public embarrassment.

In a five-year diary begun in 1940 with only four lines allotted for each day's entry, Irma nonetheless managed to chart the progress of World War II. "War and Its Victims, 1933–1957" details how, although seventy-one years of age in 1942, Irma refused to sit idly at home. Instead, she punctuated her busy days by becoming a certified Red Cross nurse's aid, volunteering in the Chicago Relief Program, and knitting socks for the war effort while listening to news from Europe on the radio.

Letters, poems, diaries, and remembrances in "Changes, 1950–1966" capture the final decades of Irma's life. During this period, Irma traveled to visit her family, sold her house, moved to an apartment hotel, and was widowed. Despite a heart attack in 1958, she rewrote a favorite family story into a book, then donated the proceeds of its sale to a nonprofit organization.

Spatial considerations prevent the incorporation of all Irma's writings into a single volume. I excluded many accounts of innumerable small events, sicknesses, family dinners with guest lists, and menus. I included enough material, however, so the reader could learn who Irma was, as well as the forces and events that had helped to drive and shape her, and come to appreciate why it was more than mere procrastination that caused her to put aside her ambition to become a writer until "later," always later.

The stories in the early chapters of this book are constructs — whole cloth woven from various entries and remembrances Irma made throughout her life about a specific subject or subjects. I have therefore supplied the dates for each quotation from Irma's writings in the appropriate chapter notes. For example, there are no diaries earlier than 1891, but during the 1950s Irma composed letters to her then two-year-old great-granddaughter Betsey (1956–1973), recounting family history and genealogical data. This letter-writing strategy was a literary device that Thornton Wilder had suggested Irma use to jog her memory and to enable her to begin putting something on paper. These letters, however, frequently shifted into ordinary diary entries, so they never really worked as the foundation of the autobiographical work Irma envisioned. They, along with the material her family provided, did, however, provide a solid basis from which I could reconstruct Irma's early years and the pivotal historical events she and her family had experienced.

Each quotation and excerpt used in this volume has been dated insofar as possible, with additional information, clarifications, and corrections included in chapter notes where required. For the sake of consistency, I have standardized both Emily's and Irma's entries so that they show the day of the week and date, where known. Where I omitted material, I have placed ellipses. Inconsistencies, misspellings, abbreviations, outmoded punctuation, and nonagreements between subject and verb have been retained. Data added for clarification of in-text references or translations of foreign words have been bracketed. Where shortcuts such as "&c." were employed, I have substituted "etc."; where ampersands were used, I substituted "and" for the sake of modern readers' convenience. However, I retained both Irma's and Emily's irregular punctuation and run-on sentences because I felt they show the stream of consciousness typical of personal diary entries and composition drafts.

I believe that I came to know Irma very well. I understood her fierce pride in our native city, Chicago, almost instinctively; I could relate, by virtue of my own life circumstances, to her love of family and her desire to become a successful author. Moreover, I made a conscious effort not to overexplain what she wrote, or to impose any particular interpretive framework upon her data. I grounded this decision in the ethnographic writing tradition and in the philosophy that is succinctly summarized on the dust jacket of the anthropologists Lawrence C. Watson and Maria-Barbara Watson-Franke's 1985 book, *Interpreting Life Histories: An Anthropological Inquiry* (New Jersey: Rutgers University Press):

Life histories are retrospective personal accounts . . . recorded as texts. This method has a long and noble tradition in anthropology and has been the basis for many classic studies. . . . Most accounts of life histories . . . depend on *constructs from the anthropologists's own world* (the etic approach), and therefore do not emphasize the subjectivity of someone else's life in its own cultural context (the emic approach). Watson and Watson-Franke are most critical of the psychoanalytical and the structural-functional etic approaches. With each of these, the life history becomes an illustration of predetermined categories brought by the researcher to the field. . . .

As an alternative to the etic approaches, Watson and Watson-Franke urge researchers to drop prior notions of personality and society and to give precedence to the subjective experience that an individual conveys in a life history.

With the foregoing in mind, I should note that Irma, by her own admission, was "nobody famous." That phrase defines *what* she thought about herself, but does not say much else. I hope, however, that Irma's story, presented in her own words, will enable each reader to reach an understanding of *who* she actually was.

Acknowledgments

I owe enormous thanks to the family of Irma Rosenthal Frankenstein for enabling me to complete this book. Irma's grandson John provided information about her relationship with Carl Sandburg, then put me in touch with his cousin, Ferd. In turn, Ferd gave me Irma's set of Emerson books with her marginalia and commentaries. These books became another rich source for understanding and interpreting some of the comments Irma made in her diaries. Ferd also put me in contact with his daughter, Nancy, who kindly sent copies of the inscriptions Thornton Wilder wrote in books he had given to Irma. Next, Ferd introduced me to his mother, Irma's daughter Ruth. Ruth spent three days filling me in on family details, in addition to supplying me with an invaluable booklet in which Irma wrote about the early years of her marriage. Without Ruth's generosity, a goodly chunk of Irma's life would have remained a mystery. Ruth also facilitated contact with Irma's "most favorite of cousins," Dick. He sent a newspaper clipping documenting her charitable work in 1893, along with the family genealogies he had compiled using data Irma had written herself. The newspaper clipping clarified a number of Irma's early journal entries that otherwise would have been inexplicable. The genealogies also helped me to fill out the history of early Chicago German Jews. Dick (who has since died, in 2002) also spent a long evening discussing Irma with me so I could be certain my interpretations meshed with his knowledge of her. To protect the privacy of the living members of Irma's family, I have used no last names but hers.

Some of the German words, phrases, and verses included in this book were beyond my ability to translate. Luckily, an extraordinarily resourceful friend, Mary Joyce Rinehart, was able to accomplish what I could not. Her sensitive rendition of Pauline Wengeroff's preface to volume 2 of *Memorien einer Großmutter* enriches the chapter note in which it appears.

Thanks are also owed to the reviewers whose careful readings of the draft version of this manuscript followed by sound suggestions helped me to make it better, and to Gail Zlatnik for her careful reading followed by sound copyediting. And, of course, I am indebted to Irma, without whom there would have been no book.

Introduction

A fairly new picket fence surrounds a certain vacant corner lot in the Hyde Park–Kenwood area of Chicago. The south edge of the property boasts the remnants of a small garden where a few red Darwin tulips and bright blue scilla defy years of neglect. Creeping Charlie and crabgrass have claimed the north edge, while mature pin oaks dot the land at random. Ghostly indentations in the hard-packed earth, the legacy of innumerable feet over the years, cut diagonally from the northwest corner to the western fence. From the street, a short cement path connects to a stoop leading nowhere.

During one of its periodic cleaning fits, the city of Chicago demolished the big, early-1900s three-story stucco house with green shutters and twin porches that anchored the property. The structure, which had become an eyesore, was not granted a second chance as a landmark, since no renowned architect had designed it, nor had anyone of major note ever owned it.

Once upon a time, however, Irma Frankenstein lived in that house. She raised three children there. She read books to them seated in a green velour Morris chair in the library, and cooked them hearty meals in her up-to-date kitchen with its fancy electric Frigidaire. Occasionally, when all her work was done, she passed the hot Chicago summer evenings reading and fanning herself under the shade of seven great oaks, while admiring the flowers that her husband, a physician, had planted.

Attached to the back of the house, rather like an afterthought, was her husband's office with its separate entrance for patients. But through the front door walked an unending stream of family and friends, some of whom were counted among Chicago's most famous and influential residents, all come to visit or dine with Irma.

Who was Irma? And why, in 1999, was I standing on the South Side sidewalk staring at a vacant lot? The answers make up two stories — one of serendipity and research, the other a tale told by an obscure Chicago woman who kept journals and diaries during much of her lifetime, a lifetime that started right before the Great Fire and ended during the Vietnam conflict.

How I came to own Irma's diaries is part of the first story.

One drizzly April day, my daughter and I blew into the wrong used bookstore in downstate Illinois. We had been aiming for a shop that advertised it stocked fifteen thousand used books. However, a peculiar twist in the street spilt us off into a direction that landed us in front of another store entirely. Well, one used bookstore is pretty much the same as another, I thought, so in we went. I quickly spied the alphabetically organized nonfiction books on the far wall, and headed toward them. On the way back, my toe caught the corner of a cardboard box. It had been wedged onto the bottom shelf of a bookcase that held volumes of no particular interest to me. I pulled the carton out and read the yellowed paper sign taped to its side: "Diary Collection — ENTIRE BOX ONLY $50." Normally, I never look at things like that, but since this box had literally tripped me up, I took a moment to paw through the dusty jumble. There were small booklets, some of them the college "blue book" examination kind, others lined notebooks marked ten and fifteen cents, and a single zippered five-year diary. Most of the journals, perhaps twenty or thirty by my quick count, seemed to have been written in the same legible hand. Many were dated — 1898, 1910, 1915, 1924, 1938 — with a few having Chicago addresses. I glanced at several of the entries: a synopsis of what she noted as "Jno. Dewey's *Art As Experience*," a mention of Ella Flagg Young, a poem or two, but mostly what appeared to be simple daily records. Hmm, might be something interesting here, I thought, flipping more pages. Carl Sandburg, "my good friend, Thornton Wilder," Ralph Waldo Emerson, the University of Chicago? This is incredible, I thought.

"Do you know anything about these diaries?" I asked the shop owner.

"Had 'em for about fifteen years," he answered. "Bought 'em from the widow of a bookseller who had 'em for about ten years. Guess he got 'em at an estate auction or something. Been through 'em all . . . 's nobody famous."

"Oh, well. It'll be fun to read 'em, anyhow. I like historical stuff," I commented while plunking down my credit card. With the purchase completed, my daughter and I headed for the car — the treasure box hugged tightly against my chest.

What happened after I returned home with those diaries reads like a detective's log. Irma's journals, her book of days, required one full year to transcribe. Typing was coupled with forays into newspaper archives, used bookstores, and several libraries. Reconstructing the direction and shape of her life lured me first to visit the Chicago homesite where she had lived for forty-six years and next to the cemetery to view her grave, then to identify the famous people she casually mentioned she knew, and eventually to interview some of her descendants. It was not easy to get a fix on a woman who, despite her long and active life, never warranted more public notice than a short obituary in the *Chicago Tribune*.

The second story unfolds in Irma's own words, taken from letters, journals, and diaries she wrote at various times throughout her life:

Books really are magic things. I've wanted to write one ever since I could read one.[1]

I have been promising for years the persons who have confidence in me to write "my book."[2]

[But Carl] Sandburg once wrote me that poetry is my medium — rather[,] verse — Sandburg's advice, at the time, sent me to the depths of despair in which there was one gleam — because, I'd love to do something with words — Yesterday, however, I baked cookies instead of writing.[3]

Zona Gale [told me] one time, when I had shown her something I had written, "You are so excited in the presence of life that you have to write about it." She said this too had been her experience.[4]

Writing is a joy to me — just writing — like breathing.[5]

I am writing because I have been fortunate, because I love to write and because as one transforms a landscape, a human likeness, a folk song, into something beyond reality, it takes on a life of its own and begins to "soar and sing" as R. W. Emerson says.[6]

I doubt if I am an artist. I just love to write.[7]

Writing is a partnership between the reader and the writer. The gifted reader has a spiritual adventure, sees new vistas opening up, hears the music of the spheres, discovers what is back of reality. To discover the truth back of reality — that's good, even if I, myself, wrote it.[8]

I have often heard that the life of a writer is a lonely one. Perhaps I never became a writer because my life has not been a lonely one. My labor has not been solitary. The persons whom I have loved and who have loved me, have rightfully claimed much of my time and energy. They have made my life significant. One writer says "There may be a more flowery path to success in writing than to choose a life of solitary labor." Possibly then, I chose the flowery path, thinking always that if I have no time to have the loveliness of the flowers enter my spirit, a solitary path without beauty would have been endurance rather than living.[9]

I used to think, long, long ago that I wanted to write a novel. But novels—well, you make them up and I think it is much more interesting to look around and see what you can do with things as they are.[10]

If I were writing a novel, Chicago would be the hero.[11]

There are persons I know who are constantly urging me to write my autobiography.

Thornton Wilder wrote me that he had seen some [of my] notes toward an autobiography and he has *urged me before.*

I once asked [my cousin], "Why do you want me to write my autobiography?" [He] hesitated, and finally he said, "Because of your attitude toward life." Until that moment, I did not know that I had an "attitude." Perhaps if I do write it, the attitude ought to come out clean and distinct, like some sort of theme or plot.[12]

Sometimes I think a good way to write an autobiography would be to make portraits of the important persons in our lives and tell how their influence played into ours. Maybe that's the way of a novelist.[13]

Writing an autobiography could be like listening to the echo of our more active and intensive days. And would they be "one grand sweet song"? Maybe. Because all the weariness and the frustrations are gone — and what one was, and saw and heard and did — and would one go on singing even when one wept, in aging, over the fresh tragedies in one's life?[14]

Hume compressed the account of his life into twelve pages[;] I should much prefer the long version of my own.

My book would have . . . the laughter of little children, the wedding march, the fragrance, not only of the lilacs, [but] the lilies of the valley and the roses from our garden, the round strains of my son's beloved clarinet, my mother's pride, but [also] the aroma of the Thanksgiving turkey roasting, and the hubbub of the family party and an echo of the family arguments on politics, on how to bring up children and how not to bring them up.[15]

My book should echo the love of a child for an heroic mother, an inspiring grandfather, the loves of brothers and sisters, friends, husband and children, and grandchildren, and even great-grandchildren.[16]

I have lived through the time when the greatest emancipation for women in human history has occurred; I have seen the greatest advance in human ingenuity, the greatest mechanical discoveries in a span of a little more than half a century, that has ever happened in the evolution of man. I have been a part of the growth of one of the most amazing cities in the world. And last, and by no means least, I have had the richest life of any woman I know. Not the richest in point of material wealth, for I have at times been far from wealthy and yet have never experienced actual poverty — but I mean the richest in the loves and the opportunities that can come to a woman.[17]

I am not a famous person. I have made no great contribution to society as a whole. My life, the life of an obscure person who has found living, with all its trials and partings, [has simply been] a stupendous adventure.[18]

Here, in the twilight of my days, I shall look upon [writing my autobiography] as an adventure, amid the noise and the confusion of living life to the full, to find the music, the hidden music too, in my life that started in the dimming past so very long ago, and seems to me, as I look back at events I could neither avoid nor understand, it seems to me that, as the sun is setting, it has been a sort of symphony with variations of love.[19]

I've started, and written, my autobiography many times — It never satisfies me — and always, living gets in the way of writing.[20]

Irma

Remembrances of Chicago, 1871

Between 1835 and 1860, Chicago evolved from a small trading post to a military fort to a town with potential. Then, during the 1860s, it developed into what some called the "most American of cities."[1] The leap from town to city occurred because Chicago's location, on the shores of Lake Michigan, on the banks of a navigable river, and in the center of the continent, made it the ideal hub from which to move goods, supplies, and people in every direction. Stagecoach lines and railroad terminals carried an almost continual stream of visitors and settlers to this inland port. A large number of hotels, most notably the Palmer House and the Tremont, opened to serve them. Theaters, among them the outstanding Rice and the McVicker's, went up to amuse them, while the advent of Crosby's Opera House heralded the arrival of real "culture." Chicago boasted about its daily newspapers, its raised wooden sidewalks and new waterworks, and about hosting the 1868 Republican convention at which Ulysses S. Grant was nominated for president. It even bragged that its citizens were "paying more for fire insurance than was collected for state, county and municipal taxes."[2] The city was prosperous and growing.

By 1870, Chicago's population pushed the three hundred thousand mark. At this time, German and Irish immigrants made up the bulk of those who had come to work in the city's factories, lumber and shipping yards, rail depots, slaughterhouses and meat-packing plants, warehouses, and commercial enterprises.

Wealthy business owners, mostly transplanted easterners, built their mansions along Michigan and Wabash Avenues. The less wealthy, primarily European immigrants or first-generation Americans, built or bought smaller houses on the streets west. Only a few urban pioneers lived to the south and north of what is now known both as Downtown and the Loop.

When the Irish arrived, they settled the Near West Side of the city.

Then when large numbers of Germans arrived, they took over the formerly grand area around Fifth Avenue between State and Van Buren Streets, eventually spreading south into Bridgeport. The streets north of Chicago Avenue and west of Wells Street to Ashland Boulevard quickly turned into another German enclave.[3]

Irma Rosenthal was born in Chicago on July 25, 1871. Her mother and father, Betty and Abraham, both German immigrants from Frankfurt am Main, had met at a charity bazaar in 1868.[4] Late in her life, on August 25, 1953, Irma recorded the story she had heard from her parents:

Some discriminating person put costumes on [my mother and my aunt] and made them waitresses in the restaurant. On the second evening of the bazaar, a handsome young man, the catch of the town, sat down to [my mother's] table.

The tall slender girl [who was our mother], with the white skin, brown eyes and coal black hair, set off by red cheeks but lately come from the fresh air of the Taunus mountains, which blew over her native village, asked him, in German of course, what he would like to have. The rest is history— . . . [T]he young man who was our father, stepped over to the flower booth and ordered all the flowers that were left to be sent to the restaurant booth, to the tall waitress.

Theirs was a love story Irma recounted repeatedly. Six weeks after her parents met, they were married.[5] They eventually had five children, of whom Irma was the third. When she was born, Irma's parents and her brother and sister lived on the South Side of the city. This area stretched from Twenty-fourth Street in the south to Twelfth Street in the north. Although one of the less densely settled parts of the city, it was fast becoming home to a number of Germans and their thriving businesses.

By the time Irma was a few months old, Chicago, including many of its heavily populated neighborhoods, was ablaze. Evidence points to the fire's origins in or near the O'Leary barn at 137 DeKoven Street in the heart of the German and Irish Near West Side. Whether the O'Learys' cow, Daisy, kicked over a lantern, or boys sneaking a smoke started the barn on fire, or spontaneous combustion caused coal, wood shavings, and hay to ignite has never been determined. Fire alarms went out, but through a series of mishaps involving misjudged distances, the firefighters were unable to contain the blaze.[6] The fire, fanned by a high wind, hopped from barn to wooden shanty to frame buildings. It swept east and north, skipping back and forth over the branches of the river.[7] People ran screaming from the flames and heat. There really was nowhere to go. The calamity became known as the Great Chicago Fire.

Throughout her life, Irma reflected on the stories her parents had told her about the fire. Each time she wrote about it, she recalled a few more details or added another anecdote. Her recollected story of her family's involvement in that catastrophe shares a vividness and immediacy with firsthand accounts of the fire.[8] The following narrative has been pieced together from various of Irma's journal entries spread over a number of years.

When I was born, Chicago, situated where a river emptied into a mighty chain of lakes in flat easily manipulated terrain, railroading was expanding with Chicago as a natural conflexion between trains from the North and the South, from the East toward the West. St. Louis, farther west where the Mississippi River divided the country into two, a little too far south for the climate to be comfortable throughout the summer, had been the gateway to the expanding West of the pioneer, and the refuge of the fever[-]threatened population of the South. Chicago was surpassing St. Louis as the life magnet centre in the middle of the country. . . . Chicago had grown like a mushroom, [with] hurriedly put-in wooden buildings . . . of balloon construction.[9]

The city limits of Chicago extended to 39th Street on the South Side.[10]

My father . . . had rented a house on 24th Street near Indiana Avenue.[11]

We lived in a sort of suburban district.[12]

A new centre of population was growing around Milwaukee Avenue and 12th Street, mostly of German extraction. Business was leaving South State Street where our father had his store which was then around 18th or on 22nd Street, moving as far south as 22nd and north between Randolph and Adams Streets where Field, Leiter and Company had its fine, expanding retail dry goods store, and Potter Palmer had erected a very modern hotel. In time the district became the nucleus of our famous loop.[13]

Mamma rarely went down town. Field, Leiter and Company was our leading dry goods store. Mamma rarely bought things there for people, [she] said Field, Leiter was more expensive than other stores. Many of the outlying small businesses were moving down town and the theatres were located down town. The Palmer House was the leading and the swank hotel.[14]

Three months after I was born, Chicago was a mass of twisted, smoldering ruins in the biggest fire any one had ever seen. . . .

Throughout our childhood, we heard stories of the night of the Chicago Fire [October 8, 1871]. It was as much a part of our early childhood as the one[-]armed or one[-]legged men we sometimes saw on the streets who had been in the Civil War. . . . It changed our calendar. When I was a child events happened not on specific dates. They happened either before or after the fire.

The fire occurred on Sunday night. . . . Mrs. O'Leary, late in the P.M., thought she had better go into the barn to milk her cow. It was beginning to grow dark and so she took her kerosene lamp with her and set it down in the dry straw of the cow's stall. She should have milked her cow an hour sooner. The cow must have thought so too for it was restless and kicked over the lamp. The dry straw caught fire, the wooden barn caught fire, and Chicago caught fire. Most of Chicago's rapid-growth buildings were of wood and, after a dry summer, they went up in smoke like tinder boxes. I never heard what became of Mrs. O'Leary or the cow, but Mrs. O'Leary has been famous ever since.[15]

A brisk wind fanned the flames and burning faggots were blown about from building to building. Persons had to run for their lives with anything they could save from the horrible flames and heat. Many lost everything they had, even their lives.

Terrible stories and beautiful ones were told about the biggest fire that had ever happened in the whole country. Chicago has always boasted about having the biggest things. The fire finally burnt itself out at the lake front for it could go no farther. Thousands of people were camped on the sand. The new Illinois Central Rail Road along the lake shore could continue to operate. The wind changed. Some buildings on the North side near the river held miraculously. For days the firemen and the citizens continued their fight among the smoldering ruins. The heart of the city had been burnt out.[16]

Here was this city, which had grown more rapidly than any city in the land had ever grown, a heap of smoldering ruins.[17]

Out on 24th Street the sky turned red, dreadful stories were told about the huge fire. My parents were worried about my mother's relatives [parents, six sisters, and two brothers, along with assorted uncles, aunts, and cousins] who lived across the Chicago River on the west side of the city. There was a rumor that the whole West Side was burning.

The West Side was on the other side of the Chicago River, then spanned by wooden bridges. After a while my father decided that he would try to find out if they were safe. . . .

How he managed to reach one of the wooden bridges that crossed the river I do not know. Somehow he made his way through all the excitement and fear to the West Side, found that the fire had not reached as far as where my grandparents, uncles and aunts lived, and then he turned to go back to the South Side. Crowds were lined up on the banks of the river because all the bridges had burned to the ground. Crowds were clamoring to get across to find a way to reach the shore of Lake Michigan—some swam across, some were ferried across in row boats that had been alongside the rivers or on it. My father managed somehow to reach the other shore, to reach 24th Street, and tell my mother that her family was safe. The whole might have passed in frightful suspense for my mother because she feared for her family, and for my father. Where was he? Could he have perished in the flames? When he appeared on the early morning of October 10, she hardly recognized him. He was black from head to foot with soot and dirt. . . .

At that time we had two maids. . . . The maids were called hired girls.[18]

We were not rich but everybody was able to afford plenty of hired girls for very small wages, or no wages at all; girls coming in from the country, and immigrants from foreign lands often were happy to have a home with board and lodging.[19]

People had back yards, and washing the clothes was done entirely by hand, and people hung their clothes in the back yard to dry. There was great rivalry among the maids in all the houses near ours . . . and the hired girls vied with each other to see who could get her clothes out in the yard first. . . . Our hired girls, in order to get the wash out on the lines first, had filled all our wooden wash tubs and the metal wash boiler with water before they went to bed. During the night, the water works were destroyed, and the water which our hired girls had collected in the wash tubs was the most precious thing in all of Chicago. People from the whole neighborhood clamored for it to be used for drinking.

The anxiety of that night made Mamma with the three months old baby, very ill and a food question arose. . . . Cows became scarce and babies needed milk. Perhaps they gave me unsterilized water out of the wash tubs whose contents were as liquid gold, [because] during the night the water works went up in flame. Only the old water tower, ever since, a quaint landmark on the Near North side, held its own. . . .

For years, people who lived at the time, and came through the Fire, told stories of suffering and loss, but they told more stories about hospitality among the citizens who escaped the calamity, and more stories about the heroism of those who saved lives and property. . . .

Never did a country respond more promptly . . . supplies of food, furniture and clothing began pouring into the city in streams. . . . After some hours, from nearby places, the people all around us came driving into the city as far as they dared go, with blankets and clothing and food. A brother of my mother's came from downstate Illinois where he lived [in Shelbyville] with a huge wagon-load and our back yard became a distributing depot for life-saving commodities [and] things. . . .

In a miraculous way, the rise of our family dated from the disaster of the city. Here, for inexplainable reasons, the fire largely propelled by a fierce autumn wind, left a building standing. The old water tower was one of them, and another one was the boot and shoe store of my two unmarried uncles. They had just replenished their stock, and [so], they were the only persons in Chicago who had boots and shoes for sale.

In those days the charge customer had not yet been created. Mamma used to tell about how people clamored for boots and shoes, especially boots, and offered fabulous prices for them.

My uncles were human. They often took the fabulous prices and just as often sold their precious merchandise at regular prices, and in extreme cases, of which there were many, sold below cost or even gave away a pair of boots or shoes. The great thing was they sold out their entire stock and, when transportation was re-established, easily replenished it. Every night when they came home, they emptied their cash receipts into Grandma's apron, and I like to think what fun it must have been to stack the gold pieces and silver dollars, and have Uncle Joe who was a mathematical wizard, count the receipts, and discuss their plans and hopes. I was three months old, but I've always been sorry that I wasn't old enough to play with the gold coins. . . . And, this started my babyhood and early childhood.[20]

Although Chicago had burned once before, in 1868, the devastation had not been nearly as severe. Then, despite losses totaling two million dollars, damage had been confined to a group of shops on Lake Street. Merchants had quickly set up shop on State Street, and carried on business as usual.

The Great Conflagration, however, changed all that Chicago had been. Five separate fires ate away at the heart of the city for two days before burning out.[21] The flames charred five miles of the city from Clark and Fullerton in the north to Congress and Van Buren Streets in the south. Over two thousand acres with almost eighteen thousand houses and businesses were destroyed. At least three hundred people died. Untold scores of animals were lost. Hospitals, public buildings, stores, and banks had been incinerated.

Close to one hundred thousand Chicagoans found themselves without food or shelter. In addition to the loss of homes and boardinghouses, hotels, too, had burned to the ground. There was nowhere for the homeless to go, so the railroads offered free rides out of the city for those who wanted to leave.

The city government set up temporary quarters in the First Congregational Church. From there, officials recruited five thousand special police to help in any possible way. General Sherman also ordered one thousand troops into Chicago to keep order.

Damage estimates hit two hundred million dollars.[22] Offers of assistance poured into Chicago from around the country and Europe. The

Chicago Relief and Aid Society immediately set up food and clothing distribution centers in churches and city parks. Although a few merchants, Marshall Field among them, managed to save some stock, the majority lost everything. Almost as many fortunes were lost in the fire as were made in its aftermath.

Recollections of Childhood, 1871–1888

Chicago lost little time in surveying its ruins. . . . The people around us were not talking about defeat. They talked about building and change.[1]

The spirit that . . . made it grow [again] was not made out of desperation. . . . The citizens of Chicago, who had originally come from sturdy New England, from lands beyond the Atlantic, to build for themselves, new lives, were made of sterner stuff than to sit down and weep among the ruins.[2]

We like to think of Chicago as a young giant who brushed off the ashes, rose among them and said, "Come on, let's brush away the rubbish and 'let's go.'" That was the origin of the Chicago "I will" insignia — the words "I will" on a helmet with wings on either side.[3]

Without my being aware of it at the time, my childhood was spent in the reconstruction period of our city's phenomenal growth. . . .

Chicago was invaded by businessmen, architects, and others who recognized an opportunity to build anew. Among them came the greatest architect America has ever produced, the father of the American-sky-scraper, Louis L. Sullivan, and the young lad who had worked in the office of Adler and Sullivan — Frank Lloyd Wright. On the site of the burnt out city, American Architecture was born.[4]

The old wooden, haphazard city in its venerable site was attracting the finest talent in the country to help it rebuild itself.[5]

All of this I did not and could not know but [there] was a sense of tremendous activity, resourcefulness and drive which we felt, culminating in Chicago's motto "I will" which for a period of time in my adolescence and early adult life, I adopted.[6]

This was the period of my childhood and youth, a glorious time into which to be born. . . . I was a happy little child, and that is a grand beginning to any life. . . . What opportunities were there for children born in the interregnum between the Civil War and the first World War, when there occurred some of the greatest expansions of all time?[7]

Chicago and I have lived through the most marvelous period in human history from kerosene lamps to the improved atomic bomb together, and one of the greatest of the miracles is that both of us are still living.

I heard Thomas Mann say that he considers the Middle West the true America — cities like Chicago, St. Louis, he feels are more typical of the U.S. than cities along the sea-coasts.[8]

[He said] you will not find the true American on the shores of the Atlantic for the Atlantic cities are European and neither will you find it on the shores of the Pacific which has its trace of Orientalism.[9]

Carl Sandburg called it [Chicago] "Hog Butcher to the world." But I like to think that two great universities hold it down at either end, Northwestern on the North and the University of Chicago on the South. In between on the East lies our Art Institute and our Symphony Hall and to the West one of the great medical research centres of the world. Be that as it may, I know my Chicago.[10]

[Our] rented house on 24th Street near Indiana Avenue, which is now . . . the Back of the Yards, [was] inland a bit from the shore of the Lake. . . . [It is] one of the ugliest neighborhoods of small automobile repair shops, of huge printing plants and a brewery on the near South Side. . . . But when I was born a lovely little house stood there in a neighborhood of other little houses with gardens. Mamma used to say that they called our house *Das Schlosschen*—the little castle because it looked like one. . . . It was probably a pretty little house that reminded [them] of Germany with its castles along the Rhine. . . . Thinking back about it now, I wonder if it had little imitation turrets and ornate gingerbread woodwork trimming. It was the era of bad taste in domestic architecture, what is called the "General Grant era." The thing that matters, however, is that my father must have been proud of it and that we, who lived in it, were a happy family.[11]

My mother never tired of describing the house and the garden. Along its fence there was a border of old fashioned sweet smelling mignonette, green and white little plumes, purple pansies with yellow dots, bleeding heart, white and pink Sweet William.[12]

Our parents were happy in [that house] if one can judge from the pleasure with which our mother used to relate stories of the hospitality that warmed it into a home. On Sundays our parents kept [until later] the roast goose or duck they were to have had for dinner at noon, for noon was the accustomed time for dinner, hoping that our father's friends, our mother's two unmarried brothers might drop in for a glass of beer or something good to eat. No radio, or television, not even cards whiled away the evening. It didn't while away. It passed quickly in conviviality and singing and German *gemütlichkeit*. My uncles belonged to the *Singverein* [glee club] and the *Turnverein* [German Socialist Democratic gymnastics society] that the first Germans who came to Chicago very soon organized. There was little formal entertainment in the city in that early time. Persons entertained themselves.[13]

Both my father and mother loved company. On Sundays if my mother had prepared an especially good dinner, if there was a turkey or roast duck my father never wanted to have the dinner at noon. . . . Papa too had many friends and everybody loved to come to our house. . . . My father, as most Germans do, loved music. He and one of my uncles, one of my mother's brothers loved music and they would spend the evening singing songs and telling stories and we[re] happy in just being together in this wonderful land of their adoption, America, where everybody ranked as high as everybody else, and business opportunities were opening up for them all. They must have been wonderful Sunday evenings. They stood out in my mother's memories as the height of her happiest days.[14]

[Today], a big oily garage occupies the site of the little castle, and the trolley car, which I won't describe because it is too ugly, passes the garage. We call that "Progress" and I presume we spell it with a capital *P*, but I am sorry for the children who live on Indiana Avenue now.[15]

Michigan Avenue, at that time, was the aristocratic boulevard, soon to be a street of mansions, down which carriages rolled drawn by two spic and span horses, with a coachman in livery in the box. In the case of our increasing number of millionaires, some luxurious carriages had the additional ornament of a footman. That was Michigan Avenue.

A block to the east was comfortable Indiana Avenue which helped to give the city its name of the "Garden City." I vaguely remember houses with gardens around them on Indiana Avenue . . . and I remember Indiana Avenue especially because a green street car, drawn by two horses that had tinkling bells on their harness, went down the center of the street. My especial delight was the curtains at the windows . . . edged with a trimming of the little balls that bobbed when the car rode along. . . . It was a single track car with switches at intervals. No car could make a continuous journey from one terminal to the other. At the switches one car invariably had to wait 'til the car from the opposite direction came tinkling along. In the interval you could hear the passengers talking and the conductor and driver visiting. All this I recall that vividly because I loved to sing on the Indiana Avenue car and keep time to the bobbing of the little balls on the curtains. I stopped singing when the car stood still. Although Indiana Avenue was a comfortable street, it had no claim whatsoever to being aristocratic. How could it have [been] with a street car going through? [16]

A shopping centre was developing on South Halsted Street. Our father opened his shoe store between two millinery establishments whose owners were rivals and kept the street lively. State Street between Randolph and Adams was where hotels were going up and small dry goods stores turning into big department stores, were the centre of the city. [17]

After we left the little castle on 24th near Indiana Av. I think we moved to a second story apartment above a store. I remember my older brother sitting in front of a window with a paper resting on the window sill, and having a precious lead pencil with which he put down the numbers on the red State Street horse-drawn street cars as they passed. [18]

Troubles came into the lives of our parents, but we were too little to know them as troubles. They meant changes, and mostly children like changes. We moved to the country, to Clinton, Iowa because our mother was often sick, and the country was good for sick people. Besides, our father's [shoe] business was not prospering, and many merchants who had country stores were making money. The venture was not a success. I remember little about it, except that we lived in a cold house that had stoves in it where you could heat apples that grew soft and warm and smelt and tasted very appealing; that you could throw chestnuts into the fire and they popped, that there was a big yard and we had a pump and a stray dog we all loved, "Billie Bender" our father called him. One day he strayed away, just as he had strayed into our yard and affections, and we all felt sorry. There was a river on the edge of the town and across the river was a place called Lyons, where one time a diphtheria epidemic raged. They talked about the epidemic in our house, and then it spread into our house. I came down with diphtheria and was sick and my little brother was scolded because they couldn't keep him out of the room where I was in bed all by myself and a doctor came.[19]

Death has often frightened me. We met it first amid weeping and wailing and our mother dressed in somber black, wearing a little black crepe bonnet with a long very black crepe veil to the hem of her long black skirt. Its mystery was less than its heavy grief accompanied by strange happenings and having a loved companion put into a hole in the ground. Children are frightened by a hole in the ground. The details of our father's death are indelibly recorded in my child mind.[20]

Emil, my older brother, had come home from school not feeling well [1876]. Mamma sent for the doctor. Papa was walking around the house with something tied around his neck and had difficulty in talking. The doctor came and after he had examined Emil and said he had the measles, he looked at Papa and asked what was the matter. Papa told him that he had a quinsy sore throat [an abscess on or around the tonsils], that he was subject to quinsy sore throats every winter, that in a few days, or maybe hours, the abscess or whatever it was would break, and then he would be relieved. It was very painful.

The doctor replied that in this day and age nobody should wait 'til an abscess ruptures and breaks of its own accord. If Papa would consent to have him lance it he would feel better promptly and could go back to his [shoe] store. Papa, who was anxious to go back to business consented and it seems to me that I remember a basin and a mirror. . . .

Papa however, took sick, a day or two after his throat was lanced. Emil and I had the measles. [Papa] told Mamma he was beginning to feel stiff all over, with much pain, and she'd better get a doctor. He didn't want the neighborhood one who had lanced his throat, he wanted one of his good German doctor friends. . . . How many days Papa lingered I do not know. Not many, I'm sure. By this time, Essie had come down with measles and was quite neglected. How she managed to survive without complications, I do not know. The evening came when Emil and I were being sent up stairs to go to bed. At the foot of the stairway where the banister curved into a post, with a flattened sphere topping it, stood one of Papa's best friends. He stopped Emil and me as we were about to go up and said, "Pray for your father."

We were terribly frightened, and went quietly up stairs. I think we went into a little room and did not go to bed. Still we must have slept[,] for there was a next morning, and on the next morning, they told us that our Papa was dead. There was a lot of blaming of the doctor who lanced Papa's throat. He had always recovered without lancing. They said poison from the throat must have gotten into his blood, that he died of blood poisoning. . . . He was thirty-nine years old. . . . Mamma used to tell it with tears streaming down her cheeks and that's why I remember it. . . .

Within [a period of] five weeks [my mother] lost both her greatly beloved husband and her dearly beloved mother.[21]

Mamma's mother had been an invalid and the shock and grief of Papa's death hastened her own.[22]

We were half-orphans [after our father's death]: Whoever invented the name of orphan or half-orphan should have had his ears cut off. To lose one or both parents might be hard enough, without being in some ways set apart from children who had papas and mammas.[23]

[Because] Grandpa and the uncles needed a housekeeper, what was more natural than we should go to live with Grandpa [on West Randolph Street on the Near West Side]?[24]

In the backyard . . . there was a green latticed garden house with slabs of wood for seats against the sides of the lattice walls.[25]

A little way back from the *Gartenhaus*, there was a green lattice fence separating the front of the yard from the back. On the other side, chickens ran around and there was a forbidding barn.[26]

Grandmother's *Gartenlaube*— garden house — makes me shudder. Big, fat green caterpillars sometimes crawling on the leaves gave us a feeling of repulsion and the dread that they might fall or crawl on us — as if the caterpillars could have known it, they would have liked our intimate social contact as little as we liked theirs. We didn't know that they would change into magnificent monarch butterflies after a long sleep, and they didn't know it either. Nor did we know what we might turn into after passing through our childhood and adolescence, when, unlike the big fat green crawling things, we were more awake than we ever again might be.[27]

I remember it well: we were living in a row of what were called "basement houses" on West Randolph Street close to Union Park. Each house had a separate wooden stairway on the outside leading up to the second or "parlor floor." I [used to sit] mid-way up on what we called "the steps."[28]

There were trees in front of the house. We called them cottonwoods. Our little front yard, had steps leading to the basement where our dining-room and kitchen and summer kitchen and furnace were. The front yard had a lilac bush in the center, and was enclosed by a fence of rounded wooden rails.[29]

[W]here the wooden stairway began, my older sister [played] jacks. . . . I dearly loved playing jacks and still bear a small smooth mark on the little finger of my left hand with which one scoops up the little iron stars from the time when, for a few weeks, I held the championship — later my younger brother, whose hands had grown larger than mine, wrested the honor from me, but I continued to play through spring and summer days on the stone that wore my finger smooth. Later, we played on the carpet in the dining room.

We had no so-called living room. Nobody did. The parlor was up on the second floor, and the shutters were closed lest the sun affect the long lace curtains to the floor (How I loved them!) and fade the furniture. It was as sacred as a sanctuary — although opened for parties and funerals — almost a frightening formal room.

The second parlor was more friendly. Later our upright piano stood against one wall. The register on the floor through which the heat from the furnace came up, was kept open, for the second parlor had a book case in it with rows of books behind the closed, sometimes locked, glass doors. . . .

Shakespeare and Emerson in English, in de-luxe bindings, and the German classics in cloth bindings, Goethe, Schiller, Lessing and Heine. We had an uncle who was fond of reading.[30]

[A]ll of us, including Mamma sat around a table playing lotto for walnuts.[31]

On our dining room walls, there hung three walnut frames — above the door leading into the little vestibule that led into the kitchen, there was an oblong walnut framed, embroidered in colored wools on the perforated card-board "Home Sweet Home." On the next wall another perforated card board, piece of card board embroidered, walnut framed Ten Commandments. I can still see it, especially the terse "shalt nots." "I am the Lord, thy God" occupied a full line.

Under that "Thou shalt have no other Gods but me" — another full line. Then came the 3rd commandment, [the] 4th, "Remember the Sabbath" etc. in rapid procession, one underneath the other, each one a different color. "Thou shalt not lie"; "Thou shalt not steal"; "Thou shalt not commit adultery."

I didn't know what that [last one] meant. It seemed to have something to do with growing up. "Thou shalt not covet" — "Covet" too was peculiar. I could rattle off the Ten Commandments blindfolded. . . .

Several feet away on that same wall hung a steel engraving of Alex von Humboldt, whom I respected most highly — He was a man of letters, very well dressed with a nice face.[32]

We had gas-light and burnt coal and wood in our kitchen stove. When we were young ladies, we had kerosene lamps in the parlor and entrance hall because we could have glowing shades on them. . . .

Memories of tragedies seem the most vivid, like the day I had

gone out with Mamma and upon my return, found that the beauti-
fullest doll in all the world, my wax doll who closed her eyes when
you laid her down, her pinkish wax eyelids curving slightly outward,
the pride of my heart and the dearest of my doll family, was a hideous sight. While I was out, my brother Kurt had scratched off all her
beautiful face and was chewing it. The smaller doll with the china
head, her black china hair parted in the middle, her very blue china
eyes always open and staring upon another day, had been decapi-
tated by Kurt because he had heard of some one being hanged and he
had put a string around my doll's neck and kept swinging her against
the dining room table 'til he cracked her head off. It was a very thor-
ough and successful hanging followed by the tears due to a quite innocent victim. Maybe I left my dolls lying around; [my sister] Esther's dolls never met with the gruesome fate mine did. And they
were always better dressed; Esther who has always been excellent in
sewing loved making doll clothes. I hadn't too much patience. I liked
little china dolls, all made of *chine*. You didn't have to dress them too
much and you could always keep them clean if you wanted to by
sticking the whole of them in water and I loved puddling in water.

[Once] Emil found a rope and rigged up a swing high up among
the rafters of the basement. We were told that we must not do things
like that. How Esther got into that high swing I have no idea. But
she was swinging aloft having a high old time when the rope broke,
and Esther lay on the dirty floor of the basement. Somebody scolded
and said Esther could have been killed, and so she could have been,
but she wasn't — still, it bothered me for a long time, she could have
been, and that's why I remember it.

But it did not keep us from swinging in other rope swings — the
higher the better and the "screaminger" the more fun. All children
love holding on to the sides, or standing on the seat of a swing going
back and forth with each rhythm from one way to the other going
higher and higher 'til you almost touch the sky. There's a cracking
sound sometimes or a sort of creak as the rope seems to protest — if
it holds, being a child, you expect to hit the sky — if the rope doesn't
hold, you break an arm or a leg. Childhood and swings go together.
There isn't nearly so much fun in a safe commercial swing in a frame
work, as there is in an unsafe one made of a rope with a wobbly seat
fastened on some way with notches.[33]

We children played safely on the sidewalks and in the streets. . . .
The sidewalk [was] where on hot days my brother would stop his
particular [streetcar] drivers and give to them a drink of cold lemon-
ade from the pitcher which Mamma had made. . . .

In a near-by empty lot, however, next door to Grossman's Livery Stable, our boys played base-ball, prisoner's base, one o' cat.
Girls never played in the lot, but we played all of those things too, in
our back yard and especially in the back yard of our next door neighbors. I could run fast and although I wasn't so good as my brothers at
base ball, I was the best of us girls whom they tolerated only when
sufficient boys were not around. One time, a few of us girls ran a
race around the block. I won. I know how I set my teeth at the last
stretch, and determined that I must die or come in first. It was a very
personal matter. My cousin Belle and I were rivals in hop-scotch. I
wanted to beat her, as much as I wanted to win the race. Belle was
ahead of me in school, there was six months difference in our ages.[34]

We children had no allowances. Once in a while an uncle or aunt
would give me a nickel or a quarter, but you'd never ask, as you would
Mamma or might have asked Papa. But children were not supposed
to spend money. They saved it and bought some one a birthday present, except when tempted beyond redemption they spent a wicked
penny at the school store for candy. There was a chewy brown kind,
marked into twenty little squares. They called it "20 caramels for one
cent." Sometimes my cousin Belle and I fell into bad ways. One of
us would buy the twenty caramels and the other one two big gum
drops — and then in our favorite hideaway we'd have a sinful feast.
Sometimes we were given pennies, which they said we might
spend. You could buy jaw-breakers then which with careful management might last the better part of a day. Some children bought
wax gum.[35]

Already in those days there were gangs. There was a hap-hazard
gang of a sort, headed by our cousin, a natural born leader. His gang,
the Randolph Street gang was not strong physically. A few boys were
in the gang. Most because there were other gangs than because of
any necessity for banding together. They were not aggressive did not
go out for annoying the neighbors and were glad enough to be left
alone to their intensive playing. . . . I vaguely remember that sometimes the Fulton Street gang emerged from what seemed a sort of

Hinterland back of Randolph. I never heard of any fights between it and our boys. These gangs, I fancy, were formed because the name is one that boys like and there's a natural tendency in the growing male to select a chief, or have one assert himself, and then there must be loyal followers, possibly rules drawn up and life or death pacts.

The Randolph Street gang, to my knowledge, never met to formulate a policy or swear loyal oaths. It was merely protective, like our U. S. military set-up. If other gangs attacked, they had to have some kind of unity something to attack — they never came to steal or do any mischief — they came swiftly to win, and hang around 'til they were either chased away. Or drifted back to where they belonged.

But there was a Carroll Avenue gang that struck terror into the hearts of the Randolph Street and the Fulton Street gangs. The Carroll Street gang lived along the railroad tracks [and] was tough, and might even have had criminal intentions. They stole, skates mainly as I remember, always from smaller boys, often off the feet of other boys, pocket knives and other precious possessions — lunch and money. There was that sinister word "reform school" — some of them would end up in reform school, and some of them had been inmates. The Randolph Street gang dreaded the Carroll Street gang as much as the Belgians must have dreaded the Germans. The Carroll Street gang did not always travel as a gang. It traveled sometimes in pairs, cowardly little toughs, because they never took on a fellow their own size. They stole from smaller unprepared kids and brooked no resistance.

Later the same pattern was repeated in the next generation — by different names.[36]

At the time of which I write [1878], Chicago was a rapidly growing and expanding city. Transportation, as we know it to-day was in its infancy. . . . Horses were still the power that made the wheels revolve. Street cars, which had hay in them in the winter time, and had a conductor and a driver and one horse hitched to them, went by our door on West Randolph Street.[37]

It was an up-to-date car because it ran in double tracks. Many street cars in Chicago did not. . . . Horse drawn vehicles passed our door, but unless a horse shied and ran away there was little danger for children playing out-of-doors. . . . [H]eating street cars and other public conveyances was unheard of.

Very few persons had carriages which were pulled by two horses. The drivers were called coachmen and [the] very rich or swell had both a coachman in livery and a footman in livery. There were many one horse vehicles.[38]

To keep horses was expensive. Only the richest persons could afford carriages *and* buggies. Therefore going about was limited and persons spent time in their homes. . . . [In addition,] our famous loop was not yet. . . .

West Madison Street was a business street. There was what seemed a big dry goods store, Madigans, where they sold goods by the yard ribbons, pins, hooks and eyes, thread and needles. It was not a department store. At Madison and Halsted there was a huge dry goods store, C[arson] P[irie] and Company. . . .

It seems a long time since the Randolph Street horse drawn car clip clopped, passing us children playing on the sidewalk along my pages. . . . How far west it went I do not know. Washington Park [was] a little park which was a Godsend to us children with its small lagoon and big grass plots, meadows. The street car went around one edge of the park and disappeared for us, into the wilds. As small children I do not remember ever having gone west of Washington Park, although later Garfield Park was the scene for us of the happiest of picnics.

Going east though, the Randolph Street car went through the very center of Haymarket Square, which a few years after the period of which I am writing, attained international prominence. It was the scene of the famous Haymarket riot [May 4, 1886] where policemen were shot to death and some men justly or unjustly called anarchists figured in the famous anarchist trial.

But at the time, the car went innocently through. Before it reached State Street it had gone over the wooden Rail Road bridge which preceded the wooden bridge with its rounded frame and upright girders, the very essence of bridge architecture, which spanned the Chicago River. We children were always relieved when we were safely over. What if the bridge should break in two while we were crossing it? One of our cousins who lived on the South Side wouldn't come to see us for a long time. She was terrorized every time the street car went over the bridge. . . . I do not remember ever being taken down town. . . .

I remember a jolly street-car strike [1877], before even there were bicycles. Everything that could be propelled in one direction was pressed into service if it could have a horse, any kind of horse hitched in front of it. People laughed, riding past our house, at the funny contrivances, and at how they were huddled into them. What the strike was about or who won I do not know. The fare, stationary for years at 5 cents and 3 cents for children wasn't raised. The cars ran no further. I hope the men had struck for shorter hours, for the number of hours all persons were employed, although life moved at a more tranquil pace, to our present way of thinking, was appalling. . . .

One of the greatest discoveries of mankind has been the wheel. We have lived into the time when transportation soars on wings. Transportation, in a way, is at the root of civilization. When the first man to find a hollowed out tree trunk let the waves float him away from the shore, he went somewhere where he had not been before, even if it was only to a near place along the shore that he had not reached by walking or running.

I wasn't there. I don't know how he formed or made a paddle, but the progress of mankind is a straight line, from that hollowed out tree trunk with its paddle for propelling and steering, to the gigantic fish shaped things with wings that zoom in and out of our big airport at Cicero — in the southwest part of our city.[39]

I wanted to grow up fast, and be a young lady, and wear a black silk dress with a low V-neck filled in white illusion (To-day we call it "net") and wear a red rose on my bosom where the "V" ended. Where I intended to go or what I intended to do except to be a romantic heroine who had suffered. There would be one whole year when I would not wear the white illusion or rusching, and would go into mourning a full year, perhaps even wear a black veil. This I would do in memory of my father.[40]

Gradually it came about that my older sister was seventeen and I was sixteen, and we wore our skirts longer, stayed up later, and were interested [in], and took part in the conversation about us.[41]

One day when my younger sister [Meta] and I were in the company of Mrs. William Vaughn Moody, a remarkable woman who was no mean factor in the building up of both the industry and the culture of Chicago, [we] mentioned the name of a certain woman and asked Mrs. Moody if she knew her. Mrs. Moody asked, "What is her relation to the city?" I never forgot the question.

What has been my relation to the most American of American cities? [42]

Chicago and I grew up together. [43]

The Wednesday after the fire, the *Chicago Tribune* headline prophesied that "Chicago Shall Rise Again!" and so it did. In the immediate aftermath of the Great Conflagration, Chicago developed into the city that Joseph Medill, the publisher of the *Tribune* who ran for mayor on the "Union Fire-Proof" ticket, had promised. [44] The norm for downtown office buildings became steel-frame construction. Exterior ornamentation and terracotta tiles (easily preformed from Chicago-area clay) became the hallmark of the Chicago school of architects. Downtown boomed as both a commercial and cultural center. Businesses clamored for space. With their salvaged stock and shipments from New York, Field and Leiter reopened their dry goods store in a horse barn on Twentieth Street on October 21. They moved back to State Street into a newly built store less than two years later. Potter Palmer quickly rebuilt his hotel, bigger and more grandiose than before. This time, it was also fireproof. Small retail businesses and larger wholesale houses reestablished themselves with credit loans from eastern bankers. Immigrants poured into the city to help with reconstruction and the city was happy to have them.

At about the time I write the owners of the [millinery] stores [on 22nd Street] were talking about moving down town to State Street between Washington and Monroe. They did and became big business. Papa too was considering it. Business was moving toward what later became the loop. If Papa had lived and had moved, we might have become millionaires. How I would have loved that — and would love it still. [45]

Just as Chicago was rebuilding, the financial panic of 1873 struck. The depression lasted six years, during which time bank collapses, unstable prices, rampant inflation, business closings, and the loss of jobs forced many people into homelessness once again. Those who still could moved out of the city; those who could not, camped out in city hall.

Irma's only real references to economics in the years between 1871 and 1890 were brief. She remarked that her father's shoe business was not doing well, and, as noted above, that there was "a jolly street car strike" and there had been a riot in Haymarket Square.

To understand the import of these comments requires a look at the history of labor in Chicago as it relates to immigration and industrialization. Partial crop failures in Europe during the 1860s almost compelled the migration of failed farmers, laborers, and servants. Those who could afford passage to try their fortunes in America came in droves. Since trade and commerce were fairly stagnant in the East, many of these economic refugees forged onward to Chicago. They crammed themselves into jerry-built apartments in the city, sometimes with three or more families of eight persons each sharing a dwelling.[46] They went to work in the city's newly mechanized factories and sweatshops, typically earning half the wages that skilled workers demanded.[47] There seemed to be a never-ending supply of immigrants from southern and central Europe who did not find ten-hour days and six-day workweeks onerous.[48] And many employers felt that these less skilled, hence cheaper, workers could operate the machines just as well as the more expensive specialist craftspeople they had formerly employed. The result was that cheap labor forced down hourly wages, and unemployment among the more skilled rose.

In Europe, craftspeople typically belonged to guilds or craft unions. When these workers immigrated, they brought their organizations and their membership requirements with them. The craft unions initially had some clout because business owners needed skilled workers. However, with mechanization and the influx of newer migrants willing to work longer and cheaper, the situation changed. The more recent immigrants did not belong to craft unions and could ill afford to spend time learning a trade in apprenticeship programs. They needed money, so they took almost any job they were offered, putting up with dismal work conditions.

In Chicago, the Germans were one of the first groups to apply pressure on the business and factory owners for improved working conditions. Their German Social Democratic Turnverein became the perfect forum in which to gather support for an eight-hour day. The German-language *Arbeiter Zeitung* and *Verbote*, with their huge Chicago subscriber base, were more socialist than democratic. Articles in these papers urged laborers as a group to negotiate with employers for a shorter workday and, as a last resort, to strike. These were revolutionary moves.

The logic behind the agitation for an eight-hour day was somewhat muddled. The argument ran that the reduction in the workday from ten hours to eight hours was beneficial to both the worker and the business owner. It would increase the quality of the working person's life, save wear and tear on machinery, reduce overproduction, stimulate demand for the resulting scarcer goods, and create employment for 20 percent more people.[49] Business owners and professional people felt quite threatened by labor's vocal demands. The prevailing sentiment was that the laborers' agitation for better working conditions and higher wages endangered free enterprise and the constitutionally granted right to operate businesses in whatever manner the owners wanted. The mainstream press was typically biased in favor of the owners and professionals.

Despite the antagonism of the media and the business and professional classes, the mostly German socialists whipped up broad support for the eight-hour day among workers at free labor meetings. Some even cautioned that efforts to negotiate with management were doomed unless strikers prepared for more than a class struggle by arming themselves. Indeed, their warnings seemed warranted. Chicago police had forcibly broken up labor meetings and demonstrations in the past. It was within this milieu of social unrest coupled with economic depression that the anarchists began to mobilize and to organize unskilled and skilled workers within the trade union movement.[50]

Mistakenly believing that police brutality at a melee during the McCormick Harvester factory strike the previous day had killed two strikers, disgruntled labor organizers organized a protest rally in Chicago for May 4, 1886. The meeting was to be held in a manufacturing and wholesale area near Randolph and Desplaines Streets called Haymarket Square. The meeting was peaceful until 180 policemen marched from their station house a few blocks away to disperse those gathered. While the police were breaking up the meeting, a dynamite bomb detonated. The bomb killed one policeman and wounded many others. The police fired into the crowd, killing four workers and wounding approximately twenty more. Around two dozen other officers were injured, most from friendly fire. Eight policemen and four rally attendees ultimately died from their wounds. The police arrested Michael Schwab, Oscar Neebe, Samuel Fielden, August Spies, Albert Parsons, Louis Lingg, Adolph Fischer, and George Engel, all known social revolutionaries or anarchists. These men were tried and found responsible for the Haymarket riot even though the bomb thrower was never positively identified. All but Neebe, who received a fifteen-year prison term, were sentenced to death. On November 10, 1887, Governor Richard J. Oglesby (1865–1938) commuted the sentences of Saumel Fielden and Michael Schwab to life imprisonment. Spies, Parsons, Fischer, and Engel were hanged the following day, while Lingg committed suicide in jail. In 1893, Governor John P. Altgeld (1847–1902), in an act that elicited much criticism from conservatives, pardoned the others because he felt no evidence actually connected them with the bomb.

The story of "Black Friday" continued to inspire labor activists, as well as anarchists like Emma Goldman (1869–1940), for years afterward. Following the debacle at Haymarket Square, the labor movement in Chicago gained momentum and strength so that by 1890, sixty-five thousand workers belonged to unions.[51] Chicago was on its way to becoming "the city that works."

Reflections on Education, 1875–1891

Irma attended school during a time when educational theories about learning and the practices of teaching — that is, recitation, rote memorization, repetitive practice, group work, attendance at lectures in which certain subjects were taught or principles, philosophies, or theories were outlined — were changing, and taking on a more American tenor.[1] Up until the 1890s, and, indeed for a while after, prevailing educational theories and pedagogical methods had been rooted primarily in European models. These models were based in large part upon the philosophies of Immanuel Kant (1724–1804), who saw education as the crucial component in improving life, and Georg Wilhelm Hegel (1770–1831), who believed education was a lifelong process.[2] To these, American educators added the educational techniques of Johann Heinrich Pestalozzi (1746–1827) who, having studied child development, called for "the natural, balanced, and harmonious development of all capacities of the child" and advocated "balanced growth of head, heart, and hand."[3] They also looked to Johann Friedrich Herbart (1776–1841), "the father of both the science of education and of modern psychology." Herbart's sequence for learning involved (1) preparation or development of connections between what is known and what is to be learned, (2) presentation of material in a sound psychological manner, (3) association of the newly learned material with prior learning, (4) generalization from the concrete to the abstract, and (5) use of the newly acquired knowledge to pursue more knowledge.[4] Then American educators, attending to children's needs for early educational experiences, incorporated the ideas of Friedrich Froebel (1782–1852) about kindergarten into the system. Finally, at the start of the twentieth century, educational reformers mixed in the idealism of Ralph Waldo Emerson (1803–1882), the pragmatism of William James (1842–1910), and the scientific emphasis of Herbert Spencer (1820–

1903) to create an unique American philosophical and pedagogical system called progressivism.

Progressivism was more than a political movement; it was more than an educational movement. Its approach to life and learning was in marked contrast to earlier educational approaches rooted in social efficiency, ones that emphasized classroom control and management within a structured curriculum that focused on basic skills. Instead, progressivism encompassed a concern with social life and cut across many sectors of American society. Its theories and philosophical applications were involved with the public nature of institutions and aesthetic innovations.[5] The Progressive Movement stressed two basic principles: continuity and interaction. In other words, each learning experience was to be nurtured by the previous experience, and everything learned was subject to revision based upon later learning.

Progressivism promoted independent thinking, creativity, and expression of feeling. It was geared to direct the evolution of society toward socially desirable ends. Progressivists assumed that science was the method by which this evolution could be brought about. The development of intelligence, morals, and values was considered crucial for this endeavor. Jane Addams, who incorporated Froebel's notions into her Hull House curriculum during the 1890s, helped build the Progressive Education Movement, along with the other two great American educational reformers, Ella Flagg Young (1845–1918) and John Dewey (1859–1952).

Irma reflected on her early educational experiences during this critical juncture in American curriculum history:

There's a difference between the process of learning and getting an education. Once started, the process [gets] going and it never stops — it reveals insights, vistas of beauty. It's the answer to a child's "I wonder."[6]

Quite naturally when we think of education we think of schools. Schools though give one the tools with which to carve out our educations.[7]

Education in growing Chicago would naturally be different from education in New York or in the German village where my mother was educated. Yet if education is a process of drawing [possibilities] out, it is interesting to speculate [about the differences]. . . . If the possibilities are within us, what we mean by education is exposure to the heritage of the race and to whatever environment chance may provide.[8]

Both my father and mother had come to America shortly after the Civil War. Mother had gone to a village school in Germany and throughout my childhood and that of my two brothers and sisters took constant delight in the opportunities our public schools offered us.[9]

What about our education?[10]

There was no psychology of learning [when I began going to school].[11] We were exposed to certain things and we seem to have, in some way, absorbed them. Some children thought about the things they were learning — some didn't. Going to school became a routine habit out of which you got, as often as possible. I loved having a cold or a sore throat because then I didn't have to go to school. I'm sorry to have to admit this. With my later stimulus to absorb all the wonders of education and learning, I cannot find much promise in my earliest years. Perhaps this had its advantages. When my own children came along, I did not despair of them if they were not at the top of their classes or youngest graduates. . . . I always hated school, hated being inactive and being compelled to do certain things at specified times. Routine has never been to my liking. Perhaps it was a lack of early training, perhaps something physical, who knows?[12]

I knew a 1st grade teacher at one time, who had an abominable habit. If a frightened or even a naughty 1st grader did something that displeased her, while she scolded the helpless victim she would tilt his or her head back as far as she could by placing her thumb under the victim's chin. She was otherwise a rather kind hearted person, but I wonder how many children she taught to hate school by perpetrating this mild and undignified cruelty upon them? Whether you like school or hate it, says the psychologist, much depends upon what your earliest experiences in school have been.[13]

I was [first] sent to school in Clinton [Iowa]. I'd give a great deal to remember what it was like. Was it a little country school with several grades in one room? I think not[,] for my sister, with whom I walked hand in hand to and from school was not in the same room I was. Why can't I remember my first day at school? I can't, that's all.

Did I learn anything in that country school? If I did, you'd never know it because I don't know it myself.[14]

Later, when we moved back to Chicago, I must have been put in the first grade because I know how I loved that first grade reader. It had a green cover and the first picture in it was a red box in a square at the margin of the book with BOX printed in rather large letters between the picture and the inner margin of the page. And so my education and my love of books started with the word "box." I still know how to spell it.

[The word "box" was] followed along [in] the next few pages, [with] 3 or 4 boxed-in pictures, starting with the word "box"

Box

Hat   knife

Cup   bell

Book   chair

The cup I think was blue, the hat, a man's hat, some dark color and the book, which I loved best of all on account of its color, was red like the box — symbolic, perhaps, because books are meant to be read. . . . [There were] about six words to a page. We would sing them off and that's all I know about it.

After we moved to Grandpa's we went to the Elizabeth Street School. It had only four grades. Elizabeth Street was the dividing line for children who had completed the four grades. As luck would have it, that dividing line separated our school life from that of our cousins. We lived a few doors north of Elizabeth Street on [West] Randolph. They lived a few doors south. Therefore, [our cousins] went to the Brown School, and we to the Skinner. The Brown School was more swanky; the Skinner, presided over by Ella Flagg Young, the better school — the best in Chicago at that time.[15]

We had a long distance to go to the Skinner School at Jackson and Aberdeen Streets. From Elizabeth Street north, there were Sheldon, Curtis, then South to Washington, Madison, Monroe, Adams, Jackson and a short block north to Aberdeen. On our way we passed on Washington Street some famous mansions, the Snell mansion at Ann and Washington where the famous Snell murder occurred.[16]

A block away from our street, [we] always slowed up a bit, and passed with great respect what I recall as a mansion, although it may not have been one, where Abe Lincoln's son Robert lived.[17]

How we managed to go back and forth four times a day I cannot now understand. Except on the coldest day we came home for lunch (school was out at 12 [noon] and we were back at 1:30).[18]

I think our schools were pretty good. We had the main tools, a very good foundation in arithmetic, spelling, grammar and writing. True, nobody seemed to have made an effort to discover and encourage talent as the best schools to-day are doing—physically, we had a few exercises. School contests and groups playing were not cultivated. We had singing and drawing lessons of a sort. The schools were more practical, as they should have been with our groping city evolution, than cultural.[19]

I remember very vividly two things I learnt in the Elizabeth Street School and I can still do them. Miss Peck, our 2nd grade teacher, was very kind. She had a peculiar physical defect. Her mouth was funny. It looked as if both her upper and lower lips were turned inside out. I practiced, I remember doing it, before a little looking glass 'til I could make my lips look like hers. I can still do it. My sister Esther remonstrated often. She didn't like it. Fortunately for me, my good imitation never became a habit.

The other thing I remember is our teacher, not Miss Peck, came into the room one day and showed us how to fold a paper carefully through the middle having the edges touch, and the[n] running a finger nail down the centre fold to make a sharp edge, then carefully tearing the paper in two, making a clean, sharp cut. In my four years in the Elizabeth Street School that is all I remember learning.[20]

One memory however brings another. Remembering the multiplication table, I suddenly heard the sound of slate pencils scratching and jotting on slates. Then I recalled how we used slates and not 'til after the 4th grade did we use paper for written work. The slates were oblong, bound in red felt, with slanting black cords, laced through holes in the wooden frames of the slates to hold the felt in place. Our school desks, of course, were in rows, and everybody had to have a slate rag ready — almost never clean. When the slate was covered with writing you had to clean it off. To clean it off, you needed water or spit — the teachers preferred water, and on every school desk there stood a bottle of some kind, with water in it, having a cork with a hole through the centre. If there is a greater joy than having the teacher ask you to take the bottle with water through the aisle, not going straight down the aisle and shaking a little pool of water on every slate and going back shaking it on the slates of the other aisle — There was a technique: It was such a great joy, it is worth describing. You passed down the centre of the aisle, zigzagging from side to side — a jerk of the bottle on one side, another jerk on the slate on the opposite side — and so you passed through the centre, down one aisle, up the other, 'til there was water on every slate and the sound of slates pushing on the desk and one little wet rag to wipe the water over the slate and a dry one to dry it. If you didn't have two rags, the corner of one would do for spreading the water. If you were teacher's pet you often filled the bottle and passed the water. No joy ever exceeded being asked to sprinkle the water.[21]

I loved the smell of a new, fresh school book, that cracked when you pulled the cover back and opened the pages. Having, however, an older brother and sister, I rarely inherited a brand new school book. From me the brown school reader and the faded blue spelling book descended to my brother Kurt at whose hands they met a timely death. . . .

I remember the smell of the school store where we bought pens and pencils, [foolscap paper], blank books and other books and where the none too dainty candy counter stood near the door where children going in and out had to pass it. Back of the school store, the family that kept it — had a shoe repairing business. The smell of the glue and the leather and dirty hands mixed with the school supplies and candy in a unique perfume, which, thank heavens, we had never encountered elsewhere. Still, it didn't affect the taste of twenty caramels for a penny or a big red, long lasting jaw breaker.[22]

[In those days] foolscap paper [had] an embossed circular trade mark in the upper right hand corner; you bought half a dozen sheets of fools cap paper for a nickel, large, ruled double sheets they were of heavy white paper, one sheet folded inside the other. You used them mostly to copy your home work neatly on them. At least you were supposed to copy it neatly. . . .

Home work was a great nuisance. Emil and Essie did theirs neatly, sitting at the dining-room table before supper or in the evening after supper. I did not always do mine on time and often sat outside on the front steps, or anywhere inside to copy my spelling or do those horrible examples of figuring out how much wall paper to use to paper rooms which I would never see, or care to see. I was always scolded for writing, as they put it, on my knee. I like to do it to this day. Did not the great Alexander von Humboldt [write on his knee as shown in] the only picture in the house outside of family portraits and the moralistic Ten Commandments? What was good enough for Alexander was good enough for me. If he could do it why couldn't I? It is true, his notes looked neat. Mine didn't. My ambition in regard to home work was not to do it well, but to get through with the darn thing. . . . The scoldings made little impression.[23]

Somewhere in the 4th grade [my sister Essie] had copied every one of her examples in arithmetic with their right answers in a ruled composition book. I was one grade behind her in school. When I caught up with the 4th grade, I sailed beautifully through my homework every night by simply copying her examples and handing them in to my teacher. I don't know how I got by. Perhaps I am still paying the penalty when the bank and I don't agree about my checking account. The bank seems to be a better subtracter than I am sometimes.[24]

Irma attended Skinner School from the fifth through the eighth grade.

Mrs. [Ella Flagg] Young, our principal, who left Skinner School after my graduation, was a wonderful educator. She was elected or perhaps appointed, to be the Superintendent of Schools for the whole of Chicago. Later she was a member of the faculty of the University of Chicago Educational Department. John Dewey, America's greatest educator, and Ella Flagg Young were associated in some most important reforms in education.

Mrs. Young was a little masculine sort of human. She had flashing, penetrating eyes. Sarcasm was one of her weapons. . . .

Many years after my sister and I were married, some one arranged a re-union of Skinner School students at Mandel's [department store] in honor of Mrs. Young. She had been appointed to an important position in Washington in the State Education Department. The room was [filled] with remembrances of all that all of us owed her. Her sarcastic smile had given way to a friendly one. When she came to our table, to shake hands and to greet separately each former student, she stopped a moment, regarding my sister and me attentively and with a smile said, "I don't know who you are now, but you were the Rosenthal sisters." Pretty good, we thought, to remember our names for over a quarter of a century.[25]

While at Skinner School, Irma learned a number of intentional and unintentional lessons.

Fifth grade was fractions. Sixth grade was decimals, [and the] French and Indian Wars. Seventh grade was American History through the American Revolution and into the later formative years of the country. I loved the American Revolution [and the] War of 1812. Eighth grade — The Civil War and the development of the country. We all thought we should have been lucky if we had been born before the Civil War. Then we shouldn't have had to study it.[26]

Fifth grade was a serious time of life. You had to learn fractions and write compositions and pay attention to your handwriting.[27]

Essie had to do the 5th grade over again. She was in high 5th and I was put into low 5th. We were not in the same room. In the middle of the year, Essie passed into 6th and I failed.

From the 5th grade on, . . . I had to make an effort, which I did not, to my sorrow at the end of the term, always make. . . . [I]n the 6th grade, I held a steady rank 2 for the whole year. . . .

[When I was in 6th grade,] a specimen of my hand writing was chosen to hang among the specimens in Mrs. Young's office. It was beautiful, absolutely perfect, and looked like engraving. I took great pains and probably much time to do it. But it wasn't my idea of good penmanship. True, Mrs. Young insisted that writing must be plain and easy to read. I have always felt grateful to her for that. My idea, however, what I subsequently tried hard to accomplish was that writing, first of all to be easily read, in addition be rapid and have a certain swing to it. I am grateful to Mrs. Young for having hammered into us the idea that the purpose of writing is that it should be read. . . .

[In eighth grade, Mrs. Young] taught us how to read and to write English. . . . She taught the subject called "Language." . . . She came in at 11 and the class lasted 'til 12, an unusually long stretch in what was called Grammar School. . . . We had learnt German before we learnt English and I was vaguely aware that somehow my English was not so fluent as that of the children of American-born parents. I never used "ain't" after one of our teachers told us it was not good English, and I never said "you was" when I learnt that "you were" was correct.[28]

Ella Flagg Young was a strict and witty teacher.[29]

We stood in awe of her. . . . [She] rarely praised, she was exacting; I think we were afraid of her, but she was fair. Discipline, which in classes that were much too large, was never a problem in Mrs. Young's 8th grade language class. Somehow we sensed that we were privileged to have her for a teacher and she countenanced no waste of time to establish order. We felt, what I know now, was an integrity.[30]

She taught me never to say anything if I had nothing to say but if I did have something to say to express it as simply as possible.[31]

If one [of] us got up with the expression "I don't think," with a peculiar smile and a sharp admonition, she would burst out with, "If we don't think, sit down!" We had to become positive thinkers. . . .

One of [her] unforgettable admonitions was "Never use a big word if a little one will do."[32]

She taught me further how to write a correct English sentence and when and where to begin a new paragraph. . . . I may sometimes have forgotten to put [it] into practice. . . . [When] I entered a freshman class in English composition at the University of Chicago, I rose to the head of the class because I knew to put into practice when to begin a new paragraph.[33]

After I left the 8th grade, I am sure Mrs. Young's influence did not leave me. If, at any time, I took a written exam, I passed it. . . . Sometimes I think, that all that I am, which may not be much, I owe to Mrs. Young.[34]

Writing compositions reminds me of two lessons about letter and composition writing I learned at this time.

One of our unmarried uncles who lived with us had gone to Europe on a pleasure trip. We had to write letters to him. I still remember sitting at the dining room windows, my sheet of foolscap paper lying on the window sill pestering Mamma with "What should I say in my letter?" Mamma said, "Tell him what you're doing, about your school, anything that you think *will interest him.*" It was a good suggestion.[35]

Much as I owe to Mrs. Young, I can never forget that I owe, in the delight I have had in writing, to one of my fellow 8th grade students. Our grade teacher, not Mrs. Young, asked us to write a composition and gave out as our subject the waste basket that stood always to the right of her desk. She said she would read aloud the composition she considered best.

In our class, there was a slender blonde boy whom I adored from a distance. He had traveled and all children long to travel. He wasn't rough. Good English seemed natural to him. . . . Herbert Stone, the blonde, slender, aristocratic member of our 8th grade class, the son of Melville Stone, the publisher I think at that time of the *Chicago Daily News*, later the founder of the Associated Press, Herbert Stone could tell the class in beautiful English of a trip he had taken South with his father. Herbert actually spoke to me several times and sent me into the 7th heaven. He told another member of my class that he thought I was a nice girl. Thereafter I worshipped him more than ever and every subsequent hero of my imagination I named "Herbert."

On the particular afternoon of which I write we were all very busy, squinting at the straw waste basket on the platform, holding up our rulers, guessing its dimensions and putting them down, describing its form, telling about its color.

Our teacher looked through the compositions while she gave us a recess — then she took from the top of the pile Herbert Stone's composition. Somehow Herbert had made the basket come alive. It liked where it stood. It liked our teacher. It felt sorry when our papers were so bad that they were thrown into it. It hated to disagree with the teacher but some of the papers it thought were not bad enough to be thrown away, for after the room was quiet and all of us had gone home, it often read the papers. It cited examples from some of the good papers thrown into him [when] the whole class had to throw its papers away because they couldn't be kept. I remember it didn't like gum thrown into it, or apple cores and it wished ardently that it weren't a *waste* basket. . . . We had described the basket as a thing — Herbert Stone had given it life.

Along with the technique Mrs. Young hammered into us, Herbert Stone's 8th grade composition [was] my most valuable lesson in what college students call English composition.

Herbert Stone became a writer. At the time of his untimely death due to the sinking of the S.S. Lusitania by the Germans, he was the Editor of the *House Beautiful* Magazine. I had always intended writing to him, hoping that my letter would not be thrown into his waste basket. After the sinking of the Lusitania I regretted keenly that I had never reminded him of our 8th grade compositions.[36]

After being graduated from the Skinner School again there were dividing lines. . . . When I was graduated, . . . I had a notion that I wanted to study Latin. The Latins were sent to a small building some where on Desplaines Street. . . . Students who were to study German were sent to the main High School at Ogden Avenue. It was in the heart of what is now rapidly becoming the greatest medical centre in the world. At that time there was already a medical school and the Presbyterian Hospital was close by.

But some persons considered it risky to send young girls to the big West Division High because people said it was dangerous for them to be close by the Medical School. They said the embryo medics would bring skeletons and other awful things to the windows to frighten the girls and then try to pick up flirtations with them. Perhaps this happened. My sister and some of the girls I went with had been going to the West Division for a year, and after completing my first year at the Branch, I would be going too. There were always girls who would flirt and some of them, no doubt suffered, and had dire troubles on account of it. We didn't. Maybe we were too dumb; perhaps we were too decent. . . .

I worried through Latin and Algebra from September to February and then I took sick. I hasten to add not from over work in school. . . . [In high school], a chum of mine sat across the aisle from me. At a quarter to 12 every morning, the school store got a batch of fresh cream puffs, and long twisted sweet rolls that were [made] with the most delicious vanilla icing dripping over them. My chum and I lived too far away to go home for our luncheons. We both were given an allowance for dessert to supplement the sandwiches we brought from home. We could hardly wait 'til the morning session was over, and every noon we ate our very freshly baked cream puff and warm sweet rolls showing through a top layer of shining icing. . . .

I ate an indigestible lunch every day and I laced my corset too tight because I was proud of my wasp-like waist, which was very stylish. And so, being delicate as my teacher had said, I became dreadfully anaemic and too sick to continue school for the rest of the year. . . .

After a vacation extending from February to September, I wanted to go back to school. To try to make up [the] Latin I knew would be useless. We couldn't afford private tutoring. And even if we might have afforded it, my family had never approved of my taking the Latin course. What good would it be to me? Girls were expected to get married and take care of their homes.

My sister too for some inexplicable reason had left in midyear in the first year of her high school attendance. Mr. Wells, the principal of the West Division permitted her to enter her 2nd year as he was sure that she would have no difficulty with second year German. He said he would help her to make up her algebra.

He allowed me to go into second year German, [and] worked a little with me in algebra in his office after school hours. Why he and I gave it up, I do not remember, except that he put me into Mr. Hicks' room who he said was tops as a teacher of mathematics. I did not dislike Mr. Hicks but he seemed dreadfully old and dry and thin. I am sure he must have been all of forty [years old]. I was exposed to geometry and trigonometry at which I did not do too well, because I preferred writing verses on the blackboard and writing long, very long, letters to my cousin at college. . . .

The great romance of my life began when Mr. French, our teacher of ancient history entered the room, at the first hour after lunch, while long, narrow Mr. Hicks inflicted himself and his tiresome mathematics on some other class. Mr. French was young. He had a lovely brown mustache and he spoke beautiful English. . . . Whether it was Mr. French being young and having a lovely mustache and liking my little weekly essay, which every member of the class had to hand in every Friday, I do not know. I do know that I entered a new world — a large, expansive, exciting world beyond my beloved U.S. My new world was luminous with growing knowledge of the arts of Egypt, Greece and Rome. I knew a little about the bible, not too much about Palestine — nothing . . . except their names about Egypt, Greece and Rome.[37]

Irma loved to read, but she discovered that

[a]t that time there were few children's departments in libraries and the flood of books for children [that exists today] was a mere trickle.

I really loved the few books I had, loved sitting at my desk and writing and although I had been taught, as all girls at that time were taught, to embroider and crochet, I exasperated my family by never working at my embroidery when I was alone. I remember an afternoon when I wouldn't take my lace parasol and go calling with my sister and one of my cousins because I wanted to study something. They were a little impatient with me. But they were generous enough to feel sorry when they returned and found that I had been compelled to entertain a casual visitor for whom I didn't care especially, all my precious afternoon.[38]

Our early reading, unguided, all but left us wrecked on impossible unrealistic shores. . . . [O]ne of our uncles brought us Grimm's and Andersen's *Fairy Tales* which I read to a music inaudible to every one [but] myself. Andersen's "Ugly Duckling" is Cinderella transposed into Andersen's fairy land. Louisa Alcott brought us down to earth where we wept naturally over the situations brought about in a real world, and rejoiced normally when the sun came in at the window. But instead of situations with no discernable foundations, Louisa Alcott's stories were built up out of the common garden variety of courage in the lives of persons we could recognize. Our copy of *Little Women* we read literally to tatters, often on the floor and Jo, Beth and Amy with Marmee and Laurie were friends who entered into our daily conversations.

A cousin of ours from Shelbyville, Illinois, . . . was important in my young life. She read love stories and brought them home and left them lying in the little 3rd floor bed-room where she and I slept in the same bed. And she always brought home a lurid sheet called *The Family Story Paper*. I doubt if ever one good story was printed on its cheap paper, with illustrations of grand beribboned young women wearing hoop skirts, languishing on sofas, before which knelt handsome young men in frock coats and puffed ties, pleading for their hands in marriage.

I read these stories avidly on the sly. [My uncle] had forbidden my brothers to read dime novels and us girls to read love stories. But [he] went to business day times and often at night to his club. We could hide the books when we knew he was around. *Skinney the Tin Peddler* was my brother Emil's favorite. He chuckled aloud when he read it. The [Horatio] Alger books had not been written.

Essie and I reveled over and wept through *Thorns and Orange Blossoms*, a copy of which I still have bound in paper for which I paid 10 cents. . . . As I remember it, it is a Cinderella story, just one of the millions of Cinderella stories, each one set in its own matrix. The jewel in the matrix is never bad. We all love Cinderella and, in one way or another, have been Cinderella. It depends on how the story is told and who is in it.[39]

A great thing happened to me at this time. My younger brother had as a reading and study assignment in his 8th grade, Emerson's *Essay on Self-Reliance*. I read it — and re-read it and my life changed. I had often wondered why I was alive. I was easily overawed by superior persons and it took me a long time to grow into Emerson's statement that "You have the same right to be here, as Cape Cod has to be there." Since those young, hopeful, wishful days I have continued reading *Self-Reliance* and shall probably continue to read it and the rest of Emerson's writings as long as my joy in reading lasts. I owe more to Ralph Waldo Emerson for a rich life — at this time still richer by far than that of any one else I know — than to any other one cause.

We were somewhat high-minded young persons. [Another] cousin was fired with an ambition to go to college. His people wanted him to succeed his father in his father's excellent book bindery business — but he was determined to get an education and prepared himself at home for the University of Michigan at Ann Arbor to which some of his friends went. I had always imitated [him]. I was in love with him throughout our childhood. His ambition to go to college inspired me. I borrowed the books he would lend me and later I bought them myself the little science so-called primers, which have been my prized possessions all my life. It is amazing that I passed many an exam from having mastered them. Ill health interfered with my getting a high school diploma and I felt ashamed of being, as I thought [myself], more ignorant than most of my friends who had their diplomas. I remember all the years I consoled myself with the thought that the best thing any high school or college could do for me was to show me the way to go on by myself.[40]

After leaving high school, Irma found work teaching.

Over 60 years ago [ca. 1888 at age 17], I took a teacher's examination in the rooms of the Board of Education. I had completed two years of study at the West Division High School. A friend of mine and I had memorized lists of presidents — capitals of the States and much such useless lumber, for we had been told we would be asked questions on such useless lumber. The day of the exam, we met Miss Margaret Haley . . . in the halls of the school where the exams were held. I remember her saying, "Girls, answer every question put to you. If you don't answer it, you've lost; if you do you might succeed in getting it right in whole or part." It was good advice.

I passed the examination, was assigned to a school as a cadet, and began my career as a teacher in the public schools of Chicago. I was sent into the room of a first grade teacher who, I thought was cruel to her little students. The second grade teacher whom I helped a little was stupid, I thought. I asked to be sent into the room of the third grade teacher who seemed bright and alert and had no trouble with discipline. She was not well and I spent most of my time in her room trying to understand her techniques. I came to the conclusion that her children were interested because she herself was so much alive.

After a few months I was assigned to a second grade room. . . .

One of the first things Ella Flagg Young did as Superintendent was to tell us teachers that we were professionals not mere maids and she abolished the wearing of white aprons, or any kind of aprons, in our class rooms. . . .

In a whole year I attended [only] one teacher's institute meeting where Professor Jackman spoke to us about the various parts of flowers. . . . The only lesson in pedagogy I had ever had was that I should know each day what I was expected to teach and to keep one lesson ahead of my class. And so, I learnt by trial and error. Where I was interested, my class of twenty children was interested.

The subjects, naturally, in the 2nd grade, were exceedingly easy. On the last day of school, on a June morning, the children gathered around me. Many of them hoped that I would be their teacher in the next year in the third grade. It was tremendously encouraging. . . .

Looking back over that year, I wonder how I did it. Our principal came into my room. He said to me "You are a born teacher." I didn't know what he meant, but as I closed my door I had a powerful experience. I looked back into the room, and it seemed to me that in that room that there had been some kind of tremendous force, growing, like sap that pushes its way up in a tree against the forces that would pull it down — that would naturally pull it down. That force had pushed its way through in the growing minds of the children. I couldn't have chopped it; I could guide it — guide it rightly or wrongly. But greater even than the combined force of the children I knew there had been something in me that had grown and expanded. I knew that it was more important to develop personality than to teach arithmetic and spelling.[41]

About this time [1892], the new University of Chicago opened its doors on the Midway. Its policy was most liberal. Unclassified students were allowed to enter and receive credit for whatever work they did and could, after they reached a specified age, take as much or as little work as they chose and have their credits entered toward a degree.[42]

I passed entrance exams easily in subjects that to-day are classified in the University as The Humanities. In fact, I was an unclassified student at Cobb Hall, the first building erected on the campus before even Cobb was entirely built. There were not many colleges in those days for women. Among all the girls I knew, there were only three who had college ambitions. They were rather brilliant girls and I did not feel myself in a class with them. There wasn't at that time, a woman's college in Chicago, and the majority of persons were still prejudiced against what was known as "the higher learning for women." . . . Broadminded as my mother was, she opposed my going to college. . . .

[B]ecause I wanted to go to college I was called a blue-stocking and there was a dire prediction in the family that I'd never find a husband.[43] Yet I was the first of the girl cousins to marry and my education whatever education I was able to pick up did me no harm — because whenever I did not know how to do a thing I could always look it up in a book.

I loved my classes [at the university] with as intense a love as I had hated learning the preliminaries that made it possible for me to attend them.[44]

Just as I have been reading Emerson all my life, I have felt the continuing influence in my life of the University of Chicago since [the] day it opened its doors within walking distance from our home. . . . Much as I owe to books, my major education, however, came from just living.[45]

Later in my life, when I became a mother, and still later when I became the president of a large woman's club, I knew that my success was due to the lessons I myself had learned.[46]

Getting educated has been the supreme adventure of my life.[47]

I grow more and more sure that to live an intellectual life adventuring into books, learning constantly, growing kinder and more tolerant — is the only wise, sure way of living.[48]

I should hate to think that my education stopped when I left the last class I attended at the University of Chicago.[49]

We pass through all the experiences that life offers to us and round out the end to where we began. The greatest of all our abilities, is the ability to learn. We may stop going to school when we have completed a set curriculum, but the curriculum of life goes on.[50]

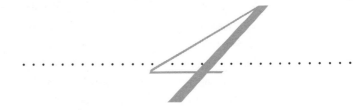

Grandpa and Emerson, 1876–1898

In our home, before my father had died, we experienced no religious observances[,] for our father and his brothers were among the first of the liberal minded Jews of Chicago. . . . [After my father died] we . . . moved from what had been our parents' home to what was considered Grandpa's household.[1]

If the training of a child begins with its grandparents, I was very intelligent in the choice of mine. I loved my mother's father deeply. He was the greatest influence in my early adolescence that probably helped me to be what I am. . . .

Grandpa . . . was intelligent, well informed, genial, or what the Germans called *Gemütlich*, a completely untranslatable word, never too much good at making a living, and he was above all, extremely religious. By trade he was a book-binder, not a good business man, for he often stopped to read the books while he should have been binding them.[2]

To Grandpa I owe my understanding of religion which I could never have had if I had not seen him live the poetry of it. Grandpa understood how earnestly I tried to be good. The recollection of it was the first great success of my life.[3]

I know I sometimes went on Saturday A.M.'s with [Grandpa] to his orthodox German synagogue on May Street. The blocks between May Street and wherever the synagogue was on May Street from our house at Randolph and Sheldon Streets were very long. Riding on the Sabbath Day was a sin. Sometimes the little girl who was I and the old man who was grandpa in our best clothes, walked alone — sometimes Mamma and the other children came too. The little girl, holding Grandpa's hand, trudging along beside him, must have given Grandpa some hope that his precious religion might pass on to another generation. I wish I could know what was in that little girl's mind beside her complete trust and sense of security in Grandpa and in God. Sometimes she asked God for special favors, when someone was sick or went on a journey — to make the sick person well, or keep the traveller safe. But I know, for the most part, she was a little anxious about God, she did not want to offend Him not because of any fear of punishment but because she was so very anxious to please Him. God was kind and reliable. He was not omnipresent. She often forgot about Him, but on the instant she could find Him if, or when, she needed Him.[4]

Grandpa observed the Jewish dietary laws. . . . Before a meal Grandpa recited a blessing. That, not being the head of the household, I could not do. But Grandpa said a longer prayer that seemed to us children interminable, a very long one after meals. That one I could read in a German prayer book we had. Before we came to live with Grandpa, we had been taught a German night prayer. That one I always said. It began "Ich schließe meine Augen wieder [und] denk an Gott mein Hüter" [I close my eyes again (and) think of God my guardian]. I liked the sound of it, but hardly ever thought of its meaning. I went religiously to Temple and had so great a veneration for our big, German bible and our prayer books that I never allowed even a piece of paper to be laid on them. Always I removed anything that some other person had placed there.

Perhaps I developed other taboos. I do not remember, but by and large, if Grandpa said a thing was wrong, in my eyes, it was wrong. Among other things Grandpa took a nap every afternoon from 1 to 3. It was wrong, during those hours, to make a noise that would wake Grandpa. To awaken parents or grandparents was a sin. To this day, if I can help it, I never awaken a sleeping person.[5]

To a cousin, Irma wrote that in addition to not awakening her grandfather, there were other rules: "[H]is prayers must never be disturbed, and no one was allowed to sit in his chair."[6]

In [Grandpa's] household, by daily observance, we learned some valuable lessons. Today, among our contemporaries, there are almost none who know the picturesque quality of the outward observance of an ancient faith founded by an agricultural community, that supposedly as shepherds, had wandered long years through desert country. The new moon, the return of spring, the early and the late harvest[,] the return of a longer sunlight and the lengthening of the days are the foundation out of which the Jewish holidays, described in the richest literature the world has ever known. And, at the return of autumn, before the great harvest Thanksgiving holidays, ten days set aside for meditation on happiness, good cheer and sin. That . . . day, devoted to the contemplation and reformation of the sin, is the holiest day in the Jewish calendar, so holy that it is a day set aside for fasting and mourning and praying [and it] would be intolerable if it were not soon followed by the joyous harvest festival of Thanksgiving and preceded by the happy joyous festival of the New Year.

All of these festivals have their specialized symbolic observances and their specialized prayers. I observed them all, perhaps a little more seriously or solemnly than the other children because I was at that stage of pre-adolescence when white was white and black was black, and it was all or nothing.

And then came the heartbreak.

When I asked Grandpa and Mamma who were more observers of religion than students of religion, "Why? Why must I do this?" or "Why must I not do this?" And the answer came back, "Because the bible says so," or "the prayer book says so."

"But why do they say so?" And the answer here was, "Don't ask so many questions." But I went on asking them in my mind. And I determined to find out.[7]

When the answer was the bible says, or the bible commands this or that, I became an avid reader of the bible without understanding much about it. . . . I must have asked innumerable questions. Later when my own children began to ask questions, I did a great deal of studying so that I could answer them at least with an attempt at intelligence.[8]

Irma learned Hebrew, taught at the Zion Temple Sabbath school beginning at the age of sixteen, wrote a weekly column for the paper the *Sabbath Visitor*, and contributed to the *Jewish Voice*. She continued to teach in Sabbath school until the birth of her first child in 1899, yet she never considered herself religious in the same sense that she thought her grandfather had been.[9] In fact, in 1891 she mentioned that she had just finished reading Emerson's *Essay on Courage*. Somehow Emerson's writings always seem to put me in tune with the world. . . . [I]t seems to me he wrote that just for *me*. I always want to go to college harder when I have been reading Emerson. I try to read one essay a week in place of going to Temple. Our people think I've grown to be frightfully irreligious and I think I'm more religious than I was before tho' in a different manner. I've always had to suffer one way or another through religion. Either I was too religious to suit the people and now I'm not pious enough. Somehow I can't strike the happy medium in these matters.[10]

It was around this same time that Irma first became active in a charitable organization, a relief agency. She continued to be involved in social and philanthropic causes throughout much of her life, most likely because of her grandfather's influence and her early religious upbringing. She explained the background to her commitment in terms of "training by example."

What drew me close to Grandpa was that I wanted to be a good girl. We thought we were bad children because we made a noise, and I wanted, above all things, to be good. Grandpa was considered a good, religious man and so, possibly I attempted Grandpa's brand of goodness, as I have attempted many other brands throughout my life[.] (My best friend once said that I had an ingrowing conscience) where or how I acquired a conscience I do not know.

I am not aware that I wanted to please Grandpa as much as I may have thought the road to goodness lay through imitating my good grandpa. . . .

One of the high spots of my childhood came one afternoon, after Grandpa had had his nap, when he said to me, "I want to speak to you alone." For a moment I was frightened. He pulled me toward him, took a silver dollar out of one of his pockets and said to me, "I want to give you this, because you are a good girl, and I want you to spend it for something you want for yourself."

We children had no allowances and rarely had more than a few pennies which we hoarded. To have a whole dollar, to have Grandpa say I was a good girl, was one of the supreme moments of my life.

I consulted my sister. Together we went over to West Madison Street and I bought myself a small string of tiny little pearl beads to go around my neck, and a pink ribbon with a fancy edge to wear when I should not be wearing the pearls. I still have a few of the pearls and a little piece of the pink ribbon I bought over seventy years ago. I could never bear to part with them. What I bought for my sister I do not remember. I had a guilty feeling about not giving the whole dollar to "the poor" but Grandpa had said I should buy something for myself. If you want to be good, you should always carry around with you a guilty feeling because there are so many things you want to have, and you want to do, that weren't good when your particular brand of goodness denies you the self-gratifications that, in the long run, for your own development might be better than Puritanic self-denial.[11]

Irma's comment about feeling guilty for not giving some of her windfall to the poor is understandable within the context of the Jewish Talmudic concept of *tzedakah*. Its roots lie in the Hebrew word *Tzade-Dalet-Qof*. It means justice, fairness, or righteousness. Frequently applied to benevolent acts or charitable deeds, such as giving money to help the poor, it is more than that. *Tzedakah* is a moral obligation, a duty. Reform Judaism believes that *tzedakah* and *tikkun olam* [repairing the world] are almost as important as the Torah, or Bible stories.

A Chicago newspaper article from 1893 demonstrates the extent to which Irma and one of her cousins took that concept to heart by working to relieve the misery of some of the urban poor living close to them in ghettos.

DIED OF STARVATION — WHAT TWO WOMEN FOUND

Destitution among the unemployed. . . . Such was the discovery yesterday of Miss Foreman and Miss Rosenthal whose names have recently become public in connection with the charitable work of the Kopperl relief agency. While some people are trying to decide the best means of relieving the distress of the poor in Chicago and others are holding aloof for fear of giving aid to the undeserving, Miss Foreman and Miss Rosenthal are going into the houses of the needy and relieving their wants. Although the work done by these self-appointed dispensers of charity has but recently become public an investigation shows that they have for more than a year been engaged in visiting the sick and poor, giving money and clothes to the destitute. . . . Accompanied by Mrs. Kopperl and their uncle . . . the young women went on a tour of the 12th Street district where many people are out of employment and in need of food.

By helping the poor, Irma obeyed the commandment to perform *mitzvot* [good deeds]. Her good deeds were part of the larger social movements begun between 1890 and 1900. This decade saw the rise of settlement houses and the establishment of church- and religious-based service organizations, all of which were geared toward helping new immigrants and the urban poor assimilate into American society, feel less disconnected within the ever-growing cities, and get training and jobs.[12] By 1890, many American cities had become crowded and filthy, even in the wealthier sections. In *How the Other Half Lives* (1890) Jacob Riis, the Danish-born New York journalist, wrote a particularly powerful exposé of governmental corruption, open sewers and drainage canals, sickness, poor or nonexistent services, increasing racial tensions, and ever more immigration into the city centers. Conditions were deplorable, and in the summer of 1893 a depression began. By the time it ended, four years later, approximately fifteen thousand businesses had failed, six hundred banks had collapsed, fifty railroads were bankrupt, and 2.5 million Americans were unemployed.

After 1859, Chicago Jews who needed assistance could turn to the United Hebrew Relief Association or to private charities run by temples or funded by wealthy individuals.[13] However, it does not appear that charity was extended to all the poor regardless of religion or ethnicity until Jane Addams brought the Settlement Movement to Chicago from England. During the depression of 1893, one Chicago institution, Hull House in the Nineteenth Ward on the Near West Side, figured prominently in relief efforts. In fact, Hull House became the district bureau of the Central Relief Association. The women of Hull House, led by Jane Addams and her friend Ellen Gates Starr, dispensed food, coal, and clothes to the poor, who lived mostly on the Near West Side of Chicago.

Hull House, as stated in its charter, was "to provide a center for the higher civic and social life; to institute and maintain educational and philanthropic enterprises, and to investigate and improve the conditions in the industrial districts of Chicago."[14] The settlement workers considered Hull House to be an extension of home and, as such, a valid outlet for the volunteerism which many nineteenth-century middle-class women practiced.[15] As the rationale for Hull House women's public reform efforts, Addams argued that "[r]uling a city was enlarged housekeeping, and women, the traditional housekeeper, should take over. The men of the city have been carelessly indifferent to much of this civic housekeeping, as they have always been indifferent to the details of the household."[16]

It was within this milieu of social consciousness that Irma, raised within a religious tradition that stressed service and good deeds, moved. According to her diaries, Emerson, Ruskin, Darwin, and Spencer, besides her grandfather's teachings, profoundly interested and excited her when she was a teenager.

Like so many American-born Jews of her generation, Irma joined a Reform temple when she became an adult. And, as the years went by, she became more inclined to read Emerson than to attend religious services. However, a deep sense of moral obligation to help others, and social values that were both Emersonian and Jewish, always underlay her apparent nonreligiosity. She commented, "Although the forms of religion, its static quality when misunderstood, have often offended me, I appreciate the values, which in the course of evolution have helped humanity to pull itself up by the bootstraps."[17]

By 1910, Irma noted, she owned "60 volumes of Emerson, more than 5 ft. long." She dipped into those volumes for inspiration throughout her life. In a very real sense, then, Emerson's words became another model for her conduct and for the numerous books she started to write but never finished. Emerson, she wrote,

exalts what he calls "the moral sentiment." And why not? Religion is founded on it largely — the supreme achievement whereby human beings can live together is the code of "The Ten Commandments" and Society can exist only if it observes them. If then the nucleus of Society is the family — for better or for worse we had better pay attention to how to keep the family as a unit, what does each family stand for — and since fundamentally the family should be based on the love of two persons of opposite sexes whose love branches out to include the children who come into being through the love of the first two in their love for one another.[18]

Emerson preached his gospel in the present — God speaks now. The measure of a great man is in bringing other men to agree with his opinion.[19]

This A.M., for a few minutes, I went back to the reading of Emerson's *Representative Men*. When I am a little weary of other reading, I can always wake up by reading something of Emerson, or William James.[20]

If you always force yourself to do what you ought to do, and do it in the way you honestly believe is the best way instead of listening to your inclination to shirk responsibility or consult your comfort or convenience you will very materially strengthen your character and your judgment.

Whatever you do in life keep in an ambition-arousing atmosphere. Keep close to those who are dead. . . [to those] who are anxious to do something in the world. You will catch the spirit of your environment.[21]

Throughout her life, Irma often struggled to align Emerson's ideals of truth and beauty with the biblical teachings and Judaism she had learned as "rules." For example, on one occasion, she reflected that

[i]ntervals of work, of prosaic reality, divide our moments of beauty. And it is only in flashes that real exaltation alights in our soul, we grasp it for but a fraction of time, and it is fine. But the hope that it will come again should never die out in our hearts. Gerson Levi told me that for him the beauty of the belief in God lies in this particular fact, that we experience God only at intervals — we are not sure — we lose God.

Somehow it suggests to me the biblical phrase: "The hem of His mantle." We would cling to it always but God must be fine. He has work to do — and I presume if we do ours we shall meet our Fellow-worker sometimes in the most unexpected places. . . .

When we really feel beauty — when it sinks into our soul — then we are tranquil — then we have arrived somewhere — perhaps we are nearing the presence of God.[22]

But at other times she framed her idea of beauty solely in transcendentalist terms, as she did in May 1924, following a concert.

The forces that be — you may call them God if you like — have created this universe of sight and sound with its phases of beauty — and a bit of that creative urge is in us when we try to reflect this beauty in another medium. I do not know how it is done — 'tis another miracle, I think . . . [part] of our reluctance to let the finer things of life fade away, fade into nothingness.

However much Irma relied on Emerson's transcendentalist sayings and essays, she never relinquished her Jewish faith or respect for its traditions, as evidenced in her 1934 account of her mother's death, and her discussion of the High Holy Days.

To-morrow it will be six months that my mother died. My mother's death made a profound impression on me. Every now and then we have come up with not truth, but what is better stated as *a* truth. In forty years — the biblical forty years — our family had not known the experience of death. After about 4 years of the ebbing away of her strength, a pitiable thing to see, she fell quietly and softly to sleep — no struggle at the end — she fell asleep as I have seen tired babies fall asleep. Esther, Meta, Victor [Irma's husband], Ruth [Irma's daughter] and I were in the room. We were all very quiet. Esther turned to me with a catch in her voice and said, "Let's say *Shema Yisrael*" and so Meta and Esther and I said *Shema Yisrael Adonai Eloheinu Adonai Echad* [Listen, Israel: Adonai is our God, Adonai is One!]— She probably did not hear us. We hoped she could and not be frightened. She moved her lips once a little but not as if she wanted to speak. . . .

I wanted to hold her hand but felt self-conscious about it. And so I stepped to the head of the bed, Meta stood at the foot, and I sat down on something that stood near, and stroked her forehead — stroked her hair that had always been lovely. I think Victor and Ruth and I were there about twenty minutes before the end came. And perhaps the real end . . . lasted five minutes. . . . Her last breaths came softly and easily. We dreaded a struggle. But there was none. There was none.

She wasn't cold — not right away. . . . And then Victor and the nurse began doing things as they do for dead people. I heard Victor say, "Straighten out her limbs," and the nurse did. She seemed inert, and helpless and something —[23]

Then, in a letter to one of her grandsons, dated Friday, September 9, 1949, Irma wrote

I have missed you. Perhaps you do not know that to-day is *Rosh Hashanah*. Mom [Irma's daughter Emily] and Laurie [Irma's grandson] came in last night after they had been to temple and wished us a

Happy New Year. I was not thinking of the so-called religious aspect of the holiday, but I am thinking that life would be rather drab if we were never to have special days or celebrations. The Jewish holidays are events in families and some nuances were recalled to my mind by the day's events.

We talked, too, about our brother Emil, who died fifty-eight years ago on the eve of Rosh Hashanah. A Jewish custom is to have what they call Jahrzeit for the one who was held dear, and if you go to temple or have a service of your own, you say the Kaddish blessing. Did you ever read [your uncle's] exposition of the Kaddish, an interesting, historical piece of writing. Fortunately you do not know these customs from [a personal] experience [of death], as we did. Religious Jews kindle a light and do not let it go out for 24 hours in memory of those who are gone. I like that custom. I put on one of the little side lights in my room and all day, either in my consciousness or my subconscious I seemed to have sensed a gentleness that was my brother's attitude toward us girls. . . .

Maybe the significance of religious holidays lies in just such remembrances as I have noted above. Don't forget that while Freud has called attention to the frustration in our subconscious, in the as yet not completely explored subconscious, there must be too fulfillments that cross the threshold into consciousness in our best moments. I do not remember if this occurs in the Rosh Hashanah service, or maybe it is only on Yom Kippur when there is a prayer about inclining the hearts of the parents to the children, and the hearts of the children to the parents. Perhaps many a Jewish family remained intact when they lived up to it. In the very nature of our lives families must scatter, but the bond remains, and whether it is tinged with bitterness or glowing with grateful memories, it is somewhat of our own choosing. For [if] living can be an art, and the very first principle of any art form is selection, which shall we choose? [24]

Young Love, 1891

In 1953, Irma mused about the summer, more than half a century before, when she had accompanied her mother, brother, and uncle to Atlantic City for a two-week rest cure. Back then, Irma was considered "delicate" and her mother "sickly," and her brother Emil suffered from what may have been a tuberculosis related back problem.[1] Sea breezes were believed to invigorate, so this resort spa seemed an especially alluring destination for midwesterners.

Atlantic City became a booming resort and spa in the 1880s, and by 1891 there was a real demand for hotel accommodations during the hot summer months. Modern luxury hotels, such as the Lafayette and the block-long United States Hotel, went up in large numbers to serve the wealthy. Smaller boardinghouses, too, opened throughout the town in response to the increased tourist demand.

The New Jersey seashore offered a welcome respite from city heat. Bicycles, boats, and fishing equipment could be rented for the day. Crabs and clams were free for the taking. Swimming was safe along the eight-mile beach monitored by professionally trained lifeguards on duty from 9 A.M. to 5 P.M. While the sickly sat on hotel verandas, the younger set bowled, danced, bicycled, and rode electric cars. But best of all, the wide wooden boardwalk was punctuated with numerous amusement piers that jutted into the ocean at right angles from the boardwalk. Carousel rides, magic acts, vaudeville-like variety skits, as well as solid family entertainment such as Gordon Lillie's "Original Pawnee Bill's Wild West Show," amazed and delighted vacationers of all ages.

All summer long, a narrow-gauge train line carried tourists and convalescents across the bridge connecting the mainland to the island resort. During the Gay Nineties, Atlantic City was *the* place on the Eastern Seaboard to promenade, to dally, to dance, and to fall in love.[2]

How fresh and vivid it grows for a few moments as I recall it. I was young, nineteen years old to be exact. I must have been pretty because I had very white skin, very dark hair, and a slender figure. And also I was very, very serious, greatly troubled about life, and destiny and what it was all about, and most eager to study everything. I hoped I was pretty, but to admit it even to myself would have been sinful vanity. Sometimes some one would admire my hair, or my eyes, and people used to say I had a nice complexion, and one of my sisters liked my hands which have since grown a little less white but more capable. I still remember how tightly I drew in my corsets because I was proud, secretly, of my slender waist. I presume the girls in our family were moderately "stylish" for we could afford good clothes, but I was much more concerned about my character than about my appearance.

And then I met him. Mother, and my older brother who was very ill, and I, were at a fashionable watering place by the sea. I was sitting on the huge veranda of the hotel as he and his sister came up the wide stairs leading to the lobby, carrying their bags. I looked up from my book long enough to think "What a handsome fellow," and then I went on with my reading. The handsome young man undoubtedly wouldn't notice me. There were many attractive girls at the hotel much more lively than I was. I always regretted that I was not livelier. In the afternoon, however, after dinner, when there were very few persons on the porch, I saw him come out from the lobby[,] look around, and then to my great amazement, walk slowly to the empty rocking-chair next to mine. My heart beat wildly. What a pity that there was no one to introduce us. To speak to a young man without being introduced would have been the extreme of boldness. I wanted to very much. But I was sure he would have been shocked — he would [be] thinking me a bad, brazen person and so I could never have hoped to win his regard.

To my astonishment, though, after a short interval, he began to talk to me. Instantly I fell in love with his voice — it had a peculiar inflection [and] I have never forgotten it — As if he might have been a fine singer whose speaking voice had the quality of prose music. Now that I think about it Ronald Coleman speaks like that.

"I understand," he said, "that you come from Chicago."

"Yes," I answered.

"I have a friend, my college chum, who comes from Chicago — I wonder if you know him." He mentioned his name.

"Know him," I answered. "Why yes. We've been to picnics together — he was my partner at a wedding." I am sure I blushed crimson at this stage, because I had often been teased about him.

I must interrupt my story a minute to tell why I had been "teased" about this young man's college chum. One autumn before his chum left for college, he sought out my mother and asked her if he might correspond with me while he was gone. My mother replied that she would not approve of his writing to me, that I was only sixteen, and that it would be better if I kept my mind on my school-work than if I thought about young men. That was why our crowd teased me. Fancy a college fellow, in those days, asking a girl's mother if he may be allowed to write her sophisticated sixteen-year-old a letter and have her answer it.

This very handsome young man, with the strangely beautiful voice and English accent, was asking me if I knew Jack who had the boldness to tell me one moonlit summer evening while we were walking through Jackson Park on our way to the street-car, having in some strange way fallen behind the rest of the picnic crowd, that he liked me — and I was too confused to answer.

"Yes," I was saying, "I know Jack."

The handsome young man gave me a strange look. I heard him say to himself in a questioning way—Dark hair, white skin, brown eyes—quiet, studious . . .

"Do you . . . ," he began. His searching look, I recall, embarrassed me and no doubt, I blushed again. "Do you happen to know a young lady named . . ." and he mentioned my own name.

I know that I hedged for a moment. For a long time afterward I regretted that I did not play with him a bit, get him to tell me all he knew about the young lady before I told him that I was the one.

I recall, however, that I asked, "How do you happen to know her name?"

"Jack and I roomed together all the time we were in college. He used to tell me he was in love with her. It bored me dreadfully. He was never sure that she cared for him but being in love with her didn't keep him from going out with other girls." . . .

If my heart had not been beating so furiously I knew I could have played along with the idea of telling him that the young lady was an acquaintance of mine. Have him tell me all about her and then finally, when I might have said something uncomplimentary, I might have declared "I am she"— or "her."—I was very particular about my grammar. I presume I should have said "I am she." If I could have declared it of course [in a] dramatic manner. It would have been fun. But when your heart is running wild you are frightened and you blurt out things.

We talked all afternoon. My mother scolded me at supper time because I had not come up to our room at 4 to change my dress. It was shocking. I had to hurry to change from my blue and white striped "blaze suit" into my tight rose-colored satin with white lace trimming.

All I recall of the afternoon's conversation was that we discussed books we had been reading and that once when I said something about our mutual friend, Jack, which I cannot for the life of me remember, the handsome young man said sarcastically, "That's water on his mill." I had never heard that expression before — and it made an impression.[3]

An undated entry written sometime during 1953 perhaps explains what triggered this memory, if a true memory it was. One of Irma's cousins had recently run into a handsome white-haired clergyman with a remarkable voice, then either telephoned or wrote to Irma about the encounter: "They discovered that they had many mutual friends. Finally my cousin said, 'I'm surprised that you do not know my family. Your paths [must] have crossed sometime [since] your professions are the same.'" Then she scribbled, at the bottom of the booklet following her story, that the man had apparently asked, in his still remarkable voice: "Tell me again the names of some of [your cousins]— their names as girls." "My cousin mentioned, among others, my name. He repeated it, and then added, 'She was a sweetheart of mine — once.'"

Irma's actual diary entries for that summer of 1891 only hint at the great emotion and the unrequited young love revealed in that tale. Before her journey, however, she recorded the following:

Tried to economize on clothes this spring as a preparation. Don't know how far I succeeded. . . . Had a brave week lately. Had a tooth extracted, confronted Uncle Joe with an argument after a scolding, called on Uncle Julius and did a number of other things I was greatly afraid of doing. I often try to do things I'm afraid of doing, just for the practice.

Am learning to swim, and can ride the [women's high-] wheel [adult tricycle]. Enjoy both.

After my week of bravery I put in a week mainly devoted to philosophy, Darwin and thinking.[4]

Following that entry, she began to chronicle her activity-filled days in Atlantic City.

Monday, July 6, 1891
Took train for Atlantic City. Arrived 6:45. Met Emil at depot. . . . Went to our room. Had supper. Took a stroll on board walk with Emil and Uncle. Great place. Met the C. family from Philadelphia on walk. Came home. Retired.

Tuesday, July 7
Met Emil 8:30 for breakfast. After breakfast, sat on veranda. Wrote letters. Took stroll to beach with C's etc. Watched uncle and Gus go in bathing. Had dinner. Took nap. Trunk arrived 4:15. Unpacked. Took walk to beach with uncle and Emil 'til supper. After supper called on C's at U.S. hotel. Beautiful hotel. Went into hall and danced.

Thursday, July 9
Weather nice. Breakfast 9:00 — Wrote letters. Went to beach with C's. Took first surf bath. Went in with uncle and Gus. Breakers [a] little strong. Liked it very much. Wasn't a bit frightened. Felt fine afterwards. Dinner. Felt tired. Took nap. Rode out to Inlet with Emil, Mamma and Gus—Very nice place. Met uncle there. Took ride to other end of car-hill. Atlantic City a great place. Never had imagined any place like it. Came home. Dressed. Supper. Read. C's came. Went into parlor. Met some Southern girls. Talked etc. Took walk to beach with C's. Went to Schaufler's garden. Came home. Wrote. Retired very late. Had good time all day. Saw a queer fish. (Flounder I believe it was.) Also saw a boat that had been thrown upon the coast by the water. The more I see of this place, the better I like it. Sorry Essie isn't here.

Saturday, July 11
Put on a respectable dress and attended services on Atlantic Avenue. Sat in pavilion on the beach and read a few prayers while everybody

went bathing. In the P.M. went to the Inlet with Clara, Gus, Emil and Miss S. Changed dress. Supper. Talked to Dr. K. Attended hop at "the States." Few gentlemen there. Gus only person I danced with. Came home 11 P.M. . . . Sat out on porch and talked 'til 12.

Sunday, July 12
Read and talked. Was introduced to Rabbi F. of Denver by Mr. C. Went to Inlet with Rabbi F., Clara and Mr. C. Went out into ocean on a little steamer. Sea-sick after being out about 15 minutes. Dinner. Went out on veranda to read. Was introduced to Rabbi Levi . . . by Rabbi F. Talked to Rabbi Levi about 2 hours. Spent very pleasant afternoon. Also spoke to Dr. K. for a while. Had a discussion (Dr. K. and Rabbi Levi had the discussion) on the best way to teach miracles to children. Changed dress. In the evening sat out on porch and talked. Clara and Gus over. Like Rabbis F. and Levi [but] fear that they know a little too much for me to feel comfortable in their society.

Monday, July 13
Wrote letters after breakfast. Rabbi F. left. Went down to beach and watched the bathers. Talked. Dinner. Stayed out on the porch. Talked etc. Dressed. Supper. Sat in parlor and talked. Rabbi Levi came in. Had very interesting talk. Mr. Levi left. Took walk with Mamma. Mr. Levi returned. Sat out on porch and talked to Mr. Levi . . . 'til 10:45. Retired. Very favorably impressed with Mr. Levi seems too good and handsome for safety.

Tuesday, July 14
Rain. Couldn't go to beach. Felt very sorry. Clara here. Talked to Clara and the girls all morning. Went bowling in the P.M. . . . Mr. C. won game. [I] made [the] lowest score (zero). Mr. Levi very nice. Came home. Supper. Dressed. Went over to "the States." Felt blue. Don't remember when I felt so blue. Mr. Levi [was the] cause of it. Danced little. Walked home with Mr. Levi and sister. Talked little while. Retired.

Wednesday, July 15
Felt very little better. Sat on porch. Went down to beach. In the P.M., went up to room with Miss Levi. Dressed. Walked out to Inlet with girls. Mr. C., Emil, Mr. Levi also in party. Received *Israelite*. Felt

highly elated over what it said about the prayer-work I helped translate.[5] After supper, took little walk with Miss Levi. Sat out and listened to a discussion on marriage etc. between the girls, Uncle Joe and Mr. K. [W]ent in. Talked to Mr. Levi little while. Retired early. Very blue yet. Am very happy that Mr. Levi will leave tomorrow. He doesn't like me any better than any of the other girls and is entirely too dangerous.

Thursday, July 16
Arose early. Took stroll on board walk. . . . Talked to Mr. Levi 'til breakfast time. After breakfast, waited for Clara etc. Went to beach. Went in bathing. Had good time. Misses and Mr. M., uncle, Mr. Levi, Mr. C., the Richmond girls and Miss F. all went in together. Had group tin-type taken. . . . Dinner. Took little nap. Sat out on porch and talked to the girls and Emil. Mr. Levi and sister left 5:00 P.M. Very happy and yet very sorry that they went. Dressed. Wrote letter home. Supper. Talked to Emil and Minnie S. Went over to "States." Had long, confidential chat with Clara. Clara in same boat in regard to Mr. Levi. Are girls silly? Felt relieved after talking to Clara. Mamma, uncle, Mr. and Mrs. S., Minnie, Miss O. and I went to Hockheimer's. Very tired. Came home, very late. Slept better than I had slept for a week.

Friday, July 17
Breakfast. Wrote long 12 page letter to Esther. Clara came. Went to beach. Had picture taken in bathing costume with uncle. Dinner. Talked to Emil and Minnie. Went up to room. Fixed up drawers, trunk etc. Wrote etc. Dressed. There is nothing like work. Forgot all about Mr. Levi in working around. Dressed. Supper. Talked etc. Read etc. Hop here. Went into ball room short time. Sat out on porch and talked to Blanche W. Stayed down in hall 'til nearly 12:00. Retired.

Saturday, July 18
Raining hard. Couldn't go to Temple. Sat in hall and talked. Read. Read prayers etc. Dinner. Took nap. Slept from 3 to 6. Dr. R. from Atlanta, Georgia called. Supper. Dr. R. sent me some flowers. First time such a thing ever happened to me. Went over to "the States" to see Clara. Didn't care about going into ball-room. Came home, late. Retired near 11.

Tuesday, July 21

Arose 6 A.M. Breakfast 7. Went out to Inlet with party of 22 — 15 girls, 7 young men. Had delightful sail on Inlet and went crabbing. Caught 10 crabs in entire party. Came home 11:30. Went bathing. After dinner, wrote letters. In the evening went over to "States" with Emil for a short time. Came home. Sat out on porch. Mamma not well.

Sunday, August 2

Talked to several people. Mr. W. and Tillie and Nora W. called. Went bathing. . . . Dinner. Sat out on porch and talked to Mr. H. and Mr. B. all P.M. Went up stairs at 6 o'clock. Dressed. Supper. Talked to different people etc. Took a stroll on board-walk with Mr. H., later sat down in one of pavilions. Came home at about 10:30. Sat out on porch and talked 'til 12:00. Retired. Mr. H. is about as nice a person as I have ever met. Perhaps a little nicer.

Monday, August 3

Arose later, as usual. Wrote letters. Clara came. Went to beach with Clara. Sat down in sand. Took walk along the beach. Went back to hotel. Sat out on porch. Dinner. Talked to a number of people. Went out with Miss M. and the youngest Mr. L. Tried the switch-back and carousel, watched a base-ball game. Went to Atlantic Avenue, did a little shopping — deli pickles — and had a good time in general. Came home, changed dress. Supper. Sat on porch and talked to Mr. B. and Mr. H. Went to "States" and called on Mrs. W. with Mamma. Came home at 10 o'clock. Took walk with Mr. H. Went to board-walk. Rode on carousel and toboggan-slide. Hurt one of my fingers a little bit. Was caught in the rain. Had on thin slippers and thin stockings etc. Sat down in carousel place for a while. Mr. H. was fortunate enough to find some one, who lent him an umbrella. Went back to hotel. Talked for moments and retired at about 11:30.

Wednesday, August 5

Sat out on porch as usual and talked to a lot of people. Went to beach. Dinner. Went out to see Pawnee Bill's Wild West Show. . . . Enjoyed it quite well. Dressed. Supper. Talked etc. Went to concert at "the States" with Mr. H. Concert over at 10:00. Went to board-walk with Mr. H. and Mr. Hamburg from Philadelphia. Came home 11:30. Retired 12:00.

Thursday, August 6

Sat out on porch etc. S. family left. Went to depot. Went bowling. Met large party in bowling alley. Mr. Joseph H. kindly instructed me in the art. Bowled with Mr. B., Miss L. and Miss G. of Philadelphia. Mr. B. victorious. My record [was] 134. Called for Mamma at Kipple and McCaren's. Came back to hotel. Dinner. Sat out on porch. Blocks left. Sorry. Went to see them off. Took little stroll on board-walk with Dr. P. and Ida N. Wrote letters. Dressed. Talked. Supper. Sat on porch with the girls. Took little walk. Sat out on porch with Ida N. and the Messrs. H. 'til 11:30. Had lunch in writing-room. Retired 12:00.

Friday, August 7

Arose about same time as usual. Had a conversation with Mr. H. 'til about 11:30. Went to beach. Took Mamma to Kipple's. Sat down in the sand with a lot of people. Called for Mamma. Dinner. Sat out on porch and talked for a while. Wrote letters. Spent some time in Mrs. M's. room. Dressed. Supper. Stayed down stairs in hall and talked etc. Went in to hop with Mr. H. Enjoyed it more than any other hop down here. Took little stroll on board-walk with Mr. H. Retired 11:30.

Saturday, August 8

Emil not well. Stayed up stairs with Mamma and Emil. Went to services. Dr. Philipson spoke. Came home. Stayed with Emil. Dinner. Sat out on porch all P.M. Dressed. Supper. Stayed up stairs a-while. Went to board-walk with Mr. H., Christine H. and brother. Saw Morris' Illusions, rode on the switch-back, carousel etc. Came home. Sat on porch with Mr. H. . . . Retired 12:45.

Sunday, August 9

Emil no better. Stayed up stairs all A.M., packed etc. Dinner. Sat out on porch. Went up stairs 'til 4 o'clock. Came down. Went out to beach and sat on sand with Mr. H., Christine and brother. Had tin-types taken. Came home. Talked etc. Dressed. Supper. Stayed on porch little while. Went to Galbreath's drug store with Mr. H. Stayed up stairs with Mamma and Emil. Mr. H. came up stairs to see Emil. Went downstairs with Mr. H. and had a farewell talk on the side porch. Retired 12:00.

Wednesday, August 12

Had breakfast on dining car. Slept 'til we arrived in Chicago. Arrived 10 A.M. Here endeth a memorable trip East.

After that wonderful summer interlude of flirtations and flowers, Irma returned to Chicago, to teaching and attending college classes at the University of Chicago. No diaries survive until those of her December 1893 trip east to visit relatives. That two-month journey took her to Baltimore, New York, and Washington. She attended plays, crossed and recrossed the Brooklyn Bridge just for fun, and visited statehouses and art museums. She even shook Mrs. Grover Cleveland's hand at a White House tea, but there were no romances. By that time, she had already given her heart away. On Friday, September 4, 1953, she recollected how she first met Victor, the man she would eventually marry.

I was introduced to him one Sunday P.M. [in 1887] by a cousin of mine. His younger brother, who was handsome even up to his eightieth year was a member of our crowd. All summer long he had spoken about his big brother, who was going to be a doctor and was then visiting relatives in the East. When fall came he would bring him to one of our parties or picnics.

Fall came and the big brother came from the South Side where the two brothers lived with their family, to the West Side where we lived. When my cousin introduced us something should have clicked. Nothing did. Although he was good looking, with his reddish hair and intelligent gray eyes, he wasn't nearly so handsome as his younger brother who was a true blonde.

But it happened that I walked with the big brother from my cousin's house to our house, a distance of barely two blocks. For want of a better topic, although there could have been none better, we began to talk about school. He was attending the South Division and I the West Division High. He had roamed around the woods in Pennsylvania where his parents and brothers and sister lived, until he was ten years old when the family moved to Chicago. He made rapid progress in school. He was older than most of the students in his classes and therefore could advance quicker. He said science was fascinating but he had always liked history, too — and both of us took keen delight in learning ancient history, most especially did he like anything pertaining to Egypt. I loved everything pertaining to Greece.

It was a pleasant conversation, but I did not think too much about it afterward. The big brother began coming to the West Side every Sunday with his handsome younger brother. It was too far to go home for supper. And they often had some light supper with us. But that wasn't strange, anybody who wanted could stay for Sunday night supper. Very soon the lad who was to become a doctor grew to be one of my older brother's staunchest friends. They had much in common. They were very serious, both of them striving hard to become educated, both of them very conscientious in their desires to help their families.

We had a literary society that met every other Sunday. The members supplied the programs. We played piano solos, recited poems, wrote essays to be read at our meeting — danced when the meetings were over and in general were the happiest group of young persons any one had ever known. My older brother was the president of the society — a boy named Toby was the vice-president, our friend Emma was the recording secretary — my older sister [Essie] was a corresponding secretary and a cousin a treasurer — a goodly portion of the membership held office.

It was moved and seconded, and was passed that the society publish a literary journal. Our red-headed friend was considered a smart fellow, and so without any reference as to whether or not he could write, he was elected Editor.

It was moved and seconded, and passed that the Editor should have an assistant editor. I shone in the society, but not as a writer. I could play the *Misere* from the opera *Il Trovatore* with feeling, I think, because it made me very sad but it was the only piece, besides chopsticks and a duet . . . which I played with my cousin Belle, [that] I could play. Everybody said I played beautifully and I believed it.

I might have played better than I now remember because I had great patience and will power at the piano and practiced for hours at a time when no one stopped me. . . . I might have become a fair musician if I had been properly guided and been allowed to practice.

It turned out afterward that we had the worst piano teacher in Chicago. If my sister and I were budding geniuses, we were nipped in the bud. Still, our [literary] society, gave us opportunities to appear in public.

I had no idea that I should not be elected to any office as my brother and sister already held office. The assistant editorship went begging. We went home, and the gang came for supper. The editor-in-chief of the journal to be launched asked my sister, "Which one of you girls is to be my assistant?"

Great God! Didn't he know that it was I? I was never so hurt in my life. I did most of the work on the journal. I presume it was excellent practice. The paper was not too bad.

Irma kept only a single sample of her work for the literary society. It is dated Thursday, September 20, 1888.

HOW WE SPENT OUR SUMMER

Our ever kind and considerate executive committee has given me this extremely difficult subject upon which to write an essay. In the first place this was what is commonly called a *Sützba* [chutzpah, i.e., nerve] for the committee has no right to dictate their subjects to unfortunate people that must write essays. If it had been how I spent my summer I would simply have taken my diary and read to you what has been recorded there for the last few months, or if the names Bertha F., Frank R., Esther and some others were inserted in the place of "we" I could perhaps give you some idea of what some people did during the summer, but the "we" makes it difficult. I do not know how most of you passed your time during the past 2½ months and therefore have very little material upon which to go to work.

Many years later [1898], I married the editor and I've been doing most of the work ever since.[6]

My memories have come to keep me company.[7]

Marriage and Children, 1898–1906

One day in a long, long ago, . . . [Victor] was a young man with whom I was very much in love because he seemed so manly and reliable and intelligent, — handsome too, but not like an Apollo, more like some Rodin statue. I was young too, and slender, and he was in love with me because he said he would rather talk to me than to anyone he knew.

[Victor] said that some time he would like a house with a garden around it, and in one part of the house a laboratory where he could keep his precious microscope, and continue to mess around with his specimens of health and disease. He loved chemistry and physics, and had a scientific mind. If he could have he would have been a research man, but he had always been compelled to make a living to help his family. Even as a little boy, he sold newspapers, raised mint in his garden, and sold bunches of mint wherever he could, and ran errands for people, so he could earn some money to give to his mother who needed it.

Such talking together made me love him all the more, and I hoped I was good enough for him because we had promised, in the far distant future to marry each other. He was a senior medical student at that time. I was earning a little money by writing and teaching, although I was not a full fledged school-teacher and never became one.[1]

During our long engagement, my husband served his internship at one of our larger hospitals [Michael Reese], and then borrowed money to spend a year in post-graduate work in Heidelberg and Vienna. It was a trying year for both of us. . . . After his return we waited almost another year before we were married, for there were few patients, office rent to pay and a debt hanging over us. . . .

And then came one of the great adventures of my life — my marriage to the young M.D. who had been my brother's best friend. I was the first of my group to wear the wedding veil that in turn was worn by my best friend, my older sister etc. I loved the glamour of being a bride.[2] We were married in November [1898].[3]

We found [a] new apartment, near 45th St. which was then "way out South," moved the office into our home thereby paying very little more for rent than my husband had been paying above a drug store 10 blocks nearer the centre of town.[4]

[For our honeymoon] we rode to Evanston on a street car, remained there one day and visited Victor's old haunts at Northwestern University, specifically the biological laboratory in the basement of the science hall, the first building on the Northwestern campus. Then we returned to Chicago, had dinner at Rector's and went to our apartment . . . —[a] very elegant apartment where we had the first electric light and hot and cold water on tap always — the first among all the persons that we knew. Entire cost of our wedding trip was $10.00.[5] We had $180.00 left of our entire fortune, part of which had been wedding presents.

Our first breakfast, the morning after we returned from our honeymoon, consisted of some old, stale dry *schnecken* [rolled sweet bread] Mamma had given Victor the week before, washed down with a pint of milk the milkman had left us to try. Never has any meal tasted better. But we really needed a hot dish, freshly prepared for subsequent meals. . . . I resolved that if I had to cook, I'd try to be a good cook, and, furthermore if any one should be in the kitchen while I was cooking, that person would want to eat what I was preparing. I would never taste the soup or gravy without washing off the spoon, taste it again for a further judgment, that if I had to wash vegetables I would wash them very clean, in other words, that the process, as well as the end result would be appetizing.[6]

We were very happy. Everybody came to see "our flat" because we had the first electric lights, the first telephone and the first constant hot water of anybody we knew.[7]

Financially our first year of marriage was difficult and anxious and profitable.[8] . . . We had a telephone put in, on the wall in our hallway next to our bed-room [so Victor's patients could call]. I became its slave. . . . I taught Sunday school and had to get out, but, from Sunday night to the following Sunday A.M. I did not leave that telephone. We couldn't afford to miss a call.[9] Patients too began to come. Calls came in over the telephone.[10]

We never spent an unnecessary penny.[11] Our whole family rallied to our support. . . . Week-ends we went to Gramma's and had Sunday dinner always at [my aunt and uncle's house].[12] [My aunt] gave Victor and me ice-cream every Sunday . . . and believe me, every Sunday we had a good dinner.[13]

And while I felt that doing the housework in [the] apartment was not quite so irksome as it had been at home, I still did not like it. Before I was married, after we had moved from the West to the South Side, we had one maid. Essie and I did the daily dusting together. Then after I had registered at the University of Chicago for a class in English Composition, we had a division of labor. Essie did the bedroom floor and I the parlor floor, for that could be dusted earlier than the upper rooms, which had to be left 'til the beds were pulled apart and aired. The stairway was my job. It was a tremendous burden to me because of my inexperience. I never saw beyond it, and it always had to be done the same way. I arose early, did my dusting before 9 o'clock because I had a morning class, and the two things that made an impression were that if I were in a hurry I could skip the rungs of the chairs, but I couldn't skip anything on the staircase and that it seemed to me that I should be dusting that staircase forever. All of this might have been trivial, and probably was, but it is my state of mind about it that I remember vividly. I loved books, study and writing so intensely that [I] begrudged the time spent in other ways. And I did not then realize, and couldn't realize it, that life is ever changing and that it is only in the drabbest life that the same stairway would have to be dusted forever.[14]

I loved having company and quite as much as I delighted in the persons who came to see us, I was astonished that they came — that we were important enough to have some of these guests visit us, especially the older ones, like my aunts and some of Mamma's friends. One time, long before I was married, I heard Mamma and Mrs. Felsenthal (one of our neighbors) comment on a visit they paid somewhere and one of them said, "She didn't even offer us a cup of coffee!" [15]

And so I was very careful that no visitor, afternoon or evening caller, left my house without offering them refreshments. Whether or not my guests enjoyed what I offered, it made me feel very hospitable.

One guest in particular taught me the most valuable lesson I learned about cooking. Not that she taught it to me, but it was what occurred while we sat in our living room talking. A strange odor of something burning permeated the apartment. We remarked about it. It grew more pungent. I felt sorry for the neighbor whose dinner was probably burning.

I felt vaguely conscious of an urge to go through the long hall into the kitchen to see what else might be happening to a chicken I was cooking, but I didn't go. It might not be polite to my visitor. When the odor of something being scorched grew so pungent that I could no longer excuse myself, I went into the kitchen. The chicken was coal-black and sizzling, the kettle was ruined, and I stood among the ruins with feelings I cannot describe and a rule of action formulating itself in my mind. I resolved then and there that Rule Number One in cooking would hereafter be for me, when I think anything cooking or baking ought to be looked after, to go *immediately* to look, no matter who might be in the living room. How much that rule saved me in disappointments, money and clearing up a most disagreeable job, I cannot estimate.

The first time I prepared a roast, Victor was sick in bed. Essie had come out to visit us. I had bought, the day before, a piece of lamb for roasting. The man at the meat counter took advantage of my inexperience.

Essie was sitting in Victor's room, where I had been darning Victor's socks, when, scared half to death I went into the kitchen, turned on the gas in my stove, and put the meat into the oven. I went back and forth from our bed-room into the kitchen innumerable times. Every time I came near or went past our bed room door Victor fired some rolled up socks at me. Essie and I concluded that he couldn't be very sick, if he took such delight in pestering me and decided we wouldn't wait on him for supper. The roast lamb began to smell very good. . . . About the middle of the afternoon I made a fundamental discovery. I burst into Victor's room, Essie was there, and announced that to my great surprise I wasn't roasting the meat at all — *the stove was doing it.* Although there wasn't much to eat on it, it tasted wonderful. Essie and I brought trays into Victor's room. We wouldn't let him get up and we three had a merry dinner together. The next day I baked some potatoes just for the fun of having the stove take over. And thus began my evolution as a cook, instead of the literary person I wanted to become.[16]

Cooking proved fascinating. Baking a cake was exactly like writing a theme. You assembled your ingredients, as you assembled your ideas, then you put them in order in the right sequence. So far, so good. The oven did the rest, and the outcome was in the lap of the gods, just the way the subsequent history of your theme is precarious — I always thought of the kitchen as my laboratory and if I had cleaning to do, I told myself that the progress of civilization rests on cleanliness. Dusting and sweeping the particular place that needed it, was contributing our share to civilization.[17]

Every now and then as I grew more efficient and learned to cook better, I liked inviting the aunts for lunch, or the whole family to dinner. In the beginning, they were always surprised that I, who loved books and learning and spent more time studying and reading, than the other girls in the family, was really amounting to something.[18]

In an undated entry during 1953, Irma noted:

I have . . . often been told when persons have been in my kitchen, that they like to watch me cook. Mamma was an excellent and interesting cook. When, some years after our marriage, she said that I was a better cook than she was and quoted a German saying that the pupil had surpassed the master, I felt an inner satisfaction, a recompense for the inner irritation that chafed because of the time consumed in the preparing and disposing of meals. But I always thought, in conducting a home, that they were very important.

Summer came on. It was a very warm one. Our living room faced west. At night there was sometimes a land breeze coming into our front windows from the west. Originally we had Victor's office in the little room next to the living room and our bed-room was very small and in the centre of the apartment. Its one window opened onto a court. There was no possibility of any wind currents coming in through its one window, and [when] the warmest days came we moved the office into the middle room and our bed room into the living room. That gave us some relief from the stifling heat and often at night when I could not sleep I walked to the front window and sat in the Morris chair which Rudolph [Victor's brother] had given us for a wedding present.

Almost our entire apartment was furnished by our relatives and friends' wedding presents. Some of them I have had all my life and have thereby remembered the persons who gave them to us. Others irritated me because they seemed to me, who knew nothing at that time of interior decorating, to be in bad taste. Some things we selected ourselves, bought with money given us for that purpose.

I appreciated sincerely all our wedding presents, and was surprised at the thoughtfulness of some persons who sent us things whom I had never suspected of being interested in us. I really felt most grateful. It was the cut-glass age, and I was proud of my precious collection. Everybody loved cut glass when it had been newly brushed with soap and water and I had set my table with my new embroidered linens, newly plated silver, cut glass bowls, water glasses and receptacles for sugar and cream; my mother was even more proud of my table than I was. The cut glass . . . caught the light [and] shone like diamonds with tiny rainbows. I never had, and I never wanted, a solid silver table service.[19]

It was good that I never wanted it for in the early days I couldn't have afforded it and besides, I've always regretted the time spent in taking care of unnecessary possessions with all the books in the world I wanted to read — The books that I had time to study and to read seemed to side with me. Some of them taught me that a dinner party, however important or attractively set [a] table might be, is not dependent on its silver and cut glass. Dinner parties had been a matter of course throughout my childhood. . . . As we grew up dinner parties were synonymous with holiday times, and dinner parties, after I was married and throughout my life, have been in my blood. Many a dinner table have I set that I thought was in itself a picture, not always conventional, but always as lovely as I could make it —

but the important things at a dinner party, I am convinced, are the food and the guests.

In our living room, we had a green tufted upholstered couch[.] I lay on it often in the evenings when Victor read aloud to me. The frame of the couch crossed at the top in a scroll and made a natural head rest. The wood was imitation mahogany. The big Morris chair which Rudolph had given us seemed very elegant to us. The back of it was adjustable to a slanting position — By arranging a brass rod with barbs on either end into the brass notches which were attached to the back of the frame work, the back could be adjusted to a slanting position, or made level with the seat. This was an important piece of furniture in my housekeeping. Many and many a time we let the back down to clean it, many a time we put a pillow on it and slanted the back to be comfortable for a temporary invalid, but best of all, for the forty-six years we lived in our [second,] beloved house [on Ellis Avenue], it stood under a lamp next to one of the entrances to our living room and curled up in it a child with a book wandered through fairy-land or the child grown older wandered through magic experience in literature. Many and many a time I sat sewing in its depths and when later a phonograph stood opposite and an embryo music critic [Irma's son, Alfred] conducted with a ruler a symphony or opera we both were listening to, I sat in that chair under the lamp.

The big chair under the lamp was our intellectual throne for many and many a year. Only on several occasions did some one sit in it who wasn't either learning or listening or both. It was a hospitable chair comfortable and always quietly upholstered in green, or black with two gold stripes through it, or dark red to harmonize with the Oriental rug and the draperies in our historic living room in the house that became a member of the family, beloved by all of us who had lived, learnt and laughed and rarely wept in it. When the chair was new it had a dark green velour covering and harmonized with the tufted velvet covering of the couch.

Among our wedding presents was an ornate imitation Verni-Martin French table.[20] I had never before heard of Verni-Martin. The original Verni-Martin pieces were beautiful and appropriate in French palaces in the 17th or 18th centuries, but [not in] our little living room, kept subdued, because I did not know enough about interior decorating to touch it up and make it look right with color harmony and contrast.

It was so obviously an imitation, and so out of key with our books and our bank account, that we sent it back to the establishment where it had been bought, and in its place bought a quiet, comfortable chair that could associate with the big green one and the sofa — This might have been of minor importance had not the relatives who had sent the table, visited us one day when we were out. The maid told us that without being invited, even against her protest, they went into every room in the apartment looking for [that] table. When they could not find what they had been looking for they seemed very angry and left in a huff. I had never liked them, and they did not like me. They said I was a snob because I never went with them to the vaudeville shows on Saturday P.M., and because I didn't play cards. I thought the Verni-Martin table had been a blessing in disguise. Needless to add that these were some of my new in-laws, not very close ones, but distant ones whom I found it good to keep at a distance.

The inevitable happened. I took sick. I was alarmed because I was pregnant. Having a baby and taking care of it was going to be an additional expense, and while Victor was making enough money to pay our expenses and to put aside something every week so that we could pay back the debt we owed our uncles for his European education, we both were much impressed with the statement Marshall Field made to his employees, "You don't get rich from what you earn, but from what you save."

Pregnancy, being perpetually tired and remaining in-doors too much laid me low.[21] I took cold, and had a fever. Mamma came and said I must have a maid, even if she had to pay the maid's wages. The family was frightened for it was during her first year of marriage, when Emma was pregnant, that she took cold, had pneumonia and died.

And so I got a maid — where from or how, I do not remember but I shall never forget her.[22] I paid the maid the munificent salary of $2.50 per week. She washed and ironed and scrubbed and completely scorched and all but ruined my new kitchen equipment of which my mother had been very proud.[23]

Adjusting to a household of my own, taking care of my things, becoming an important member of the family not just one of the children, watching the telephone with a little teaching and a little writing, all of it in an atmosphere of love, the astonishment that even older persons came as guests to our apartment, sketched against the anxiety of pregnancy, made up the first months of my married life. Accidental pregnancy must always, I think be fraught with anxiety. I felt like a captive of Nature for her own purposes.

The summer [of 1899] had very many hot days and on the day before the very hottest one, on the first day of September my battle began. I did not know it was to be a battle. I have confidence in my own bravery and found consolation in the thought that every person who walked the earth must have been born and most mothers survived.

And when the battle did begin, for battle it was, at first it seemed no worse than the menstrual cramp[s] I had sometimes had. They seem[ed] like a knife cutting through one's inside, . . . but, when hour after hour the cramps continued each one longer than the one before, until they reached a peak of agony where I no longer seemed a human being and every little while the nurse had to change my gown so wet it was from perspiration of a hot day and the effort to give birth it seemed to me, I was no longer human [but] a ball of agony. The doctor, who had been Victor's superior sat at the foot of my bed, a big, silent Buffalo Bill looking man and who, in all those hours of suffering never said a word of encouragement, consulted now and then with Victor and said one time, "Do you know now, Mrs. F., why they are called *labor* pains?" . . . (the M.D. [was] supposed at the time to have been the best in the city, and because he had been Victor's instructor, and Victor being young had an exalted respect for him and would have felt it presumptuous to have attempted to interfere).

Finally, I begged my young M.D. husband, begged, and begged him, to end this awful suffering. I didn't care how. It had been going on for hours and couldn't grow worse. It could only end. The last I remembered was calling out twice, "O, Victor dear, give me *enough* chloroform, please give me *enough*."

When I came to, I was mildly surprised that there was a world and I was in it, without pain. . . . Later they told me that my baby could not have been born in the position in which she lay when labor began. If I had not had the anesthetic, the outcome could have been fatal to one or to the two of us.[24]

They showed me the helpless little creature all wrapped up in her soft blanket, with the little forehead bruised where the forceps had held, I remember words formed themselves "O, the poor little thing!" But the next moment despite the pain and exhaustion, something stiffened in me and I felt she was a challenge to all the strength I might regain, the intellect I had and whatever goodness there might be, or might come to be, in me.

Nothing that I had ever experienced, not even falling in love, expanded my horizon as my little baby did now that I was really aware of her. She was hardly a day old when I began to think of the neighborhood she would grow up in, the school she would attend. All of a sudden the neighborhood and the school took on a vast significance. It must have been around the third afternoon after she was born when I began to feel physically very bad. I accidentally heard my young doctor husband say to Essie, "I'm afraid she's running a fever." Fever in child birth I know is often fatal.[25] I did not want to die. When Victor and Essie came into my room I was crying. I did not want to leave my husband, and my helpless baby, and have Mamma plunged in grief again. Victor consoled me, "It is probably only your milk coming into your breasts," and that was all it was.

I have always been a squeamish person — much too squeamish for my own comfort. I hated being an animal — so many things were happening — a baby tugging at sore breasts.[26]

My Aunt Rose brought me four whole bars of Baker's sweet chocolate after Emily was born. She said chocolate is good for nursing mothers. Who ever had four whole bars of chocolate at one time?

The baby, it seemed, had brought a gift of good fortune. Victor's practice increased. We had more money. The hardship we expected in paying for my nurse, giving the doctor a present, for M.D.'s do not send bills to each other, and other extra expenses of our baby's arrival we met easily.

Before she was born I remember being on our back porch one day with Victor when we heard a baby crying. It worried me. "How do you know what's the matter with a baby when it cries?" I asked Victor.

He answered, "A baby has different kinds of crying. You can tell, whether it's crying because it's tired, or hungry, or in pain. And when it cries and you pick it up and it stops, you knows there's nothing wrong, except that it wants attention."

I soon learned.

I thought Victor was very cruel one night when the little soul cried and stopped the minute we picked her up.

"You've got to train her," said Victor. "You're not strong enough to be up with her all night, and I've got to sleep when I can." . . . Doctors made many more house calls at that time than they do now. After an active day, Victor was often called out at night.[27]

After a few nights when she cried less every night, but always seemed to wake up at a certain time, she must have concluded that she had landed cruel parents who were not in sympathy with her idea of night life and, until early A.M. the three of us could sleep.

And when she slept in the day time I loved standing a moment or longer at the baby basket all lined with the daintiest of lace and blue ribbons and looking at the beautiful little creature, breathing so softly that often I bent down to listen to note anxiously if she were breathing — wondering, hoping, planning. A new love, the deepest I had ever known totally different from the love I bore my young husband, yet intensified because it was a love we felt together. If there is anything in all nature, softer, more beautifully formed, more delicate and flower-like than a little baby's hand, I have never seen it. I used to touch the little hand gently.

To my astonishment the whole family awoke to something new and lovely in all our lives. When she was a few days old and Essie came to my bed-side and said, "Wouldn't you like to name her Emily after Emil [who had died in 1890 at age twenty-two]?" it seemed as if that was the only name that could be for her.

She was a family possession, I soon realized. The presence of the little baby filled the whole apartment with something beautiful and warm. When Mamma came, or Essie and Meta, or Kurt they no longer came to visit me, their first question was about the baby.

She must have been about six weeks old when Meta came one P.M. and after playing with her a little, I sternly announced that it was time for one of her naps, and we'd better put her in her basket in our middle room where she would be undisturbed. We did, and she cried. But I said, "I'll let her cry. I've got to train her so that she senses I mean business even in the daytime when I lay her down." Meta agreed. She seconded me strongly. We were going to be adamant. We left her and went forward into the living room, listening, anxious, but firm.

After a short time, her crying ceased.

Both of us were elated. "See how easy it is to train a baby if only you are firm enough," I said.

And Meta agreed.

But, in a little while, as all young mothers do with their first babies, I thought I'd better take a look. All young mothers of first babies have visions of a baby strangling itself by getting tangled up in its blankets, or turning its head so as to interfere with breathing. I knew very well that she was too tiny and too helpless to change her position yet I made many little useless trips, from where I happened to be to where I had placed her.

I tip-toed to the middle room, peered into the door, and there in a rocking chair, sat Essie, who had come in the back way, heard the baby crying, had taken her up and out of her basket-bed, was holding her with the little head resting on Essie's shoulder and Essie's one hand gently patting her back, singing "Rock-a-bye-baby." . . . Both Essie and the baby were the two most contented people in the world. . . . I called Meta to see how we were training the baby.

The first time we took her out, we went down to Mamma's. Victor laid the cover down diagonally, . . . laid the little bundle down in the center and wrapped the brown cover around her like an envelope, with the flap thrown over the little face. I was afraid she wouldn't be able to breathe, but he had it loosely thrown over her head — such a precious bundle! The family made a joyous event of it, which did not surprise me at all. What had surprised me was the family's attitude of possession. . . .

We went down to Mamma's to spend the night on the day before Thanksgiving and my little baby's basket stood between Essie and me in the room where I had spent my girlhood, it was Essie who was awake every little while, looking into the basket, to see if the baby was all right. By that time I had grown a little less apprehensive. On Thanksgiving A.M. when I gave her a bath in front of the grate-fire in the living-room in a big china bowl, the whole family stood around. She could splash a little and that was wonderful, and she made funny faces and sounds and they marveled that I really could give her a bath. But Essie dressed her. Essie loved dressing her. Essie loved making doll clothes.

The baby herself — a breathing, hungry, warm, moving little creature, perfectly formed and perfectly beautiful had seemed a miracle.

But the miracle was only in its beginnings. To have a tiny, naked baby on one's lap and after a few weeks when you gently rub a bit of oil and pat a few puffs of powder over the tender pink skin, and there is a little sound of satisfaction, to watch for its first smile and to get it, and to go on watching as day after day slowly there are new developments in an intellect that is beginning to dawn and take hold, recognition of those about it, the curiosity with which it examines its hands, later its little toes as it is cooing in its crib — all these are a part of the miracle. Everything is an event — when you can sit the baby up — when it can sit up by itself, then turn over without help, as it learns to creep and toddle and makes its wants known and pushes its aversions aside. It is conscious growth, expansion, life — and it is in truth, the great miracle of the universe and its mystery — for in the expanding (growing) intellect and abilities [and] power of the baby, consciousness dawns and greatness has its beginnings.

A baby grows articulate; speech develops. Plants and animals have their limits, beyond which they cannot develop. The intellect of man may be collective co-operative through speech, singly it may soar and reach heights in its own sphere of consciousness undreamed of. A dog remains a dog; it can attain to nothing else. . . . [T]he poet might be right. It might come "trailing clouds of glory." A baby's smile, communicated into its eyes, at the [point] when recognition begins . . . is a true miracle.

And so that beautiful little body, each part retaining the roundness and the beauty of a child's growing body, united with the unique charm of babyhood and childhood, made as one with our growing community life and filled our lives with a new joy in companionship and a new interest shared.

I remember Emily, when she was a few months old, sitting in her high chair at Mamma's table, while we older ones of the family were gathered around having dinner. What there was for dinner, or who was there, did not seem of so much importance as little Emily pounding with a spoon on the tray of the high chair, emitting sounds which no one understood, but every one could interpret. Having a happy baby at the other end of the table from where I was seated, having her between Kurt and Meta, each one of whom wanted to hold her or play with her, added an interest and a joy to the family dinner like no other guest, distinguished or merely loved, had ever done. When we left the table I realized that I had hardly taken my eyes off of her all through the dinner and that there was a glow in my heart because she was mine.

She learned to walk early. She was about a year old when she could toddle between two chairs, then take a few uncertain steps alone. (We used to laugh heartily when she should have been creeping with her hands and knees and, instead she moved along on all fours and could go backward as rapidly as she could go forward.) And finally she could walk across the room into Victor's arms when I set her down. We decided to surprise Grossmutter [Grandmother]. The next time Grossmutter came for a visit, when we were upstairs in the big bedroom and Grossmutter was at one side of the room and I at the other, I acted quite unconcerned when I set her little feet down on the floor, held onto her 'til she had an assured start and off she began to toddle across the floor toward her Grossmutter whom she loved. Grossmutter gave out a little scream, but Emily undaunted, pursued her uncertain way toward Grossmutter's arms and with a happy look of triumph was caught up in her arms and hugged. Essie stood by, an astonished and delighted spectator as I knew she would be.

Everything in those years clustered about the living and the welfare of the little creature we had been so fearful of welcoming. As those beginning years went on I remember little else, except that Victor's practice began to expand and what Dr. Otto Schmidt had told him grew more and more to be true, when Dr. Schmidt said, "At first, as you finish with each patient, you wonder from where the next one will come, and then there is a next one, and your practice begins to go by its own momentum."

Our landlord, noticing that more patients seemed to be ringing our doorbell, raised our rent. We had been paying $32.50 a month. . . . [On the first] of every month, promptly at 8 A.M. he rang our door bell and then he stood in all the austerity and meanness of ownership. It both infuriated and amused us. He could have waited at least, 'til 8:30 or even the second or third day of the month! Once in a while, just to plague him, Victor wouldn't pay him 'til the second day. We always had the rent ready — would have had it ready, even if there had been nothing to eat in our ice-box and he knew it.

Our lease ran for a year and a half. At its expiration our landlord tried to raise us to $40.00. He noticed that the location was good for

Victor's practice. He raised no one else in the building which had six apartments. We didn't like him and it made us angry.

Shortly afterward when Mamma came to our house for luncheon one noon, she said she had seen a lovely little grey stone house across the street that she wished we could rent. We told her that we had seen it too, and that it was not for rent but for sale.

"Why don't you buy it then?" she asked.

"Buy it?" Victor answered. We looked at each other thinking that Mamma had suddenly gone out of her mind. How could we buy a house?

Mamma persisted. She knew that Victor had received some fees for his surgery and that we had been very careful about spending money, as a matter of fact, in the year and a half that we'd been married we had saved nearly $1500.00, a small part of that had been wedding presents and I had earned a little bit. We never spent big fees. We tried to live on the little ones and put the big ones aside as savings. Victor, all his life, no matter how little he had or earned, some way, had managed to have something in savings. He used to say that he went in debt with himself and the debt to himself was always his savings. . . .

There was a bit of advice, too that Dr. Oliver Wendell Holmes had given to a young doctor in a book. . . . We all read it and in it Dr. Holmes had told a young M.D. to hang out his shingle in a good neighborhood and sit down and wait for patients to come. In a good neighborhood they would be good ones who could pay for services, whereas in a poor neighborhood more patients might come, but the doctor's fees would necessarily have to be small and sometimes there might be no fee at all.

It was good advice. To-day the practice of medicine has changed completely. Rarely does a doctor have an office in his home. He is much more dependent for patients on his telephone, on other M.D.'s with whom he shares an office and dependent on his hospital affiliations. Before the telephone became universal . . . people called a doctor from their own neighborhood.

Young doctors depended greatly on the recommendations of their patients. Victor had been vaccinating some persons in the neighborhood and one evening one of the patients [called, one] who knew little about him except that he was young, up-to-date and had had excellent training including study in Europe which, at that time, was considered the best qualification. The man who sent for him had been to see a chiropodist and[,] since the chiropodist had taken care of him, had a pain and swelling in one of his toes. Victor recognized immediately that the patient had an infected wound. The infection spread up the patient's leg with amazing rapidity, and in a day or two the whole leg was swollen, and the patient had a case of blood poisoning.

Both the family and Victor wanted consultation. Two top ranking surgeons thought the patient's leg must be amputated. Victor was against it. He was sure that by constant attention he would be able to save the patient's life and his leg. He was not in favor of giving the patient a general anesthetic.[28]

After the patient had recovered he often took delight in telling me how Victor had chucked him full of whiskey, got him drunk, and the three M.D.'s removed a huge quantity of pus and left him in care of Victor. No patient ever received better attention. Many times a day Victor ran into him to cheer him up and watch that leg and although it took a long while for it to heal completely in the end the patient made an excellent recovery and was very proud of retaining what he called his "hand carved leg."

The patient was wealthy, genial, talkative, and very grateful, and became our very best friend. Victor's reputation as an excellent doctor spread to the patient's entire family and to their relatives and friends — and Victor's reputation was established. For a doctor beginning his practice, it was an ideal case. It was every young doctor's answer to a prayer. The patient paid Victor a handsome fee which was no small part of our $1500.00.

We had a desire to remain in the neighborhood — At that time 45th Street and Vincennes were considered pretty far south, but the neighborhood was growing rapidly, the surroundings were lovely and the class of people we had as neighbors was very good.

Mamma's idea that we should buy the little stone house across the way [, which] was one of a row of houses called modern at the time, did not seem quite so fantastic when we began to think about it seriously. My uncles, Mamma said, would take the mortgages on the house and our $1500.00 could be a down payment. Paying interest on our mortgage and trying to buy it so that we would own the house outright would be the very best incentive to save.

It was a lovely little house. The former owner was a contractor who was fond of beautiful wood. The woodwork throughout the house had been treated like the finest of furniture. There was plenty of room for us and our baby and a maid.

We moved into [that] lovely little, grey stone house — one of a row of houses. On one side of us lived Dr. Hulett, on the other a genial big man with a wife who was forever cleaning — boasted to me one housecleaning time that she had scrubbed every inch of woodwork in her house with soap and water and a nail brush. The women on both sides of me were better housekeepers I thought than I was. . . . To me housekeeping and home-making were never quite the same thing. One was basic and necessary — the other, the poetry of life, the things for which the basic techniques had to be gone through with. I think I inherited from my mother the pleasure I have always found in a "party-table" and often I used to say to myself every meal ought to be a party.

But scrubbing the wood work could well be left to others. If it weren't done I had a guilty conscience about it, but once I turned it over to some one else, I didn't inspect too closely or watch the person doing it. It was off my conscience and there were more fascinating things to do. Still one could make a game of it, in a way. On the rare occasions when I couldn't escape such jobs I could divide them into squares, or other designs or try to learn better and quicker ways of doing them. . . .

We had a week of excessively hot weather in the middle of May. The little garden, back of our house . . . was in full bloom — mostly I remember the pansies and the flowering, delicate flowering of some of the low fruit trees. At twilight, Victor and I would walk in the garden, with little 3½ year Emily scampering around and prattling in that dear baby voice — and I was very large and heavy and uncomfortable.

At the end of the week, on Sunday A.M., Ruth was born. When Ruth was a few minutes old, [my cousin] called up and wanted to know if she could come over. Somebody told her that we had a new little girl at our house, that had just arrived and was only a tiny baby — and that she had better not come that morning. [She] immediately told her father (my uncle) about the new baby. He called up Grossmutter and congratulated her, and she did not know why. And so he told her she had a new little granddaughter. She was very much excited and came right over from where she lived, across the street. . . . [My nephew] had a cough and Victor wasn't too pleased about Grossmutter coming over — but she just had to come and it harmed nobody and I was very happy to see her.

Grossmutter thought that Victor would be disappointed because Ruth wasn't a boy. Maybe he was for a second — but, inside of a week, he was 100% her Daddy.

She cried for twenty-four hours and that disturbed me no end. I had an English nurse, Emily Mantle, who sang English lullabies to her [like] "Chick-a-biddy bye," and quaint things — a big, strong, friendly, plain young woman of whom we all grew very fond — she and our Emily were lovely friends. She used to take Emily with her on her daily walks and often she went into the neighborhood of 45th and Greenwood where a former patient who had a garden lived. She and Emily would come home laden with pansies, huge ones and Emily Mantle would put them about my room, spread out on platters with a little water underneath them. I remember lying in bed, quiet, just happy and content, looking at the individual pansy faces. I nursed Ruth, as I did all of my babies, and that pansy contentment was good for us both. She was a beautiful baby, her big brown eyes radiated contentment and comfort. . . . I have always had a guilty conscience about buying extravagant things — and I still remember that one day when I was in Field's, I couldn't resist a beruffled lacy bonnet for baby Ruth, which had soft light blue pompons dancing in the lacy ruffling that surrounded her soft baby face.[29]

The two little girls completely filled our lives in a way, although my family and friends have always been very important to me. . . .

Of Ruth's babyhood and her growing into a little child, Emily's entering kindergarten, and later [Alfred], I seem to recall that the busy days passed[,] the seasons came on and when they had completed their cycle [we] entered upon a new season — snow and ice and cold, the buds unfolding. Summer in full, and then autumn leaves which we pressed with a fairly hot iron between two layers of wax-paper. We loved doing them and decorating our sun parlor with them. . . .

I always fancied that each of my babies brought its special easement of our living. When Emily was born Victor rode around on a bicycle calling on his patients, but patients began to be more plentiful and even before Emily came, I had to have a permanent maid, and when she was a few months old we moved into our own house.

With Ruth came our horse and buggy and an additional maid. . . . We had Nellie, who wore brown and white striped dresses with brown and white checked aprons, when she was not wearing white aprons. . . . Her mother did our laundry work, and we had a little high school girl, Lilian, who took our baby out. It was a happy time in my life.

Victor selected a horse with the aid of a veterinarian at the Stock Yards. She was a young, beautiful, spirited animal. We thought she ought to have a name. Emily suggested that we call her Grossmutter which Emily thought was a compliment to her grandmother, whom she dearly loved. We felt it was hardly an appropriate name for a young horse. We let her choose another name and she chose "Dolly." Dolly soon became a member of the family. She was a beautiful horse, slender legs, coal black body and a white star on her forehead. She was a very friendly, affectionate creature. . . .

They were lovely, those two little girls and we were happy driving around in a doctor's buggy with a beautiful horse. A few automobiles, horseless carriages began to appear in the streets. Our horse shied and reared whenever a horseless carriage making a terrific noise approached from the rear and we were often frightened.

One day in driving out with Victor while he visited his patients, we saw a room which seemed to have no walls, only windows. It struck our fancy. It was in the home of one of the Rosenwald's.[30] We made some inquiries and decided to have one like it built above a sort of stove-room extending into the yard back of our kitchen — the roof of the room could be covered and be the floor of the sun-room. The walls I remember were Georgia-pine, what there was of them, just enough to hold the windows that made three sides of the room, with its entrance into the back bed-room where Victor had his office. . . . The sun-parlor, the second of its kind on the South Side was our children's play room and the scene of their parties. For parties we always had.

After the sun parlor was up we moved the office into our front living room down stairs and used the second living room between the front one and the dining room, as a reception room for patients. It was a very bad arrangement but a great relief no longer to have patients trooping up stairs to the second floor where our bed rooms were.

Victor and I occupied the front bed-room, Emily and later each baby as it came, occupied the little room next to ours. In the centre of the second floor, overlooking the court between our house and Hulett's was the small bedroom, which our maid occupied.[31]

Ruth and Alfred were born 2½ years apart at [the grey stone house], Emily 3½ years before Ruth at [the apartment]. These were very busy days.[32]

The Hyde Park–Kenwood neighborhood where Irma and Victor lived after they were married lies eight miles south of downtown Chicago in a green oasis bordering the lake. In pre-fire days, Hyde Park had been a township. Later, it was granted village status. By 1889, it had been annexed into the city proper.

It had broad boulevards, clean water and air, and no industry. By 1894, food markets and small specialty stores moved in on 47th Street and Lake Park Avenue. The area was advertised as exclusive and convenient. Hyde Park–Kenwood residents were primarily Caucasian, Protestant members of the middle and upper classes. However, a few prosperous Jewish families were also beginning to build in the area.[33]

The University of Chicago attracted intellectuals, and the open spaces lured people of wealth to build houses. Apartment buildings and luxury hotels had been constructed in anticipation of the 1893 world's fair to be held in Jackson Park on the lake. The city was accessible by train, cable cars, or steamers from the 53rd Street pier. By the late 1890s, "pressure for housing, both for university people and Chicago's constantly growing population, resulted in extensive development of row houses and apartments."[34] Speculators and developers built many of these multifamily structures; building tradespeople constructed others for investments.

At that time most medical students and doctors just starting their practices borrowed money or worked at odd jobs to supplement their incomes. Oftentimes, young doctors worked for pharmacists while building up their practices.[35] Although Victor never did this, he did borrow from Irma's uncles to finance his postgraduate study in Germany, and to pay the rent on his first office. In that era, hospitals were for the poor; hospitals were also unhealthy and unsanitary places where people did not often go by choice. Doctors and surgeons who treated private patients made house calls. When he first entered practice, Victor rented office space in downtown Chicago, but discovered that he could save money, and make house calls more efficiently, if he set up an office in his home. He borrowed Irma's younger brother's bicycle to make those house calls.[36]

A doctor's success was judged not necessarily by how many patients he had, although this was indeed a good measure, but by the quality of the horses and buggies he drove.[37] In one sense, then, driving around in the neighborhood with his wife and children in a buggy symbolized both Victor's material success and his stability and social position as a family man.

Irma's comments about homemaking, housekeeping, sunlight, and sun porches appear to be simple recollections of her first apartment and house and of her early years of marriage. However, they actually tell quite a bit about American social customs of the 1890s.

Some social historians have suggested that during this period education was rapidly becoming universal, and with education came "taste" and a love for beauty, such that the educated homemaker's main preoccupation became the decoration and care of her home. However, the education was, perhaps, not so much that of the traditional sense of school-based learning, but rather, through books. Literacy was on the rise, and one of its effects was that more women were reading. One of the early shapers of the movement to establish standards of taste was the novelist Edith Wharton.[38] Following the complete renovation of her cottage called Land's End, Wharton collaborated on a book with the Boston architect and designer Ogden Codman Jr. In their enormously popular volume *The Decoration of Houses*, they suggested that both architecture and home décor should be simplified. It stressed that harmony should exist between building and room design and furniture.[39]

The discovery of germs also affected housekeeping practices and home décor. A *House Beautiful* article of October 1899 announced that "[m]icrobes lurked in heavily carved surfaces and deep-piled materials; sunshine and fresh air, as well as soap and water, were microbes' enemies."[40] Out went the old ornate Victorian settees and fireplace festoons, off came the heavy room-darkening draperies, and open flew the windows. Easily washed ceramic tiles in kitchens and baths were installed. Sunlight was allowed to pour into sun porches and other living areas. Cleanliness, sanitation, and simplicity of design became the watch-words for the up-to-date woman. Of course, the homemaker's next thought was about raising a family in a healthy, clean environment.

A few years later, Irma and her family moved to another house on Ellis Avenue, one which Irma dearly loved. It "stood in the midst of a flower garden . . . and had many windows . . . where light came in." She called it her "dream house," and it "grew to be more beautiful in reality than either of us could have imagined in the far distant past when we were young."[41]

[I]t became a member of the family for so much living was done in it, that it seemed to come alive and have a life of its own. When the children had gone to establish homes of their own, sometimes as I walked down the front stairway and saw the living room, where the piano stood silent, and the phonograph rarely sent its masterpieces of music into the room, sometimes it almost said the words, "Where are they?"[42]

Children and Learning, 1910–1912

During the first decade of the twentieth century, American cities continued to grow at an unprecedented rate. Many immigrants from Europe and Asia, as well as rural Americans, arrived in urban centers looking for better education and work opportunities. Unfortunately, they often found themselves and their children embroiled in social problems bred in filthy, overcrowded slums, where crime, gangs, truancy, and juvenile delinquency were rampant. Contemporary critics and social reformers placed much of the onus for a wide range of urban problems directly on the disorganization of the slum communities. They also blamed slum-based gangs and juvenile delinquency on the loss of parental control. Children who were arrested were sent to reform schools or incarcerated in adult prisons; neglected or dependent children were sent to orphanages.[1]

To assist parents who worked, reformers and social workers often established playgrounds and recreational programs with supervised activities. The Boy Scouts, Girl Scouts, Girl Guides, and Boy Pioneers organizations were started to teach nature lore, health craft, handicrafts, and citizenship, as well as to keep children entertained.

When Irma's children were born, middle-class parents had many resources to provide their children with activities. There were dancing classes, piano lessons, summer camps, plays, concerts, and, for Jewish children, Hebrew and Sabbath or Sunday schools. Middle-class parents kept their children busy, and, most often, their mothers were not employed outside of the home so could supervise them relatively closely to make certain they did not get into trouble.

Still, even for the middle-class parent, there were no books on child rearing. Much of the practical information about babies, their care and feeding, was passed from woman to woman. However, because of increased mobility, urban-fostered anonymity, and other factors, there was a general shift among the more educated middle-class women to asking doctors' advice and attending lectures on child development.

Sometime during 1908, Irma heard a lecture about children's literature that had a profound impact on her subsequent behavior and child-rearing philosophy. She revisited that 1908 lecture twice in her journals. On Monday, January 26, 1931, she wrote: "I always thought 'the personality of the mother' was a great thing in child training. Professor McClintock of the University of Chicago had said that. . . . A happy adjusted, *adjustable* mother would still be better for [children] than a sad one."

Then, on Sunday, May 9, 1948, Mother's Day, she commented:

The most significant remark that ever was made to me was at a club meeting where Professor McClintock of the University of Chicago had delivered a lecture at the Isaiah Woman's Club on Fairy Tales for Children. During the question period I told him that I do not like the wicked step-mother, the fierce man-eating beasts and the malignant witches that filled my childhood with terror. He said that children are not unduly frightened by these things, that in *Alice in the Looking Glass* when the Queen commands "Off with his head!" No child is frightened. I did not agree. *Alice in Wonderland* is a whimsical fantasia which young persons enjoy and do not take seriously, but Grimm's *Fairy Tales* while they have in them such gems as "The Ugly Duckling," which was one of my childhood favorites, are full of cruel and terrifying stories. "Hansel and Gretel" may be a classic, but I never could see the enjoyment, in opera, on the stage or in a book of wandering children being forced into an oven and asked to stick out their fingers so that the malignant witch might know if they are properly roasting. These are German stories and no doubt the Nazis got some of their brilliant ideas from them, particularly in regard to the ovens. Professor McClintock finally admitted that an imaginative child might be harmed but that most children will read or hear such tales one minute and forget them the next. Perhaps they will forget them the next minute but at night when the lights are out and the house is still, they are afraid. We argued and argued as did the little bird and the duck in that delightful tale of Prokofiev which cannot possibly frighten an imaginative child however much it will feel sorry for the duck, . . . and finally Professor McClintock said (Finally, I think as much to silence me as anything else), "In the raising of children the one factor of greatest importance is

The Personality of the Mother!"

That made a profound impression on me. I thought of it all the way as I walked home, a distance of ten city blocks. "What was I?" "What had I been?" "What could I have become?"

At home were my two little girls, aged eight and five and their little brother aged two. Certainly, I must never fail them. I must grow more efficient, better educated, kinder, more understanding and patient.[2]

During 1910, Irma planned to construct a book she tentatively called "Nursery Ethics" around quotations collected from a number of her favorite authors, along with proverbs and aphorisms. She also attempted to set out the codes by which she would raise her own children, and the notes she made mix her own ideas indiscriminately with those of others.

NURSERY ETHICS

Build therefore your own world. As fast as you confirm your life to the pure idea in your mind that will unfold its great proportions. [Ralph Waldo] Emerson

MARY EMERSON[3]

All men, in the abstract, are just and good; what hinders them in the particular is the momentary predominance of the finite and individual over the general truth. The condition of our incarnation in a private self seems to be a perpetual tendency to prefer the private law, to obey the private impulse, to the exclusion of the law of universal being. The hero is great by means of the predominance of the universal nature; he has only to open his mouth and it speaks, he has only to be forced to act and it acts. All men catch the word, or embrace the deed, with the heart, for it is verily theirs as much as his, but in them this disease of an excess of imagination cheats them of equal issues. Nothing is more simple than greatness; indeed to be simple is to be great.

Scorn trifles — lift your arms; do what you are afraid to do. Sublimity of character must come from sublimity of motive.

The most elevated ambition a man or woman can cherish is to be a perfect parent.

The principle underlying every line in this book is *justice to children*.

Child's own point of view consistently ignored.

When they are surrounded by impulsive people, who are swayed in their treatment of them by the feelings of the moment.

It seldom enters the head, even of a fond and indulgent parent that there is an inevitable obligation upon him to be kind.

The child [is] an undeveloped man.

A horse trainer does not resent the restlessness of a creature with sensitive nerves.

The endeavor of a parent should be to make stern demands of himself, to be sympathetic and patient, to bring about the correct relations of the child toward himself.

In family government the difficulty far often lies with us rather than with our children.

"Let bitterness not enter into the heart of a mother." Egyptian proverb.

What sentiment do we wish to inspire in the young mind toward ourselves, love or fear?

Idiosyncrasies are always unpleasant, but they are not always criminal!

It is a mission for which the parents would do well to prepare themselves by the practice of a *rigid self-control*, and the cultivation of a *patience* and *tact* far beyond what they have ever needed in any other relation in life.

Children are much scolded merely for being inopportune.

Unkind thoughts. Follow each [with] severe punishment and widen a breach between parent and child.

Disapproval should be in proportion to the amount of intention in the act, not in proportion to the disagreeable effect produced upon beholders.

It is a radical error to be careless of provoking children. All emotions are latent, and it is desirable that [those] we wish to remain weak should be allowed to remain latent.

All the most cautious and learned guardians of youth from Socrates down to Rollin, advocate environing a child with silent care, keeping him out of the way of temptation, and coming to preserve in him innocence and purity of mind as long as it is in our power to so shield him.

Scolding is the dread of childhood. Fretfulness is too common.

There is a wide difference between offending the proprieties and deliberate wrong doing. We wish above all, that our children should grow up honest and upright. Well then we must be content to let many things slip.

How frequently people find themselves doing and saying precisely that which they had resolved not to do and say as if some impulse overruled their judgment and intention.

Pitifully commonplace living.

A wise woman [is one] who values the welfare of her child more than the opinion of the world.

There is no doubt that a large part of the naughtiness of children does not begin as naughtiness but is converted into *it* by injudicious treatment. We have no first conception of how constantly we balk their harmless wishes.

Much of the naughtiness of our children comes from the artificial lives we make them lead. We substitute our own mature, educated tastes for their simple infantile ideas and so force them too early away from childhood.

We correct them not nearly so much for being bad, as for not being what we prefer to have them. Judicious letting alone that is necessary for the healthy growth of little ones.

While we make behavior and not virtue the object of our training.

A child is the true idealist.

Let him believe and trust, let him retain his faith in human nature, and accredit goodness to his companions as long as he can.

The vacuity that is like a disease among a certain class results from the suppression of natural activities in their forefathers.

This power of waiting for the good momentarily dimmed is the basis of fine character.

Don't aim at controlling every detail of a child's life. Leave him liberty in small things.

HERBERT SPENCER[4]

Gradually lifting a child out of his position of helplessness and dependence into the position of self-sustaining manhood or womanhood.

The law of evolution.

Some children remain babies a long time.

Parents do not sufficiently excuse forgetfulness and inattention.

The unfolding of other faculties give[s] them conscious delight and we ought from the beginning to address ourselves to their intelligence.

The parent who has a high ideal of his duties will make his care of his child a progressional education.

The parent must either be benefactor or foe.

The critical attitude is easy to assume, hard to relinquish and by indulging ourselves in it we come to dislike persons who jar against our nerves.

"We instinct them too nicely, we torture them and lose their love."

ROUSSEAU[5]

If a parent will recall the experiences of a single day it is probable that he will find that most of the reprimands with which he has visited his child have been for faults against usages; faults which if left alone would in time amend themselves —

The law of evolution, in child training — suppression of the undesirable traits brought about chiefly through strengthening the desirable traits.

Infinite patience, unfailing kindness are qualities to cultivate.

HORACE FLETCHER[6]

Courage is a birth right. Voluntary workerhood is the bravest of all arts common in life.

Whoever teaches a child to be fearless, builds greater than she can ever know, for fearlessness in one inspires courage in many; and as courage inspires strength and causes action, there is no end to what might grow out of the fearless influence of the frailest and physically weakest of women, and any young mother, in the quiet and seclusion of a modest home, can set in motion vibrations of strength and fearlessness that may result in the building of a great city or the invention of some world-emancipating tool of progress.

"We require such a solitude as shall hold us to its revelations when we are in the street and in palaces for most men are cowed in society." Ralph Waldo Emerson

I have observed that when people are impressed with a sense of the real importance and the necessity of a pursuit, they find time and energy to engage in it.

When the baby ceases to be a pet, he sometimes becomes a nuisance —([put in] chapter on development of character).

Just as we permit him to use his muscles as he acquires control of them we should respect his growing mental powers and resign our authority in each instance when he shows that he has attained judgment enough to decide any question of conduct correctly.

It is not in intellectual *toils* that human beings gain self-knowledge and the ability to formulate definite purposes.

The power to continue and compare is the most valuable faculty of the mind. It is essential that it be exercised unrestrainedly; by each person for himself. If the exercise is by manipulating of objects we call it experimenting, and if only dealing with ideas, we call it reasoning.

What is the most obvious failing of the ordinary man or woman? Poor judgment. Hamilton observed that it is suicidal to distrust the evidence of our faculties. But evidence depends upon the normal condition of perception.

The function of parental government is to protect the child and prepare it for independent life.

In the training of the young, confusion, trouble and discouragement are the rule not the exception — Commonly the entrance into life is the beginning of a warfare with those where duty is protection not aggression.

Man alone makes a failure of governing his offspring. For the reason that his government is an intelligence with nature.

CHRISTIAN LARSON[7]

Create a strong desire to transform, refine and improve everything with which you come in contact, and the finer consciousness will develop steadily.

We can make ourselves over absolutely, we can change and improve everything in ourselves and our environment and proceed in the realization of a great superior destiny.

The whole world of power is ready to build for the man who is thoroughly permeated with the desire to be more and accomplish more.

Character without ability — negative goodness.

With character and ability, any one can attain.

Divine presence felt at all times. We are helped by a higher power.

Faith knows that the goal can be reached. . . .

Faith is not blind itself — it is not belief at all. Faith is of live conviction.

The average person does not try to be himself but tries constantly to imitate. Every event that transpires in daily life is an opportunity, but we must have the insight to see it and the power to employ it.

He can who thinks he can. The secret is persistence. Pay no attention to temporary failures.

In the mastery of fate one of the greatest essentials is to *prevent* environment from impressing the mind and to prevent this your mind should be filled with your own ideal impressions. Keep your ideals. In this connection the *true* use of the imagination becomes extremely important. Every thing that we imagine we could impress upon the mind. Therefore through the imagination we can work ourselves into almost any condition or state of being.

The habit of permitting everything we come in contact with to impress our minds is responsible for a great deal of misdirected effort.

Every seeming failure is not necessarily a real one.

"The great secret of all secrets is to live your own life in your own world as well as you possibly can now." Larson

This is very important, because by learning yourself to be at your best in little things, it soon becomes second nature for you to be your best in all things, and when you are called upon to do something of exceptional importance, something that may seem very difficult, you are fully equal to the occasion.

Make yourself the best of your kind whatever your sphere of action may be, because by so doing you are not only increasing the number of great minds in the world, but you are adding immeasurably to the world's welfare and joy.

Making tangible in real life what the visions of the soul have revealed in ideal life.

The average person is full of artificial desires — desires that have been suggested by what other people possess or require.

You will realize that since it is in the present and the present only for which you are living you will concentrate your attention upon the living of life now.

> We have honeyed words for the stranger,
> And smiles for the passing guest;
> But we vex our own with look and tone,
> Though we love our own the best.

Irma also laid out lists of important things to put in her book, along with various rules of conduct.

HOW TO THINK CORRECTLY:

Negative	Avoid Prejudice
	Excess of emotion
	Excess of pride
	Excess of fear
	Excess of sympathy
	Excess of admiration
	Emotion has a rightful place in all true thinking
Positive	Importance of method
	Art of Concentration
	Laws of Evidence
	Distinctions
Importance	Be sure of facts
Of Health	Similarities
	Laws of association

Irma intended to weave the quotes and thoughts she jotted down into a book for other mothers to consult. She never finished this project.

Among the papers and diaries she kept was a small quarto leather ledger labeled "Emily's Diary." The accounts begin in 1909, when Emily was ten years old, and continue through 1912. In it, one can see the effect that Irma's educational efforts had on her children.[8] While reading Emily's entries, one is immediately struck by the similarities to Irma's journals. In both there are lists of guests present at parties with enumeration of gifts received, snippets of copied poems and inspirational quotes from authors read, rules of conduct, items baked or cooked, lists of books read, received, and lent, as well as detailed recountings of daily events.[9]

One of Emily's diary entries, dated 1911, indicates that she created a personal conduct list of twenty-five rules quite obviously based upon and very similar to her mother's maxims. However, she actually devised only twenty-four because of her error in numbering. Nothing shows better than these entries the character lessons Irma felt were required learning for her children to become upstanding members of society and good people.

SOME VERY IMPORTANT RULES

1. Be obedient to every one who you are expected to mind.
2. Be honest.
3. Be truthful.
4. Be noble.
5. Act as you should.
6. Do not put on any airs.
7. Go with only people who [you] think will make you better in any way.
8. Observe the manners and language of people who are considered better than you and try to improve by them.
9. Do not be silly.
10. Do not be ashamed to own up to any thing that you have done or said to any person who is honest.
11. Act as the people in your sex should.
12. Be careful of what you say.
13. Have respect for older people.
14. Be gentle to younger children than you are.
15. Do your duties cheerfully and your play will be more enjoyable.
16. Read only good literature.
17. Memorize good pure and noble sayings or poems.
18. Do the best you can in whatever you do.
19. Compare your manners with other [people's] and if they are not as good as the other persons polise [polish] them up in a hurry.
20. Use only refined language.
21. Delight in everything that is Gods.
22. Be cheerful and everyone else will be.
23. Be just and fair.
24. Love the things God loves. . . .

"My fairest child I have no song to give you;
No lark could pipe to skies so dull and gray;
Yet, ere we part, one lesson I can leave you
For every day.
Be good sweet maid and let who will be clever.
Do noble things, not dream them all day long;

And so make life, death and that vast
Forever
One grand sweet song" Charles Kinsley[10]

"Never lose opportunity to see anything that is beautiful. Beauty is God's handwriting." Charles Kinsley[11]

In the same small brown notebook from 1910 in which she jotted ideas, Irma also chronicled daily walks in the park near her house with her children. These walks were part of Irma's educational plan designed to supplement the public school curriculum.

Beginning around 1910, John Burroughs's "nature curriculum" was in vogue in Chicago's public schools, as it was elsewhere in the nation.[12] Burroughs (1837–1921) was known both as a Hudson River naturalist and the father of the American nature essay. He wrote a couple of books every year, becoming one of the most popular and respected authors of his time. As a result of Burroughs's popularity, a large curricular emphasis was placed on knowledge about and appreciation of nature. Irma's diary entries show that she was well acquainted with Burroughs's writings, evident from the following quotation in her 1910 journal:

NATURE STUDY
[by] John Burroughs

Nature study, as it appeals to us in books, fails of its chief end if it does not send us to nature itself — What we want is not the mere facts about the flowers or animals — we want through them to add to the resources of our lives; and I know of nothing better calculated to do this than the study of nature at first hand[.] To add to the resources of one's life — think how much that means! To add to those things that make us more at home in the world; that help guard us against ennui and stagnation that invest the country with new interest and enticement; that make every walk in the fields or woods an extension into a land of unexhausted treasures; that make the re-turning seasons fill us with expectation and delight; that make every rod of ground like the page of a book in which new and strange things may be read; in short, those things that help keep us fresh and sane and young, and make us immune to the strife and fever of the world.

Because she was supplementing the public-school nature curriculum which involved geology as well as local flora and fauna, Irma (and Emily, later) took "nature notes."

Saturday, March 12, 1910
Went out to Kenilworth [a suburb north of Chicago] to visit New-mans with Victor, Emily and Ruth. Brought home pussy willows, hazel catkins, crab apples (wild) which had lain under the snow all winter. Made five glasses of fine jelly out of them. Found a deserted last year's nest which we think is an oriole's nest. Saw fungus on pop-lar trees.

Saturday, March 19
Visit to Field Museum with the Geographical society. Went into var-ious departments with the curator of the department. Very interest-ing. Saw (in maps) formation of the Chicago plane.

Sunday, March 20
Took a short drive with Victor through Washington Park. The alders and birches in blossom.— Saw robins two days before in the park, on March 16 while driving through with Victor and Alfred.

Wednesday, March 23
Took Emily, Ruth and Alfred to Washington Park to see the alders and birches — poplars beginning, elms beginning. Walked [through] conservatory. Too warm to stay in the conservatory. Many interest-ing things outside.

Friday, March 25
Good Friday, no school. Emily and I planned to take a walk to Jack-son Park at sun-rise. Didn't wake up 'til 7 A.M. Emily, Ruth and I left the house at 7:40, walked to Jackson Park—Elms in full bloom. Poplars and maples beginning. The children didn't want to go home. Telephoned to Victor from the Windermere Hotel to bring Alfred

out, and to Eva [maid] to pack some lunch for us. Found some co-
coons on our way out to park.

P.M. Had our lunch back of German building.[13] The children gathered shells all A.M. Found a letter from Uncle Kurt to Emily in a book
that Victor brought out to us. Sat on a bench in front of the Japanese
houses on the Wooded Island and read and answered it. Alfred was
sure that he heard Japanese men talking in the Japanese houses.
Written on the Wooded Island — Saw some big brown butter-flies
wings edged with white, spotted edge —

Monday, March 28
Read that the butterflies we saw are the first to appear of the season, called Morning [Mourning] Cloak. Emily saw two beetles on
Friday. We left the park a little after 4 P.M. Had a remarkable, beautiful day. Spent some time near the Cahokia court house on the
Wooded Island. Saw some Grackles. Didn't know the button-wood
tree — found out.

Wednesday, March 30
Peach willow sprouted two days ago. Oaks beginning. Rain last
night. Horse chestnut buds opening and ailanthus just cracked.

Tuesday, April 26
Very warm unseasonable weather until April 21 (Friday) when a
terrific storm arose — At 4 P.M. there was darkness as of the night,
lasting about fifteen minutes — absolutely dark out of doors — one
couldn't see in the street without a light. Then came a rain and wind-
storm followed in the evening by a sudden drop of many degrees
in temperature — and by Saturday A.M. there was a heavy fall of
snow. Rain and snow alternating 'til Tuesday noon, low temperature persisting. The newspapers estimate the loss to the crops of approximately $38,000,000.00. Hope this is overestimated. Sun began
to shine this A.M. Went to a luncheon and heard Mr. J. Lloyd Jones
speak but was home by 2 P.M. and took the children and Arthur
[nephew] out for a walk. The season had advanced as far as latter
May — surely a whole month. The fresh foliage that was so beautiful
last week, looks sere and limp. Found oak catkins — frozen on the
trees, maple keys torn from the boughs, apple blossoms limp and
life-less, a fledgling bird under a pine tree on Drexel Boulevard

frozen. Emily picked it up and brought it home. Taught Arthur to observe the arrangements of leaves on the stem, whether opposites or alternates — Had a delightful time with the children. Watched the robins and the sparrows. Emily takes Nature notes diligently. Lilacs seem to have stood the cold best of all. Forsythia looks bad, horse-chestnuts had a magnificent start, the birches and some poplars seem to have been less affected by the storm than the horse chestnuts and elms. Watch for the work of the adventitious buds.

Thursday, April 28
Went walking with the children at sunset. Portions of the landscape still dreary and sad from the frost but much of the foliage etc. seems to be recovering. Our tulips on the lawn looked frozen. The three outer petals that enclose the other three are yellow and sere but three inner ones look as good as ever. Saw two more dead fledglings on the side-walks — This evening we visited our land marks on Drexel Boulevard. . . . We had a lesson on dandelions this P.M.

Saturday, May 14
Joined with Saturday Afternoon Walking Club's Sunrise Bird Walk with Emily and Meta. Left home at 4:40 A.M. and returned at 8:15 A.M. On the Wooded Island [saw] the Keel tailed black-bird or Grackle, American gold finch, Belted Kingfisher, Robins, sparrows, Golden winged wood pecker, or sapsucker, or flicker or high-hole, Ruby-crowned Kinglet, Cat-bird, Hermit thrush and song sparrow. Looked for Meadow larks (yellow breast with a dark crescent on it) Tatarian honey-suckle and choke-cherry in bloom.[14]

Monday, May 16
Saw locust and mountain ash in bloom.

That Irma shared her nature explorations with her children is clear, and that Emily, at least, took her mother's lessons to heart is evidenced by her own discussions of nature in journals dated between 1909 and 1912. These entries confirm that she did indeed take "nature notes" and also indicate that Emily, too, was familiar with Ralph Waldo Emerson and other authors Irma favored.[15]

Thursday, November 11, 1909
This afternoon I was over to Helen Southord's house. When I came

home Arthur and I helped Mamma with the bills. After we were done Mamma read to Arthur and Ruth and Alfred, the *Song of Hiawatha* while I wrote this. . . . Saturday, Papa, Mamma, Arthur, Ruth and Alfred and I went to the flower show at the coliseum. Mr. Simmons [the florist] was there and gave mamma some chrysanthemums.

Wednesday, July 27, 1910
This morning I went with Papa to the Hospital. Alfred went too. We sat out in the back of the hospital on some chairs that were there, while I read to Alfred out of Robert Louis Stevenson's *Reader* while a nurse came out on the porch and asked Alfred if she could have some of his curls, and I told him to answer her and he began crying and said he didn't want to talk. Then we went over to that little garden at the side of the hospital and picked clover. The clover had such nice long stems that I made a braided clover chain, the first braided clover chain I ever made. I wanted Alfred to wear it home but he didn't want to so I wore it. In the afternoon I went to the park with Mamma and Miss Leopold, and Mrs. Kahn, Miss Leopold's sister.

Emily recalled a trip from Valparaiso, Indiana, on Sunday, August 20, 1911:

After going 6 or 7 miles we came to a farm where a sign was which read "Honey for sale." We stopped and all went in except Grossmamma. The farmer with an Irish setter was just coming along the walk. Papa asked if we might see his bees as we supposed [they] were his. He said yes and showed us a place w[h]ere some bees were drinking. That was something new to me. I never knew before that bees had to have water. The farmer told us [that if] they didn't have this watering box the bees would go to the horses watering troff and since he had that they keep away from it. He also said that during the hot weather they used an awful lot of an amount just the exact amount I cannot remember. While we were standing a man partly a cripple came up. "This is the bee man" said the farmer at which we all said "Oh" a little surprised because we thought the farmer owned the bees.

This man showed us a part of the different partitions of one of the hives until Alfred got stung on one of his fingers and then we went in the house. Papa had asked to see some honey for we wished to buy some. We bought $2 worth of the finest honey I have ever eaten.

After we had left "The Bee Farm" and had gone about 2 miles papa got a punter in a front tire which took him 20 minutes to change and put another tire on. After that we were all right. We had a glorious trip through country roads with either farms of many acres or dense woods on the sides.

Somehow we got off the right road and came to Gary Ind. which we had avoided before but we got on the right road again.

On entering South Chicago a tire in the front was so bad that papa was afraid to run on it so we stopped again for about 35 minutes.

The rest of the ride wasn't so pleasant as I said yesterday.

On getting home I read a little and heard a little to what Aunt Esther said of what happened while we were gone and then took a bath. After supper we read a little about the bee's sting and then I went over to Elsa's.

Sunday, August 27, 1911
This morning dawned bright and fair and sunny. Just the day for a tour. But toward noon it grew hot and then it wasn't the day for [a] tour but we didn't mind that. We had our minds set on a good 100 mile run to Lake Geneva.

At last all was ready and we were off. At Michigan Av. and Jackson Bl. Papa set the speedometer back with the guide book. We rode through Garfield Park and out to Oak Park out of Chicago. Through Maywood and then turning and over the railroad passing the American can company. Then we began to leave city dirt and other things behind and were getting more and more into the country.

At last we stopped and ate our dinner under the shade of some trees. The views from there were indeed very pretty. A hill covered [with] the prettiest soft velvety green grass with a few oak trees where some cattle were grazing was one of the prettiest of all the views. Another one was a dusty road going uphill with a farm house and some kind of [illegible] house and green fields on the left and trees on the right. When we went up this hill after we were [through] we saw that there were squabs and pigeons for sale there.

In response, perhaps, to Irma's request that she think about and analyze what she read, Emily wrote:

NATURE

Verse beginning of Emerson's *Essay on Nature*

The rounded world is fair to see,
Nine time[s] folded in mystery
Though baffled seers cannot impart
The secret of its laboring heart,
Throb thine with Nature's throbbing breast
And all is clear from east to west,
Spirit that lurks each form within
Beckons to spirit of its kin;
Self-kindled every atom glows,
And hints the future which it owes.

Meaning to me is the following:

The world which is round is fair to see. There are many mysteries which we do not see.

Emily's other 1911 entries also include poems about nature from some favorite authors, such as Richard Henry Stoddard:

Summer or winter, day or night
The woods are ever a new delight
They give us peace, they make us strong.
Such wonderful balms to them belong;
So living or dying, I'll take my ease
Under the trees, under the trees.[16]

In a 1911 composition for Arbor Day at school, Emily wrote:

Nature indeed comes before all other things. As it says in one of the songs I learned when I first went to school,

"I fancy when the Earth was young
She told the birds and bees:
My children are the grass and flowers
My grown folks are the trees."

That surely is a fine thought. Are not the trees large and strong and tall while the flowers are like little dwarfs beside such large giants?

Nature always has at least some beauty one way or another in all her children. What is more beautiful than a slender elm or a graceful linden? All trees are beautiful from the large stately oak, to the small but graceful mulberry. Could Nature make them more attractive?

Again I say Nature is above all other things. We go into a deep forest. There we will see the Earths grown folks and children; or rather Natures. How cool and refreshing it is to be under the trees. How pretty the wild flowers are which grow at ones feet. How we long to pick them a[nd] feel as though we cannot get half enough. And what pity it is when we get home to find them almost withered or dead. (That is if we have a long way to go home.) It is best not to pick many but to leave them for the enjoyment of others who come along. One flower is as good as a good many.

To dwell on the trees beauties is a large and long fact. But a tree has as many uses as it has beauty. It is of course a shame to cut a beautiful graceful tree down to make lumber to help build a house or make some article of furniture. But I understand there are men who can tell whether a tree may be cut down without causing a sorry to Nature.

We make chairs and tables and play things in our manual training out of wood. Could we ever think that the wood we are sawing or nailing or sandpapering grew from either an acorn or a tiny seed or a little twig? It is almost impossible but yet it is true.

Again I say go into the deep forest and it feels cool and refreshing. Does not the coolness of the forest come from the trees leaves and large branches? The trees shade give the coolness to the forest. Its breezes also refresh us in the evening after the sun has gone down and we have had either a hard days work or hard days play.

So many uses of a tree and I cannot express them all on paper. So many beauties so many wonders from a tree. We who have a tree belonging to our home ought to take great care of it and have great pride in it.

In the 1910 Arbor and Bird Day book there is a saying that is

> "He who plants a tree, plants Hope."
> "He who plants a tree, plants Joy."
> "He who plants a tree, plants Peace."
> "He who plants a tree, plants Love."
> Is it not true?

There is a large lawn around my home, or rather my father's home. On it are seven oaks, one horse chestnut, one sumach, one mulberry, and one peach willow. The trees are very beautiful in summer and help to make the lawn look pretty.

My favorite pastime on summer mornings is to take a book and sit under my favorite oak and read. The reason it's my favorite oak is because it casts its shade in just the place I want to sit. And what more can I want?

We call our home, "Seven Oaks," because there are seven oaks on the lawn, although sometimes we call it just, "The Oaks."

Emily (Age 11) For Arbor Day [17]

Emily had clearly taken to heart the template for good writing her mother had written out in 1910:

Form the habit of writing your thoughts. Pen in hand you will be able to keep closer to a subject than by merely thinking it over in your easy chair. The mechanical element in writing assists in the power of concentration.

Thoughts and how to gather them:

        1) observation
        2) reflection
        3) reading
        4) social intercourse
        5) travel

Throughout her later years, Irma remarked time and again how much she valued the rich memories recorded in her diaries. She turned to them to refresh her mind about who she had been and what she had been thinking, as well as for the homely details they contained about her daily life in past decades.[18] As early as 1910, she had written:

THE VALUE OF MEMORY

We have to use an effort of will. Possibly the thought of practice of any kind, especially of the right kind has never entered your mind or if it has been immediately rejected as not worth while.

The materials with which your mind is richly filled as any treasure-house may have been unused or little used.

Again on Monday, January 13, 1958, Irma returned to the idea of memory. "Memory is a storage garden in which our most precious blossoms should cast their beauty over the present, emitting the music and the fragrance of other days into our present journey 'til it reaches into another past and ever the future beckons before us."

Most likely Irma conveyed to Emily her feelings about memories and the inherent value of keeping a diary as a record. Emily's diaries, which in general contain somewhat introspective reflections on the events of her life, are also full of her activities at dancing school, at parties, plays, and excursions, and of her scholastic achievements, which included writing competitions and the publication of some of her writings in children's magazines.[19]

For example, on Sunday, June 29, 1911, Emily noted that "Mamma has been sick all this week. I fixed her pillows gave her water to wash her hands and teeth and fixed her bed for her this morning. I then put my white middy blouse with the blue collor on and the white skirt on and went to Grossmammas. Aunt Meta corrected an essay I wrote on 'Flowers' for me which I am going to send to the Youth's Companion."

Then on Sunday, August 20, 1911, she wrote: "Elsa and I read a little and I discovered in Aunty Bee's paper that a wise-saying I wrote about Alfred was in it. At last 8:45 came and I went home and to-bed feeling very very very very happy."

Emily's final journal entry records another triumph:

Friday, March 31, 1912
When I received this book and when I made my first entry in it I did not think that my last entry would be such a glorious one.

Truly it is a glorious one. For am I not happy after winning the first prize at Sunday School the second time? Wouldn't anybody be? The title of my story this year is Pasach [Pesach] in Flowerland. The prize is a years subscription to the Ark.[20]

When I went to Sunday School this morning I never dreamed of the grand way in which the announcement would be made. True, it is, that I knew the announcement would be made this morning and I also had a suspicion of my winning the prize. But I repeat it again I did not think I would be made quite so popular.

"The first prize," said Dr. Stolz, "is awarded to the story called Pasach in Flowerland. It was written by Violet. Now who is that?" I raised my hand, stood up and then after the Doctor's inquiring (make believe) look I gave my name. He looked at me then at the children and then said, "Think of that! Emily F. won the 1st prize last year too." Every [one] was as quiet as could be but after that such clapping and drumming.

After school a good many people, I mean children or better still, classmates came up to me and congratulated me. I walked with Elsa T. and Arthur to Elsa's grandmothers. But I was not content until I went to Grossmammas. [I] told them about it, called mamma up on the phone, went to Aunt Roses and to Mr. Mayers.

I read another story in class this morning for class-work, which I wrote last night and which I got considerable praise on too. It was called The Character of Samson. But then I have written quite a few stories for class-work this year and have had praise on them from Miss Rau.

A good many people ask me how I do it. Really that puzzles even myself. How do I do it? It just seems to flow. I write and I write and I never think much of it until I have won something and even then I do not think to much of myself (At least I try not to).

It seems to me that I am always successful when I write from my heart. Of course my brain has to be used but not as much.

My best writings are those which are written from my heart, regardless to grammar. And then is the time I have my grammar most correct. When my whole self, mind, heart, and even sometimes body, enter into my work. Then is the time ideas pop up, and I can always make use of them. If not at that present time I can nearly always remember them afterward. A dozen or so are in my mind right now. An essay on Great Heroes where doctors and nurses are the chief and main parts, an essay or story about writing in which I call writing my music.[21]

Then again when I have writing in my mind as my music I usually have a good result. And my newest idea is a composition about writing from the heart and writing from just rules or the brain. When one writes from the heart, brain and all are included and it generally affords a good result. But let me get back to the happenings of to-day.

Grandma F. came over for dinner. Of course I had to read my essay to her and the children before dinner. Grossmamma R. was over for supper and of course I had to read the essay again and the family approved of it. But then maybe they didn't. Still they never showed any resentment or corrections.

After supper mamma and I took Grossmamma home. We walked.

Aunt Esther of course had to hear all about the day and its happenings and also what the grandmas did. I called this a grandma day.

But now it is time to close this diary. This diary which I have written in for so many years. This diary which papa gave me one summer eve when I was lying on his bed (we slept outside then already) and he was cleaning out his desk. Then I had visions of this book being complete and now it is true.

All the nice things I have stored away in here are like a story book but only a hundred times better because they are all about me, I, and myself. They are my thoughts and though they may interest other people they chiefly and mainly interest me. All my pleasant times, all my lovely good times are recorded in here and if I ever wish to write an account of my life as L. M. Alcott did I have this to fall back on. Now I must close this book and begin another just as entertaining.

Politics, Nature, and Travel, the 1920s

There is a gap in Irma's diaries between 1915 and 1921, and another void after 1921 until 1924, then a three-year break. Irma was busy raising her children, seeing her two girls marry and have children of their own, and taking courses at the University of Chicago, all of which presumably left her very little time to write.[1]

During the time for which she left no records, Russian Jews, persecuted and expelled from Europe, had fled to America in record numbers, further clogging city slums and straining welfare programs; Henry Ford serialized anti-Semitic libels in the *Dearborn Independent*; many Jews lobbied for a Palestinian homeland; the Eighteenth Amendment went into effect; Chicago became the illegal-liquor distribution center of the Midwest; and the world suffered through a horrible war.

It will never be known what Irma thought about any of these occurrences or what impact they had upon her, except for the First World War. Even then, in all of her diaries she made only three passing references to that conflict. She wrote one while in Canada in 1915, another in an undated letter sometime during the 1930s, in which she casually mentioned that Emily's first love had died in a World War I army camp, and a third following World War II.

On Tuesday, August 17, 1915, Irma wrote:

Victoria is clean, it is quiet, it is beautiful — All of these Chicago is not — . . . Just saw an ark-load of war nurses drive up to a store across the way — they seemed a jolly lot — Uniformed men all over the city — Never saw so many "khakis" in my life just walking about and harmless looking — Kilts in evidence on many of them — they look silly to us. Imagine our American boys and young men in short pleated skirts with aprons, bare knees and funny inverted colored

boat-shaped caps stuck on top of their American heads and stream-
ers going down behind.

War nurses across the way buying felt hats. . . .

Last night at the conclusion of the hotel concert — the band
played "God Save the King" and the whole company arose. We had
just come back from a walk — it was impressive.

The other day at the end of the entertainment on the boat the
Captain who had been laughing and joking announced that we
would conclude with "God Save the King" and if the Americans
wished they might sing "My country 'tis of thee." It was a strange experience — about half singing one set of words and the other half another. I was interested in the look that came over Captain Locke's
face. He doesn't believe in prayer, but it was certainly an expression of the utmost solemnity — I thought he was much more stirred
by his national hymn than we Americans were, although we all
seemed very solemn — no doubt due in some measure to these war
times.

Soldiers' encampment-training school [is] on old race-course —
Saw recruits from the distance drilling — not allowed to motor into
grounds. Afterward saw soldiers marching.

The second reference was in an undated letter found among Irma's 1958
papers: "Dr. F.'s son, Harrison was in love with Emily when he died in an
army camp during World War I. It was a dreadful blow to Emily." The
third, equally brief, was an undated entry in 1958. In it, Irma commented
that "[i]n two world wars they [the Germans] almost succeeded in wrecking civilization."

Although Irma wrote little about these major events, it was during
the 1920s that she finally realized her desire to become a "real" published
author when a poem for which she was paid twenty-five dollars was
printed. She also voted for the first time. She typed out a brief account of
this experience, crediting a local organization, the Chicago Woman's City
Club, with helping educate her in how to vote. She also managed to write
a short book titled *Walks into May* for her sister Meta. In it, she recounted
how she had argued the heritability of criminal tendencies with Clarence Darrow, talked about the Women's International League for Peace
and Freedom Congress held at the University of Chicago, and related
an encounter she had with a bookseller. And, finally, she toured Europe
twice.

Irma's poem was written in response to a lecture at the University of Chicago during which Frank Harris and Percy Ward debated the question "Has Life Any Meaning?" The poem was printed by Emanuel Haldeman-Julius in 1921 in the socialist-populist publication *Appeal to Reason*, in the People's Pocket Series.[2]

THE MEANING OF THE MOON

"The moon," he said, "is dead."
And some day the corpse of the earth will be
    another moon;
"The moon," he said, "is the skeleton at our
    feast."
Then I remembered that night
When the moon came up behind the hills
Sifting gold through the trees;
And I walked in the moon-light with a girl.
    I wonder,
Did he ever stroll through the moon-light
    with a girl,
And was the moon dead that night?

In 1920, the universal suffrage amendment to the United States Constitution passed. Irma never mentioned how she felt about its passage, although it cannot have failed to excite her, since enfranchisement was the goal of most club women at that time. In Chicago, Irma's friend Jane Addams was a prominent suffragist.

In Illinois, women had received the right to vote for school officials on June 19, 1891. Later, women's enfranchisement was extended to electing University of Illinois trustees.

The Illinois Federation of Women's Clubs had endorsed a number of municipal suffrage bills between 1902 and 1906. However, women who supported suffrage also formed a number of organizations specifically to advance their cause, formal clubs composed of serious women with a mission. The North American Women's Suffrage Association (NAWSA) was among the most visible of these groups. The Chicago Woman's City Club was another.

The wives of several members of the all-male City Club founded the Chicago Woman's City Club in 1910. The men had thought their wives' organization would be an auxiliary helping to push their husbands' political agenda through city hall, but the women had a different plan altogether. They wanted municipal ownership of garbage collection and disposal, a municipal strike bureau to settle labor disputes, a new fire prevention bureau, an elected board of education, as well as cleaner air. They also proposed that the city of Chicago preserve open spaces along the lakefront for parks and free beaches. Finally, they urged the city to take an active role to help solve the tenement problems. In other words, the Woman's City Club believed that meeting the needs of daily life ought to be one of the primary purposes of government.

In 1913, Grace Wilbur Trout of the Chicago Political Equality League pressured the Illinois Speaker of the House William McKinley to introduce a bill permitting women to vote for presidential electors and all local offices not specifically mentioned in the Illinois Constitution. The bill passed; Governor Dunne signed it into law on June 26, that same year. Illinois women could then vote in the April 1914 elections.

Following the passage of the 1913 suffrage bill, the Woman's City Club, the Political Equality League, the African-American Alpha Suffrage Club, more than 130 ethnic women's organizations, the Women's Trade Union League, and the Wage Earners' Suffrage League pushed women to register to vote at a huge outdoor rally attended by ten thousand women. At that rally, the leaders urged women to declare a party affiliation, to vote in the primaries, and to work for their party's candidates. Jane Addams had, at an earlier date, reminded women that their first job would be to "translate human needs into political action."[3]

On June 10, 1919, Illinois became the first state to ratify the Nineteenth Amendment. Twelve months later, when Tennessee ratified it, women were finally granted universal suffrage.

Prior to the first primary vote of 1921, Irma had looked to the Chicago Woman's City Club for assistance in learning how to vote. She wrote an account of her first voting experience:

Tuesday, April 12, 1921
Eleven o'clock. Went out to vote. Took almost an hour. Victor and I voted Republican. They gave us green ballots. Democrats had brown ones. Green was the appropriate color for us. We knew a little about the candidates but there were so many of them the ballot was a disturbing puzzle. Victor and I discussed it when we came out. I was delighted that it puzzled Victor too who is a man. I told him that I did it this way. Since I had to vote, and it wasn't at all a simple affair

I thought I should adopt a system. I said to myself, "I shall be 100% American, and when in doubt I shall vote for an American." I looked at the names. I can't repeat them. They were Polish, German, Bohemian, Swedish — a few American names — but no doubt some of these were names which had been changed from Lesinsky or Roederguishkw. That system wouldn't work. I tried to recall all the recommendations of "The Woman's City Club" and I remembered some of them.

I "fell" for one poetic name, Earl somebody or other. His name was in two places. I voted for him once. So much for poetry — the art which once brought me in twenty-five dollars and has given me such joy in life. But I wonder — for all I know Earl Somebodyorother might be that fat dun-colored politician I know only by his back as it still parades up and down the street beginning at our corner. It seems to be my fate that everytime I look out that fat one is walking the other way.

It didn't take me so long to vote as it did Victor. I found a system and I daresay I voted as intelligently as most voters. But I, who am great on resolutions (which I usually do not keep) resoluted to pay more attention to coming elections so that I shall go to the polls better prepared the next time.

While I was waiting for Victor, I glanced about the room in which we were voting, in the basement of the Shakespeare school [in] the manual training room. Nothing attractive about the room. In the back sat a peaceful policeman absorbed in a newspaper which he was holding rather high before him. Six women had charge of the party. All but one seemed the bossy kind, the rather neat though-not-stylish-dressing-kind. You always think you can tell a good deal about women from their clothes. But you can't tell much. I happen to know. Sometimes one hasn't time to be fashionable. Those women interested me. I thought, looking at two of them, "Why are all politicians fat?" These two were large, fat women, the kind which spread all over the frail looking chairs they sit in. I was thinking that all politicians are fat because politics make them fat, or politics were invented for fat people. I noticed that four of them were not fat. Now, of course, there is a chance that the four lean ones haven't been in politics long enough and might wax fat in time — or else all politicians are not fat, and the proportion of fat ones to lean ones is two lean ones to one fat one. That might be a profound observation.[4]

The next set of diary entries is in book form, covering the month of May 1924. During this time Irma "resoluted" to write a book for her sister Meta, intending to surprise Meta with the book in time for her October birthday. Irma chronicles walks the sisters took in the park, around the neighborhood, and in downtown Chicago. The book also contains a short account of a conversation with a bookseller, showing Irma's continued intentions to write, mentions preparations for her trip, and gives her regrets that she was unable to attend the Women's International League for Peace and Freedom Congress, as well as some more general thoughts and reflections.

Tuesday, May 20, 1924

I have never had so long a time in one stretch in Kroch's.[5] Mr. Solle [the manager] came up to me every once in a while and talked to me. I told him how I had surveyed the History of Art in one hour the other evening in the book he had sold me Saturday — Reinach's *Apollo*. I said that when I am abroad I want to behold with as much intelligence as possible, what I am seeing. Of course you know . . . how profound my learning is, when I can do the history of art in an hour, like the speed camera in the movies. I suspected that I was making Will Solle a bit disgusted — he couldn't stand me with my superficial art talk, and so he said, "When I go to Europe all I shall care about is to eat in famous restaurants."

It was growing closer to dinner time that is why I presume he felt that way — or maybe he was so filled with rage at me that he would like to have chewed me up.

Somehow I didn't feel so sorry for him as I should have, nor did I try immediately to convert his carnal soul to the higher things. Perhaps he was in earnest. I can understand, in a way, that a man who lives among books, and knows what's in books, might prefer occasionally to know what's in pantries and dining-rooms rather than to see the things he has everlastingly been reading about come out into the open. It's all a mood. . . . — Will Solle was hungry — earlier in the day he admitted that he never takes more than 20 minutes for his lunch. I suppose when he goes to Europe he wants to sit down for long periods of time in all the restaurants and eat and eat and eat — and never think about a printed page.

I looked at many books. . . . Not one could hold my attention for more than three minutes. . . . I didn't want to read books. I wanted to write them.

And so when Mr. Solle came up to me again I asked, "Mr. Solle, have you ever written a book?"

He said that he had.

"Where is it," I asked.

"Oh, it's never been published."

"Why not?"

Then he told me that the *Atlantic Monthly* people had seen it and praised it very nicely but they found one fault with it.

"What?" I inquired.

"You see," he answered, "it is a series of letters and the *Atlantic* criticism was that it hadn't enough background."

I felt as if something had hit me. I began to wonder if this book of mine had background and if it did what is its background. . . .What I want for my background is an elusive, spiritual thing—I want my background to be the mood of the month of May.

Holmes (It is Holmes or Lowell?) said, "What is so rare as a day in June?"—much as I love June—I think it wears a perpetual smile—[but] I like better the struggling month of May, which starts, in our climate merely as a dotted light green motif set in an atmosphere of crystal winds and ends in a burst of glory in the summer breezes.

It is a struggling month, winning day by day its spring-time beauty out of clouded skies and raw winds. . . . Often I have thought this May-time, watching the struggle, May ought to know that it will win—that summer is inevitable—and so perhaps, we too, are winning. I must keep the mood and make it mine—I want the spirit of May to be the background of my book—beauty winning through struggle—ever fresh new beauty of effort and new beauty of soul. . . .

But to return to Mr. Solle.

I asked, "Mr. Solle, where will you put my book when it comes out? Will you place it here on your front counter?"

"If it belongs there," he said. "What will it be—essays, biography, poetry? Poetry rarely is 'a best seller.'"

"Not poetry," I said, "Not at present—essays perhaps—I don't know. I can't actually define it."

He ran his hands over a small obtruding counter. "Here we always keep our three best sellers."

I looked. This week they are *The Seven Lively Arts*— a book on garden flowers —I can't this moment think of the third.

"Well, maybe mine will land there," I ventured.

And again I chuckled, thinking how I was putting him on. How funny it would be if it actually did and he were selling a book which he had helped to live.

Preparations for Irma's first trip to Europe required a great deal of thought and shopping effort, as well as personal sacrifice.

Tuesday, May 13, 1924
I [did] a fool thing, perhaps — skipped my lunch and had buttermilk and dry toast. I hate the uninteresting, sourish stuff but I hate my "figger" too — then I tottered around weak and tired all the P.M. knowing what all the family would say if I were caught red-handed dieting.

I wish I could make up my mind to be stoutish and jolly. The trouble just now is that I've been fitting clothes and no one ever refrains from saying, "Of course you know your hips are so much broader, proportionately, than the rest of your figure." If they'd only say, "What wonderful shoulders you have, how like a sylph you are from your brains to your waist-line." I ought to have been one of those half-beauties in a museum who stand on tables from their waists up. . . .

Mamma said yesterday that she is glad that I am going to stay home [and not work at the Women's International League for Peace and Freedom Congress or with the Woman's Aid club as an officer any more]. She knows I must have things to do. I know she means cleaning closets and attending to all the important matters which house keepers find to do in May. (That is my sentiment)— but if I let these days escape into my dusty closets, shall I not have a dusty outlook on life, instead of one of fresh, expanding boundaries? I'll take a week of furious activity when May is over.[6]

Friday, May 16
Bud [Alfred] said that [my new] hat is "The Bee's Knees" which is paying it a most high compliment, unless it were paid a higher one and called "The Cat's Meow." To-day I thought about it and I won-

dered if Albert [Emily's husband] would call it "Spiffy." Isn't that a "spiffy" word — spiffy?

Tuesday, May 20 [from Irma's book for Meta, *Walks into May*]
On the way home on the [elevated train] you were telling me about the opening of the International Summer School [at the Women's International League for Peace and Freedom Congress] the day before, how the delegates reported, what they wore and the impression their personalities made upon you. For a moment I wondered why I hadn't exerted my powers and activities to become an "international woman." Neither of us have become women of fame or of accomplishment! No doubt we haven't the qualifications — just a certain amount of prominence has come whenever I reached out for it. But we've tried to "do our bit" (as they used to say in war times) I hope. My young people whom I have raised are not lazy, or narrow-minded. Some of us must stay at home to preserve whatever beauty has been won out of the experience of the race. You are doing your share — filling an important position not alone capably, but gracefully too. If the nations were more graceful and mannerly to one another, their hideous, dirty wars would be over.

Friday, May 23 [from Irma's book for Meta]
I did not really want to attend the International Congress. You and Essie are surprised that I have not been to its sessions. If I were taking part, if they needed me specifically, I'd be there. Of course, I know everybody who attends takes part and is needed — but, what, in the last analysis is it all for? I asked you and Essie what the women were saying and you both told me that they were talking about conditions in their various countries, pleading for a better understanding between nations, telling the old, old tales about how the poor and unfortunate of each country would fraternize with the poor and unfortunate of every other country if left to themselves — going into details relating specific incidents. I've heard it all so often and I never for a moment have doubted it. Never for the fraction of a second was I misled during war-times by the vicious propaganda which poisoned so many of our best minds. My dear! there is no doubt at all in my mind that there is a humanity which is broader than narrow patriotism — a world patriotism. The nations are stupid and some day these hideous wars will be no more just as human slavery has been abolished. Oh I know all the arguments that we have not abolished

slavery, that we have industrial instead of corporal slaves and all of that. True, but society is an intricate web of tapestry — slowly and slowly does the pattern come out a bit better each time than it was before, as we weave and weave, unrolling and letting it pass on year upon year, and year upon year. There is an organization of writers from all over the world who met in New York last week, who are saying that if books were ambassadors there would be no wars; if Anatole France and [John?] Galsworthy controlled the affairs of their separate countries we should have peace.

And so I've been thinking that I'd better be writing my book — that if humanity could walk into May and see there the stupendous struggle of nature in which we exist and are victorious in a slight degree, perhaps humanity would wake up and know that there is enough war so that the human race need not commit suicide, enough war and struggle to brace itself against and conquer.

It is such a mad, mad world such frenzy and excitement over nothing, such weaving of intricate patterns when the truest beauty comes out in clear, clear lines. There may have been justifiable wars in the past, but the last war appears so much a mad frenzy due to the excesses of our civilization that there seems nowhere any justification for it. You can't find contentment or joy in May, or even in June, unless you study a bit, unless you try to interpret with intelligence growing out of research and appreciation. Spontaneous joy I know there is when we are very young and react sensitively to each manifestation which plays upon our perceptions. From that keen joy might [. . . come] the desire to know and to understand. To transpose through study, through the intellect this sharper edged reaction into our mellowing souls as we grow older — to be able to do this is to possess the universe. . . . You told me that to come in contact with the personalities of the women of the Women's International League is a wonderful experience. I am sure it must be. I shall meet some of the delegates next week but the truth often is that we have no time to become acquainted with our personalities. . . . Don't you see through all of this that I'm simply *dying* to go to the Congress but I haven't time?

The Women's International League for Peace and Freedom had been founded in The Hague on April 28, 1915. The conference's organizers were women, many of whom were also involved in the International Suffrage Alliance. More than one thousand women attended this first congress and elected Jane Addams president. The league's mission was to secure full, equal rights for women, justice for all, and world peace through disarmament.

The 1924 congress found women from almost every nation in the world convened at the University of Chicago. They developed strategies to improve their lives and make educational, social, and political gains, and they urged scientists to support their platform for disarmament. Deciding to stay home from the congress when many of her friends were attending was difficult for Irma.

In that same month, while the women were trying to formulate ways to end war and violence, a vicious crime was committed in the Hyde Park–Kenwood neighborhood. The newspapers sensationalized it as the "crime of the century."

In late May 1924, fourteen-year-old Bobby Franks, a son of Jacob Franks, was kidnapped from outside his private school and murdered. The Franks lived four blocks south of Irma. By May 29, Nathan Leopold Jr. and Richard Loeb had confessed to the crime. The noted Chicago attorney Clarence Darrow defended them.

Why did this case receive such unprecedented attention from the media and the public? Certainly, the papers had enough other news to print. In Chicago, headline-grabbing reports of violence were common. The previous year, Cook County had 267 deaths caused by guns; gang warfare was so rampant that it was unsafe to walk the streets at night, even in residential neighborhoods surrounding the University of Chicago.[7] And, although it was the time of Prohibition, there had been 216 deaths attributed to "moonshine." Corruption was so prevalent that brothels and gambling dens openly operated with police protection.

Perhaps Bobby Franks's murder became front-page news because of the callousness and lack of repentance of Leopold and Loeb, college-educated sons of wealthy Hyde Parkers who for no apparent reason had planned and committed what was to have been the perfect crime. Perhaps it was because the story showed the working and middle classes that even the wealthy were not above getting into trouble. Whatever reason lay behind the media attention, the Leopold and Loeb affair shattered the Hyde Park–Kenwood Jewish community because all the boys were Jewish.[8]

On June 5, 1924, the grand jury indicted the two boys on eleven counts of murder and sixteen counts of kidnapping. The papers published their full confessions the next day.[9]

Irma never mentioned the Franks murder until 1957. However, in 1924 she did write about one of the central characters in the incident, Clarence Darrow, and her earlier contact with him when he spoke at one of the clubs to which she belonged.

It is interesting to consider Irma's comments about Darrow in light of her certitude that the personality of the mother was responsible for how children turn out and to compare it with Darrow's convictions about criminality.

According to one writer, Darrow held to a "mechanist philosophy: that a man was formed and his actions determined by his birth and environment, that he had no free will, thus could not be held responsible for what he did. He considered it barbarous to punish a man for a crime because man cannot control his behavior."[10]

One immediately senses that if Darrow had aired this philosophy while Irma was in the audience, he would have become involved in a debate. On Monday, May 26, 1924, she wrote to her sister Meta:

I had to stop. You and Essie had come in (Friday P.M. it was) and were telling me about the talk on anti-Semitism. There was little in it that I had not, at one time or another, heard. Do you remember the day I said to you, "I cannot any longer go to club-meetings unless there is something specific for me to do there. I can no longer go and listen and listen without acting." It was some years ago and it was you who first encouraged me to get up "in meetin'" and let my voice be heard. Do you recall the day when Clarence Darrow had spoken and you said you knew by the look in my eyes and the expression of my face that I had something to say? I can feel now how my heart thumped at the thought of getting up and saying it. And you tugged at my sleeve and muttered in my ear

"Coward! Coward!"

Without thinking further I arose and had some discussion with Clarence Darrow about criminals. Afterward he spoke to me privately and the next day sent me one of his books.[11]

It was the beginning of active club life for me. Thereafter I was seldom timid when I felt that I had something to contribute. You remember my meteoric career in the clubs 'til I laid down the important presidency [of the Chicago Jewish Woman's Aid] on account of illness. I have tried not to be a slacker.

But again I have the feeling that I cannot go to Congresses, cannot listen to numberless speeches on a variegated assortment of topics unless I have a specific work to do which these speeches will illuminate. I know that just because of my going abroad in a few weeks, it might have been to my interest to attend this International Congress but I am not going abroad to study, in forty-five days of rapid travel, the social conditions of the countries we shall be skimming over. . . . When I come back, I shall work again.

The next diary entries — for the most part, short notes — are from 1927. Irma had returned to Europe in 1926, this time with her son, Alfred; Ruth had moved to Toronto from Philadelphia; Alfred was planning to take a job in New York; and the house was in desperate need of cleaning. She commented on Lindbergh's flights, and then took herself to task again for failing to accomplish what she had intended.

Saturday, June 11, 1927

Lindbergh, who flew across the ocean from New York to Paris, arrived in Washington to-day. Over the radio I listened to a description of Washington as it was to-day with crowds of cheering, welcoming human beings thronging the streets, heard a description of the parade and heard President Coolidge's speech in presenting Lindbergh with the distinguished flying medal, and heard Lindbergh's reply. Sitting here quietly in my living room, I felt the wonder and the thrill of it all. It passes through my mind now as a vivid, marvelous poem I might have read. And the marvel of the brave flight was so much more wonderful than the fact that 25,000,000 persons not in Washington, not seeing the parade and the demonstration, could still see and take part in it over the radio. Will these things seem wonderful a quarter of a century from now? Are they more wonderful than the telephone was twenty-five years ago? The telephone to-day is just part of matter-of-fact living as is also the automobile — a few years ago we used to rush out into our yard when we heard a motor whirring in the sky and we gazed with delight at every aeroplane which passed above us. I confess that I still look at every aeroplane whenever and wherever I might see one, although automobiles are just common things, which we no longer see.

I liked President Coolidge's speech. It was simple and dignified and inspiring. Inspiring for what, I do not exactly know — but inspiring — made one feel that any boy who was decent is a potential Lindbergh. Personally, I think Lindbergh is just an ordinary person who has suddenly by chance circumstances become a great hero. Lindbergh himself would agree with me, I am sure. I am sure that he is just so ordinary and just so great. Part of the greatness of our thrills and our acclaim of the lad lies within ourselves. Perhaps that is why President Coolidge's address was inspiring. A little of our own bravery, of our own desires to be undertaking great flights, responds to Lindbergh's accomplishments. The young man is an *Arabian Nights* character and we all still love the *Arabian Nights*. Just a decent, clean chap, serious and busy and he flies into fame and into American history, acclaimed by the eminent ones of the earth, and akin to all the humble ones whose dreams will grow.[12]

Saturday, September 10
When I last wrote in here on June 11, I was in the midst of house-cleaning. I had been in Toronto [to see Ruth] all of April and most of May. Then, Ruth spent two weeks here and after Ruth left, I began putting my house in order. House-cleaning isn't merely cleaning. One puts to rights all the things which one had to get out of one's sight for future arrangement and dispersal. It took me a long time, almost six weeks, for I hadn't had a real chance to put my house to rights since before I left for Italy in April 1926. In the fall of '26 we had decorators and I left for Toronto before the house had been entirely put to rights. Upon my return there followed a period when Alfred and I refused to have a maid. Alfred took a job downtown [at the *Chicago Tribune*] and I kept pretty busy trying to save the wages of a maid. Both Alfred and I felt we had a debt of honor to pay back in economy. We each took a journey after our return from Europe which we felt, financially, we were not entitled. Bud went East on a quest of reporting a musical festival which we felt might be Opportunity, and I took Emily and Wutzsie [grandson, Victor C.] with me to Toronto. And so the house patiently kept its secret disorders until June when it seemed to me getting things to rights was like a campaign — I seemed to conquer the closets and the stow-away places one by one — but one must constantly [be] on the defensive move . . . to retain one's conquests. Everything is in order now — . . . but there is the whole winter to clear up things — I'll clear them up — but

one's heart grows heavy — the disorderly times mean living fully — the clean-up times are a disease of civilization. And thus, is one never satisfied — It has taken me four years to try not to miss Ruth. . . . I tell Alfred perhaps he will return. . . .

Three months ago, on a Saturday, I wrote in this book, thinking then, that I should not be too busy during the summer to write in here at times, and to send out some things which I have been writing for the last five years or so —

The summer has gone and although I've written a sketch or two, as far as writing goes, it was wasted. What did I do? I don't know. Just lived.

I have spent more time than usual with Mamma for she is growing feebler and irritable sometimes, and my heart aches when I notice her weaknesses.

Time passes and I never accomplish all I feel I want to. . . .

I remember reading once that "Regret is the mildew of the soul." Everybody, I suppose has regrets. What's regret anyway? It's thinking to-day that you should have acted differently yesterday. Yet how could we lead our lives with our eyes constantly on tomorrow, trying constantly to avoid to-morrow's pain when we do not know if there will ever be a to-morrow, and cannot suspect what pain never experienced before, might await us. I think it might be a little cowardly to be always trying to side-step future regret and that we might live less fully in that reality which we call to-day, were we always trying to save ourselves pain. And how do we know but that if we try to avoid the pain of regret by strolling along the river-side to-day instead of being blown along the sea-shore, we might not regret to-morrow that we missed the sea-breeze — Who knows?

Staying Afloat during the 1930s

On New Year's Day of 1929, the nation looked back at the preceding five years, noting with pride that they had been ones of unprecedented prosperity. Herbert Hoover was the president-elect; workers were earning more than ever before; interest rates were low; factories were churning out products at a furious pace. People were investing, buying, building, and traveling. Irma was no exception.

Saturday, August 24, 1929
The summer is almost over. Five weeks from today Victor and I are sailing for Spain. Yesterday I took a jaunt down town to attend to my first shopping prepatory to our journey. It seemed a jaunt because I was in a mood to enjoy it all — went to Field's first where I looked at shoes and coats and dresses — tried to get a sweater — bought a stack of heavy envelopes for filing my recipes and stories — had lunch with (interruption! maid, Betty, cleaning my room — had to pick up things — show Victor an article on anaemia from the Medical Journal) — was about to say that I had lunch with Miss Vivette Gorman whom I like very much. We had crab-meat salad in tomato, cole slaw, coffee and lemon-cream pie in The Black Cat Room at the Tip Top Inn.[1] . . . In the afternoon I had my eyes tested preparatory to going away. . . . Then I went to a shoe place to try to get fitted with shoes —. . . . Then down to Menacker's to look at coats.

Sunday, August 25
Interesting time visiting Martha N. — motored to The Northview Country Club. . . . Sat out on a sunny lawn at the club talking to Martha, Marc and Sam E. Took Martha and Marc back to their home in Winnetka, then to Ravinia where we saw *The Secret of Suzanne* and

La Vida Breve— beautiful singing by Bovi and magnificent stage settings. Took Sydney F. and his mother home from Ravinia stopping on the way to have something to eat at "Sally's Waffle-Shop" on Sheridan Road. It was about midnight and the restaurant was crowded — rather second-class food but Sydney said you are not in the social-register unless you have eaten at Sally's. Interesting psychology.[2]

Just two months after that routine entry came Black Tuesday, October 29, the stock market crash, and the acknowledged beginning of the Great Depression.

Mention the 1930s, and people invariably call up images of the dust bowl, bread lines, hoboes, the shantytowns called Hoovervilles, FDR, and public works projects. Ask people who lived through those years, and their reports vary little: "Those were hard times." From those comments and familiar media reports, it would appear the depression struck everyone at the same time with the same degree of severity. However, this is incorrect. As in the earlier depressions of 1873 and 1893, the economic downturn of 1929 affected those involved in business and finance, and the working classes, first and hardest. Middle-class people often had resources upon which to fall back and nonessential expenses they could eliminate, so they could stave off financial disaster longer.

In fact, it seems that, from Irma's diary entries between 1929 and 1931, nothing untoward was happening in her life at all. Irma traveled abroad, as she had in 1924 and 1926, entertained, shopped, cooked, read, saw movies, attended lectures, and wrote in her diary.

Sunday, April 13, 1930
And so it goes. A diary — in which one writes on August 25,— and then again on April 13 — meanwhile having been in Spain, Italy, Sicily, Turkey, Greece, Egypt, Palestine, Syria where I kept a diary of a sort, and wrote many letters —

Thursday, October 2
I don't have the sense of guilt in keeping a diary which I had in my younger years. I had a feeling that because there seemed so many demands on my time and energy that time spent in writing which showed no results calculated in terms of what I thought was utility, or in terms of money returns which might be translated into utility, was time wasted. And yet I always had a guilty feeling too because I

was not writing, feeling that recognition of some sort might compensate for meals less well prepared, socks undarned and buttons that were not [sewed on].

And now, were I tragic, I should say "Vengeance is upon me" — now I have more leisure and an almost-never ceasing pain complicated with a bit of stiffness in my right hand and arm. I find difficulty often in using a pen at all especially when I am tired. But somehow, when I keep a record of the days as they pass, I haven't so much the feeling that they are slipping away from me forever, as I have when I do not write.

Yet, how absurd! What difference does it make? They slip anyway, whether or *no* I ever re-read these lines. I used to think that when I was this age I should be old and might want to read about my younger days. I do. There was rich living and I wish I had recorded more of it — the bringing to maturity of three human beings, club work, the travels — All were interesting but somehow I find that my interest in the passing time is equally keen — I seem still to have interests, to take part in the current activities — there have been many changes. But I still seem to feel that whatever the effects Emily, Ruth and Alfred must still find me ready to serve them and their advancements (whatever advancement may mean). And house-keeping is still my job. Alfred loves this old house and Irma Betty [granddaughter, often called "I. B."] talks of it as her home. She says it is always her home that stays, no matter if she lives in Toronto or St. Louis. — So I want to keep it. Victor sometimes wants to give it up. Sometimes not — I don't know what living would be like if this house weren't always here for us.

Monday, January 26, 1931
Alfred came home for two weeks at Christmas time. We had several parties. It was a gay time. Two weeks passed which seemed like a day.

There are no surviving journals between December 17, 1931, and 1937. This gap may well have been the result of one of Irma's many "weeding-out" episodes.

Sunday, July 4, 1937
Most of the day, whenever I could, I looked over a lot of papers and stuff, recipes clippings etc. which I have foolishly been collecting for years. Weeding out most of them and I was at it 'til 3 A.M.

Tuesday, July 6
In the last few days have cleared up many of my papers and recipes and have thrown many away.

The years for which there are no journals would have covered the worst of the depression for most of America. Nevertheless, in Chicago, the city celebrated its centennial with the 1933 World's Fair, dubbed the "Century of Progress." The fairgrounds were on the Near South Side on lakefront landfill. There were wonders galore: a sky ride, flashy science and technology exhibits, artworks from around the world, and, of course, the infamous fan-dancer Sally Rand. Anyone who could afford the price of admission came. The money spent in Chicago boosted the local economy and enhanced the city's reputation. Chicago needed the help.

By 1933, industrial unemployment in the city had doubled; payrolls were down almost 75 percent from their 1927 highs.[3] Foreclosures and evictions had tripled from predepression levels. More than fifteen hundred men slept under Wacker Drive. The fair did not remedy these problems, since the depression lingered on long after it had closed, but the additional income helped city-run social service programs. Real economic advances were actually slow during the 1930s, but the hope that better times were soon coming seemed pervasive, except among the self-employed professionals.

The next set of Irma's diaries begins on February 21, 1937. The entries for the following two years are very different from any earlier ones. Nowhere else in her previous journals did she ever list expenses or figures in such detail. At no time before did she ever attempt to justify expenditures or to detail the cost of living. In these journals, however, she discusses how she made old clothes look up-to-date, and the cost of entertaining and buying a new electric refrigerator. More through suggestion and intimations, than by actual statements, Irma's journals and records build a picture of how and when the Great Depression finally hit the middle class, the devastating effect it had, and the efforts the middle class took to preserve appearances.

Tuesday, April 13, 1937
This evening I had a serious talk with Victor about our finances. Life insurance bills are due, which are difficult to pay. At present there is $185 in the bank which we certainly must keep for current expenses. So far this month, I have paid the H.O.L.C. [Home Owner's Loan Corporation] and all other bills, but must count on a big gas bill.

Saturday, April 24

I thought I needed no new clothes this spring, but to-day when I wanted to go out, I realized that my things aren't snappy (not that I need startling things)—I mean, have no look of newness about them! Well, I'm not going to get anything new because I have no money to spare, but I wish I could. I'd love to have a flowered print on a black background, and a new hat and coat. . . .

[At a luncheon meeting with friends] I wore my black crêpe waist dress, my hat from last year, suede purse and suede gloves. [I also wore] the black and white polka dot, three cornered scarf—black ground, white dots and a white rose. I wasn't out of style, I think— but my clothes haven't the feeling of newness one likes in the spring. I have a different feeling for clothes than I used to have.

Tuesday, April 27

We looked at Electrolux Refrigerators [like Essie's]—then over to Commonwealth Edison, looked at several refrigerators and then [bought] a Frigidaire—7 cu. Ft.—cost $241.00 including 7.04 sales [tax], payable monthly—($241.54—234.50 price of refrigerator— 7.04 tax).[4]

In some sense, Irma's purchase of a Frigidaire during the depths of the depression seems quite irrational. If money was tight, if Victor's patient base was shrinking, why buy an expensive piece of machinery? The purchase can be more readily understood if one reasons that, although cash might not be readily available to pay the iceman for the blocks of ice for the old icebox, the Frigidaire could be purchased on credit; there was always the hope that "next month" money to pay the bills would come in and that "happy days" would be here again. As such, the Frigidaire functioned as so much more than just a middle-class status symbol.

Friday, April 30

Right after lunch the Frigidaire came. Victor C. [grandson] was much delighted with it, as I am. Showed me how to make it work and took possession of it like a grand new toy. It is a beauty and has many conveniences — automatic defrosting and temperature control, contrivance for loosening containers for ice-cubes, lever for loosening ice-cubes, electric light inside the box. It will be a pleasure to use it and it is a pleasure to look at it. Does not take up very much room in the kitchen.

Saturday, May 1

After supper Victor C. came to sleep here. Of course he had to look the Frigidaire over wipe off the door and the outside of it carefully — We drank a bottle of coco-cola together. One glass with two straws — cellophane "straws" which he likes. Then Victor came and the two Victors admired the Frigidaire and praised it.

Having a child around enhances simple living — Children are so eager, so interested in "everything" — it has been twice as much fun getting the Frigidaire to have Victor C. around. He takes a possessive interest in it and a delightful pride in its conveniences and beauty. It really is a beautiful piece of machinery — harmonious — every part perfectly and economically adapted to its function. It is a *grand toy*. . . .

Looked over the statement from the bank to-night. We have a balance of $98.00. Last month Victor paid $140.00 on his New England Life Insurance policy. At the beginning of the month there was a balance of $185 and Victor put $250 additional in — Life Insurance, Home Owner's Loan Corporation, Gas bill (Heating) took up over $230.00 — doesn't leave much for current expenses. The Frigidaire cost somewhere around $236.00 but we have three years in which to pay it. Of course, in three years we would have needed ice in the old refrigerator. There is a possibility that my frequent winter colds have been due in part to the difference in temperature between the warm kitchen and the cold place where the old ice-box stands.

Sunday, May 2

Victor C. and I had breakfast at about 9 [A.M.]. Put my Frigidaire in order, listened to the University of Chicago Round Table on "Sweden" — tried to adjust electric cord in dining room — Did some telephoning etc. At about 3 P.M. Victor C. returned with Albert — Belle R., Essie and Rudolph came and all looked at the Frigidaire and admired it. Victor C. loves to show it off.

Monday, May 3

In the A.M., I went down town, shopping with Meta — although the reason for going down was to go to the bank. Deposited $95.00. Must pay life insurance bill of $96 or thereabouts. Went to Electric Company. . . .

Tuesday, May 4

Prepared lunch — Cooking green kern soup for Laurie — cooked a piece of brisket in the soup and prepared a horse-radish gravy to serve with it. Busy all day cooking . . .

Victor C. discovered a little can of prepared ice-cream in the A & P store yesterday. You add ½ pint of whipping cream, whipped, and put it in the ice-cube container of the refrigerator. We bought a can of chocolate and this noon, when Victor [C.] came home from school we prepared it. Victor still takes great pride and a great interest in the Frigidaire and adds to the fun of it. The ice-cream is pretty good. I was interested in the fact that as soon as he came home from school this P.M. he went to the refrigerator to see what had happened and wanted to know if he could have some. He prevailed on me to take some too, just as he wants me to take a straw and the two of us have a bottle of coco-cola, or awful cream soda, or orange soda together. He always wants me to join him in everything — and so I do most of the time.[5]

Sunday, May 16

Very interesting to rearrange space in the new Frigidaire and to defrost it. Defrosting (automatic) took less than an hour — an efficient piece of machinery that is a real pleasure to handle and work with. Wonder if it works so excellently well, just because it is new or because it is very good —

Monday, May 17

Had to go down town this P.M. to the bank, paid the electric light bill. . . . We had some strawberry ice-cream made in the refrigerator and then had some fun making real ice-cream in the small freezer. Victor C. enjoyed eating the ice-cream off the dasher.

Friday, May 21

Sallie and Essie came for lunch. Set the small table in the dining-room window with yellow luncheon cloth, my best plates etc. Had tomato juice with pretzels, fried chicken from "The Chicken Shack" with French fried potatoes and salad (cost $1.24) maple ice cream done in the Frigidaire, cookies, coffee — Then we went up to the library and read Emerson's *Essay on Friendship* and Santayana's ideas on Friendship.[6]

Wednesday, May 26
Checked over bills and made out some checks. I am very late this month.

Saturday, May 29
Laurie [grandson Lawrence] inspected my Frigidaire, ice-chopper and food containers in the refrigerator. He was much intrigued by the light in the Frigidaire, kept the door open too long, inspected the mechanism of the light going on and off as you open or close the door. He is coming here Monday. I showed him the little ice-cream freezer and promised that he could make ice-cream in it on Monday. . . .

Straightened out the house this A.M., after the party of last night, read the [Chicago] *Tribune* which contains much significant news I think over which I skim hurriedly, labor troubles, Chamberlain becoming prime minister of England and Baldwin stepping out, Wally Simpson and the Duke of Windsor making the front page again —

Thursday, June 3
Went to Kroch's to get Eastman's *The Enjoyment of Laughter* to send to Bertha F. from Essie and me — too expensive $3.75 without the tax and price of sending.

Friday, June 18
Went to a little party at Meta's — Claudia U., Agnes K., Carol S., Leola H. Miss U. mentioned teaching young children how to make things and so I showed her how to make boxes and balls out of paper. Came home at about 12:30. It is now after 1 A.M. to-morrow. There was talk this evening about the maids at The Shoreland [apartment hotel in Hyde Park] striking and Meta said the maids at the Piccadilly [apartment hotel in Hyde Park] had been on strike and they were expecting the elevator-boys to go on strike to-morrow. Agnes spoke of a new kind of salad-dressing

        ½ pt. sour cream
        2 packages cream cheese
        dry mustard
        onion juice.

Must try it.

Monday, June 28

Have a guilty feeling about having bought the latest edition of the *Boston Cooking School Cook Book*. I'll probably never need to buy another one and I wanted this up-to-date one.

Saturday, July 10

I wore my light flowered silk dress from last year and my white hat from last year. White shoes, white gloves and white purse.

Wednesday, July 28

I spent a little time at my desk sending out a few checks that had been delayed.

Tuesday, August 3

Home at about 5 P.M. Checking over bank statement, grocery slips etc.

Thursday, August 12

Went over to [Temple] Sinai this A.M. to see S. W. S. about dropping our membership.[7]

Sunday, August 22

Friday I went down town and had a rather difficult time convincing a woman at The New England Life Insurance . . . [entry left unfinished]

Thursday, August 26

We went to the bank, the Insurance Company, The Board of Trade Building — had lunch in a Cafeteria near the bank. We met two Swedish women who were very careful in wiping their dishes off. Met also a woman who was wearing a blue print dress exactly like mine. She said she had gotten hers two years ago. So did I.

Friday, September 10

Spent a little while at my desk, sending resignations to organizations to which we have belonged for many years: The Jewish People's Institute, B'nai B'rith, Sinai Congregation. We find the dues too difficult to pay. The summer cost me more money than I had and so, in order to pay some of the dues, I borrowed [from Victor's life insurance policy], unknown to Victor who would feel unhappy and excited about it — $200.00 to pay dues and other debts which I would find it impossible to meet.[8]

Saturday, September 11

After clearing up my desk yesterday I went down town to the bank and drew out $60.00 to pay Sinai — my last payment makes me grow very prosperous. I debated about resigning from The Sisterhood but concluded that when you have to borrow on your husband's life insurance (Victor would hit the ceiling at this) to pay Club dues it is time to resign from the clubs — Perhaps I *have* contributed my quota. I have been a member of some of them since their inception. Victor's income is not what it used to be — and yet in order to have any income at all we must continue to live in this big home, keep up the garden and the appearance of the house, have an automobile and live, in general, like rich people. Fortunately, I do not need any new clothes.

After attending to a few errands yesterday, I took the No. 6 bus and went to Sinai, and paid the dues in cash — one fifty dollar bill and one ten — and how I need that money! I have still to pay this month's electric light bill, gas bill, telephone bill, cleaners bill, Carson Pirie's ($13.00 for clothes I hardly *needed* but thought I did) and Victor has a bill of $30.00+ at Ortenstein's which he had foolishly allowed to run for months. I paid up the balance of the automobile insurance, Marshall Fields bill which I had not cleared up since June, club dues (B'nai B'rith and Jewish People's Institute — $22.00 — Council of Jewish Women $5.00) and, as soon as we can clean up the remainder of the bills we shall have to begin to put money aside for the next semi-annual installment of the taxes on the house — $188.00 and the premiums on the life insurance. It certainly takes money to live — the day to day living expenses for Victor and me are not heavy — but to live *somewhere* costs money.[9]

Sunday, September 12

Very rainy morning. Put on my old brown dress, my oldest black coat (I have three) — all *old* ones at that — one is two years old — one is eight years older, and the one I wore I've had since oberverscholen [überverschollen, long-forgotten] times.

Tuesday, September 14

To-morrow is Yom Kippur. We have no seats in the Temple.[10]

Saturday, January 15, 1938

Victor came in. Wanted to go to Drexel State Bank but he couldn't make it and so I hurriedly changed my clothes and walked to the bank — Deposited $50 and straightway made out a check for $47.92 for Home Owner's Loan.

Monday, January 3

I checked over the bills, looked over the bank statement and straightened out my figures. After paying taxes last month of $188.98, paying H.O.L.C. $45.00 for gas and $22.00 + for telephoning, telegrams etc., besides the regular "over-head" there is a balance of $67.53 in the bank. We must be careful. Life Insurance bills next month — Club-dues — and so it goes —

On loose papers associated with materials from 1938, Irma made the following notations:

MONTHLY EXPENSES

Home Owner's Loan	48.00
Taxes	35.00
Heat	25.00
Janitor	14.00
Water Taxes	1.50
Maid	50.00
Laundress	6.00
Electric	13.00
Gas	13.00
Garbage Disposal	2.00
Watchman	3.00
Telephone	15.00
Food	225.00
Incidentals	50.00
Stamps	
Field's	

and written on the reverse side of the page:

H.O.L.C.	48.00
Taxes	30.
Heat	35
Janitor	14
Watchman	3

Garbage disposal	2
Water taxes	6.59
Maid	60
Laundress	9
Telephone	18
	288

Monday, March 28
Saw man about selling fur coats at noon and went out to market at
about 4:30.

Monday, June 27
Felt very much discouraged. Emily had asked me for a loan of $12.00,
Meta needed $10 — didn't know how I was going to get it, but knew
that I'd have to.

Wednesday, July 20
Cleaned and dusted the whole house. Took all morning. Cleared up
kitchen too — put things to rights the way I want the maid to keep
them. Elizabeth came at 2. Intend to have her half days for a while.
My feet ached badly after I had finished — sat in the bath-tub for a
long while trying to get the "kinks" out of myself — pretty tired. . . .
Saved a little money while I had no maid — paid myself $5 weekly
and put $15.00 into a very private savings account yesterday. Really
put in $25.00 as Victor had given me $10.00 as a birthday present.[11]

Saturday, August 6
The bank and I disagreed about our balance — 7 cents in my favor. I
was so elated, as I always am, when the dollars came out even, that
my common sense told me to take the bank's arithmetic in prefer-
ence to mine and let it go at that. Still I went over the figures again
and again and always the bank had 7 cents more than I. Finally I went
carefully over the checks and discovered that a check for the Woodlawn market, marked check No. 10, I had subtracted as $14.10 when
the actual check was $14.03. Silly perhaps to have spent time and en-
ergy tracing the 7 cents, but there was great satisfaction in it, when I
found it. If we would comb our lives carefully in this way for the er-
rors we have made, could we discover them and balance our accounts in the end. My time account, or rather accomplishment ac-

count, is always in arrears. I watched myself today. I have no maid and so I had to do all the housework that was necessary.

Thursday, August 11
Essie brought me a cherry-pitter and some apricot jam and I gave her a patent bottle cover and one veal chop I did not need and so we were even.[12]

Monday, November 21
After going to bank to take out of my savings of last summer in order to pay for my shoes and coat, I met Meta at the tailors —fitted my coat —

Wednesday, July 5, 1939
    Drew $25.00 out of bank— spent for stamps $2.90
    A & P store 3.98
    Woltmann's 1.59
    Woolworth's .38
    Shoes shined (new) .10   Must pay maid to-morrow
    Bakery .05   7.50
                            9.00 [crossed out: 10.00]
                            9.97
                            7.50
                            11.50
                            25.00
                            16.50 [crossed out: 7.47]
                            8.50
    Emily for card for Zelda   1.00
                            7.50

Interesting to keep track of where one's money goes. About once a month I buy supplies at A & P store — sugar, soap, some canned stuff, salt, paper toweling — In the P.M. checked over supplies, verified bank statement, prepared things for dinner and for luncheon to-morrow when I expect Sally and my maid will be out. Seemed to have gotten mixed up in my figures. Sent $9.00 for household supplies — then counting $7.50 for the maid and $1.00 for a present for Zelda out of my $25.00 I have $7.50 left — enough to pay the maid for next week if I did not have to spend one single penny for a week. Of course not going down town and having plenty of summer clothes I ought not to be spending much in the next months. Bought supplies on June 5.

Thursday, July 6
Spent 5 cents to-day — one whole nickel. *Tribune* collector came — Victor had only $1.10 — keeping tabs on my $7.50 — Didn't feel tired so stayed up and sent out monthly checks —

Saturday, July 8
Very, very tired. Had to wait up because some patients were coming. Read for a little while. Spent 31 cents at A & P store — Andrew [handy man] 11 cents.

	Cash account	
Movie	1.10	
Andrew 11	7.50	
Supplies 31	1.52	
	5.98 balance	

Tuesday, July 18
Finished [straightening] desk — Wrote [a letter] — cleaned drawers in desk in living-room. Went down town — did some shopping then went to a dramatic reading at The Chicago Woman's Aid — wanted to hear Olga Rosenova read. Remembered her charming announcing in The Wings of A Century at The Chicago World's Fair. After the Aid Meeting went to Kroch's — then home, then marketing with Victor — prepared supper. Balanced cash account. Drew out $30.00 — must pay out $21.00 for help in the house before August 1, and so cashed check for $30. — Balance to-day $35.59. Must pay maid and laundress by Thursday.

Thursday, August 31
. . . In bed all day. Great deal of pain in my throat. When I could, read *Grapes of Wrath.*[13]

Friday, September 22
. . . When I came home, Victor had a big pickerel fish which a patient had given him. Broiled the fish. Went to bed right after supper. Heard Dr. [Thomas] Mann speak on the radio — *Yom Kippur* eve. Emily and Albert came after services.[14]

Included in Irma's diary for 1939 is a newspaper horoscope column for her birthday that year. On it she noted: "Bess sent me this." The horoscope, the only such clipping in Irma's ephemera, reads in part:

Tuesday, July 25, 1939

Afternoon and evening favor financial study and decision. Avoid worry now [through] Aug. 31 . . .

War and Its Victims, 1933–1957

In 1933 and again in 1935, Irma's son-in-law Ferd, a rabbi, traveled to Hitler's Germany to assess the state of affairs there. Following his first trip, he wrote a pamphlet, "Sentenced to Death: The Jews of Nazi Germany." Very few in the United States wanted to believe what he wrote. And why should they?

Did not German Jews, by and large, belong to the vast urban middle class? Were they not prosperous business people, lawyers, and doctors? Since they were socially and culturally integrated into German intellectual, cultural, economic, and political spheres, they were no different from other Germans. Although the news that filtered out from Germany late in 1933 and 1934 refuted those perceptions, as late as 1937 some German Jews, both in the United States and in Germany, continued to deny that Hitler was a threat or that there were real problems. If they admitted there actually might be problems, they maintained that the reports were exaggerated.

Monday, April 12, 1937
Happened to meet Jule G. who had lunch with us. Jule told us some things about Germany. She thinks 80% of Germans are against Hitler and his crowd. Said Germany and no other European country wants war. She seems to live very luxuriously and comfortably in Germany and said the stories of persecution are exaggerated. I didn't agree with her. I think she didn't like me. I quoted Ferd at times and she admitted that Ferd had been placed in situations where he would hear about things of which she and Ide and Abe had no knowledge.

In the United States, the depression continued and, as so often had happened in the past when times were bad, anti-Semitism surfaced.

Monday, August 23, 1937
Maid did not appear this A.M. Did not notify me simply failed to show up knowing too, that I am having a dinner party tomorrow evening. Called her up and paid her. She tried to recommend some one else to me. It is a pity that such things upset one emotionally. I asked her, "Do you think this is an honorable thing to do?" She replied, "Nobody, now-a-days, thinks about being honorable." Very interesting. She asked me Saturday if we were Jewish. Her husband works in a German Rathskeller. She was surprised that we were Jewish. Baked cookies — took me all morning what with telephoning, interviewing maids, Laurie's coming etc. I do not mind the work I do — in fact, I rather enjoy it, but I regret keenly that it leaves me no time or energy to write and to read.

By 1937, the European situation was becoming more serious, whether people wanted to admit it or not. Russia, Communists, Hitler, Jewish refugees, and Eastern Europe became dinner-table topics, as Irma's diaries show.

Sunday, August 1, 1937
Company for dinner. Emily and Albert, Ruth, Ferd, and Juny [grandson]. Al G. and his wife. We ate on the porch.
Discussions on politics, Russia etc. Afterwards Al G. told us about Trotsky. Ferd talked about Roumania and Poland. . . .

In July 1938, President Franklin Roosevelt presided over a conference in Evian, France, to develop a solution to the German refugee problem. Over thirty nations participated but drafted no plan or resolutions. News from Europe was bleak. War in Europe appeared imminent.

Saturday, September 24, 1938
Tried to put some closets in order. Dashed down to bank and to Woodlawn Market early in the P.M. Found Albert here upon my return playing croquet with Victor C. Cooked barley soup. Flo C. came. Essie called up, asked us to walk over to her house to see her new kitchen stove. Flo, Victor C. and I walked over and then Victor and I walked home. In the evening read and listened to news. European news very disturbing.

Tuesday, October 4
Heard Dr. [Thomas] Mann speak on the radio — "The Individual and His Destiny" — a very disturbing and troubled address interpreting world events of last week. It is Yom Kippur eve.

Tuesday, October 18
Heard Ethel Kawin talk on "The Over-privileged Child" in the A.M. Met Mrs. F. at noon. Attended luncheon of "The Round Table for Jews and Christians." Rabbi Schulman of The North Shore Congregation [Israel] spoke on "Incorrigible Europe."

In August 1938, the Mauthausen concentration camp opened, as did the Central Office for Jewish Emigration. Those Jews permitted to leave Germany were stripped of all their property before being granted exit visas. Thousands clamored to emigrate, but had nowhere to go. Some found refuge in the United States, where Jewish philanthropic organizations, either independent or allied with synagogues, assisted them financially.

Sunday, October 16, 1938 — summer weather
Elizabeth [the maid] sick. Meta came while Victor and I went out to dinner at 5, in a private apartment, where some German Jewish refugees are serving meals. Meal not particularly good. Came home, listened to radio, talked to Meta.

In an October 25, 1938, letter to her granddaughter, Irma wrote that

[i]t is morning and I have had breakfast, checked over the things in the refrigerator, sketchily outlined my day, and glanced hastily over that "Chamber of Horrors," the *Chicago Tribune*. Persecutions and expulsions of Jews continue. Now it is Czecho-Slovakia over which, defenseless, deserted by its Allies, we have all agonized in these past weeks.

What will the world be like for you, who have come up through your babyhood and childhood, in which cruelty, injustice and brutality seem to be gaining the upper hand? Perhaps it is not the Germans, not the Japanese and not the Arabs so much as the brute surviving in that animal man, despite the fact that the divine spark of his intellect might illuminate the globe.

I was thinking of two things this A.M. when I was lying in bed, not fully awake maybe. It was too early to get up. I was thinking about how Germany is crushing out the intellect of its grand country except where it can be turned to account in perfecting its colossal war machine and when she turns that iron and chemical force against the rest of the world, what destruction she will create — Will some physically weak David arise to slay the giant in a vulnerable spot? Will the intellect triumph, or are you and your generation facing the beginning of another Dark Ages? Yesterday I read an article about the German Concentration Camp where the free intellects of Germany are being broken in body, with extra brutality and revolting sadism against those who by chance were born Jews.

Dr. Mann says that out of the 17,000,000 Jews in the world to-day, 10,000,000 are *homeless*.

What I have written above reminds me of last summer when Victor C. and Laurie were spending a few days here. . . . I told them long before bed-time that bed-time was approaching — I asked them to begin to think about beginning to get ready for bed. Gradually, as time passed on, I kept reminding them — and then, all of a sudden it was bed-time, and then even more suddenly it was past bed-time. And so very gently I began to say:

> "It's time to go to bed."
> "It's time to be in bed!"
> "Please go to bed."
> "Won't you please go to bed?"
> "Won't you *please* go to bed!"
> "Why don't you children go to bed?"

Well, seven is a lucky number. I counted seven pleadings, suggestions and pleases — and still Victor kept on drawing and Laurie kept on hoot-nannying. Finally I wondered what I could do, or should do. Spank! No! I hadn't the right to, I don't enjoy it, and, well, what would be the use. You spank when you are very, very angry and you delude yourself that it's for the good of the spanked. At that, it might have done them good, but it would have upset me terribly. No, for my own good, I couldn't spank though they deserved it.

Finally I shouted "Go to bed now!" and they really looked up and then I said, and I wanted to say it very sternly, "Do you know I'm not half strict enough with you children!"

Victor gave me a look, a funny kind of look, as if he were trying to figure out what to do with me, the interfering pest — And then he said,

"Please don't! You know, Ainee, we like you just as you are!" I melted of course, and that's probably what he intended I should do. I promised not to change, if they'd go to bed *now*.

They went.

And so both of us won.

That's contrary to war, in which both sides lose. If wars could be changed to be that way — but I'm afraid Germans are strict. And being strict means that you want your own way. Of course for the other fellow's good — but maybe the other fellow is far better able to decide what is for his good, than a one track mind can decide.

Irma returned to the issues of the homeless and the approaching war on Wednesday, October 26, 1938, in a letter to her sister Meta.

Dearie,

It has been a busy day. I have just heard Herbert Hoover and President Roosevelt over the radio. I think, yes I think that ex-president Hoover's address on the International Situation was calm and sensible, cool and calculating but I believe the President's address was much more human, and equally sensible. I cannot write much this evening. Something in the President's address and in his voice when he spoke of "our people" has touched me deeply — and, dearie, I sit here weeping, and I do not shed tears easily, instead of writing. Both the President and the ex-president spoke of the imperative necessity of maintaining peace in the world! The ex-president spoke of economics and declared there can be no peace as long as tens of thousands of innocent victims of the dictators are wanderers over the face of the earth with no place to lay their heads.

And on Sunday, October 30, 1938, Irma prayed: "Unite our human confusions — fellowship deeper than that of race or nation or group — grant us thy peace —"

The pogrom known as Kristallnacht occurred all over Germany on November 9, 1938. It soon became obvious that Europe was mobilizing for war, so Americans stayed glued to their radios, listening, hoping, praying, and waiting.

Tuesday, August 29, 1939
Ferd and Ruth in and out of my room all day, listening to news about European Crisis over the radio.

By the time Hitler actually declared war on September 1, 1939, more than 50 percent of Germany's Jews had fled or been forced to emigrate. With the war's advent, all constraints on Hitler and the Nazis were effectively removed. The Final Solution to the "Jewish problem" began.

Monday, September 4, 1939
Labor Day. Finished reading *Young Joseph* by Thomas Mann. Up part of day. Feeling bad. . . . Listening these days to radio a great deal. War in Europe — frightful — distressing to hear it all while feeling so sick. . . .

Saturday, October 14
Listened to radio and cleared up things — Pres. Roosevelt on the radio, talking about the Relief Situation.

On May 10, 1940, German forces swept westward. By June, the Nazis occupied Holland, Belgium, and France. On August 8, the Battle of Britain began with Germany launching air attacks.

Sunday, February 9, 1941
In bed all day. Heard Winston Churchill speak on radio. Read a little — slept part of day.

By April 1941, Germany controlled Europe, Greece, and Yugoslavia and counted Hungary, Bulgaria, and Romania as Axis satellites. In the United States, the American Red Cross opened up to thousands of volunteers who wanted to help with the war effort. So many volunteered that by 1945 one quarter of the American people belonged to the Red Cross. Many women who could not leave home became Nurse's Aid Corps volunteers. The corps had been organized at the behest of the Office of Civilian Defense to provide community health care during a time when there was a real shortage of registered nurses and medical doctors. The volunteers were required to pledge 150 service hours annually. At the time Irma received her nursing diploma and volunteered to knit socks for the war effort, she was almost seventy years of age.

Monday, March 17, 1941
Red Cross nursing class in the A.M. Remained at [the Chicago Woman's] Aid for lunch.

Tuesday, March 18
Went down to bank and market. Essie came in P.M. Started knitting socks. . . . Knitted, sewed, radio in evening. *Cold.*

Monday, March 24
Went to Red Cross class in A.M.

Monday, April 7
Nursing class . . . Home in evening. Sewing, reading — very tired.

Monday, April 14
Went to nursing class in A.M. Down town in P.M. Came home. Raining. Victor drove me down town to make up 1st nursing lesson at Red Cross Headquarters. Home 9:15.

Monday, May 19
Last Red Cross nursing lesson. Received diploma.

Because anti-Semitism was also on the rise in the United States, the Anti-Defamation League became more active. Leaders held meetings at which suggestions were made about how to deal with prejudices in an organized fashion. Victor belonged to the B'nai B'rith, so he and Irma attended these meetings as shown in Irma's diary.

Friday, November 21, 1941
Anti-Defamation League meeting in A.M.

Tuesday, December 9
Anti-Defamation League at [the Chicago Woman's] Aid in the A.M. . . . Went out to Sisterhood meeting to hear Rabbi Silver.

On December 7, 1941, the Japanese bombed the Hawaiian Islands, Wake, and Guam. Irma made a brief note in her diary:

Sunday, December 7, 1941
Roasted ½ of a duck. Went to see Becky at 4 P.M. Terrible day. Japanese bombed Pearl Harbor at Honolulu. Everybody excited by treachery of Japanese.

Irma listened to the radio the following day as Roosevelt informed the joint session of the Congress about what Secretary of State Cordell Hull had called the "treacherous attack." Her concern over the news must have been amplified by the fact that her son and daughter-in-law lived in San Francisco:

Monday, December 8, 1941
President Roosevelt on the air. In middle P.M. drove down to 22nd St. with V[ictor], then to market on 53rd. Waited at Woodlawn Hosp[ital] while V[ictor] made call on 64th St. San Francisco black-out at night. Frightfully disturbing.

Then, on December 11, 1941, Roosevelt again stood before Congress to announce that Germany and Italy had declared war against the United States. Following the announcement and possibly constrained by the four lines allotted for each day's entry in her five-year diary, Irma jotted short entries.

Friday, December 12, 1941
Lunch at Meta's. Fussing with curtains. Worried about San Francisco — black-outs etc. Much telephoning. Looking over papers — writing to Alfred and Ruth. Down town in P.M.

Sunday, December 14
Awfully busy in house. Went to movie, Bette Davis in "The Little Foxes" then to Sherry for dinner. Home at 9:30. Radio. Letters from Alfred [in San Francisco] disturbing.

Tuesday, December 16
Home. . . . Sent article to *Reader's Digest*. War news less disturbing.

Americans were informed that winning the war required everybody's help. Part of the effort involved buying war bonds to underwrite the costs of war, and to assist the government, factories, and businesses to prepare for war. And part of the effort involved volunteerism. Irma, knitting socks and already qualified as a nurse's aid, next offered to work in the relief effort assisting both refugees and women whose husbands had gone to war. She also participated in her block club, preparing for the unthinkable — an attack on Chicago.

Friday, February 20, 1942
Down town in A.M. Meeting at the [Chicago Woman's] Aid for Welfare Work. Volunteered for 1 P.M. once a month. Skinner School Mother's Club.

Friday, April 17
Cooler. Packed things to go to Salvation Army. Wrote to Alfred. Mother's Club at Skinner School in P.M. Defense Meeting at Shakespeare School in evening. Market in P.M.

Tuesday, May 5
(May 4) Went to Shakespeare School to get ration card for sugar.
Laurie went with me. Came home.

Tuesday, June 16
Victory luncheon at church. Meta went with me. Attended luncheon
between trips down town.

Tuesday, July 14
Luncheon at Adele G's. Enjoyed it very much. Talked for a while with
a German refugee woman named Alschuler.

Tuesday, August 11
Went to Block meeting with Mr. T. in evening. Mr. T. elected Block-
captain. Beautiful cool weather.

Wednesday, August 12
Wrote letters to Victor and Laurie. Did up packages to send to them.
Meta here in P.M. Marketed on 43rd. Albert and Meta here for din-
ner. Blackout from 10 'til 10:30. Very interesting.

Tuesday, October 20
Met Emily at Chicago Woman's Aid at noon. Heard Helen Ross talk
on Psychology for Children in War Time. Home at 4.

As the war progressed, gasoline and food became scarcer. Americans
were issued ration cards, encouraged to plant "Victory gardens," and
urged not to drive except when absolutely necessary. Victor, as a doctor, was issued a gasoline ration card different from those of nonmedi-
cal persons. Controls on domestic use of certain commodities lasted
throughout the war. If people complained, they did so privately.

Thursday, November 12, 1942
. . . Shakespeare School for gasoline rationing with Victor.

Monday, March 22, 1943
Went over to 47th St. to do some marketing. Very little selection in
the markets. Radio, sewing in evening.

Wednesday, March 1, 1944
Home. Taking care of house and meals. Made chicken salad with one
chicken leg.

During the war, government propaganda urged women to fill desperate labor shortages created when the male workers went into the military. The strategies encouraged women to be patriotic and to do their
duty for the war effort, either by enlisting in the armed services or working in factories and shipyards. Few able-bodied women who could work
outside their homes wanted to be domestics in somebody else's house.
Those who did, however, expected wages comparable to what they
would have made in factories. Irma discovered this situation when she advertised for maids during the height of the war.

Monday, February 15, 1943
Advertising for maid. A few responses. None quite available. . . . In
evening two country girls called. Took up my time. In the end the
[one] girl wanted to become a nurse.

Monday, April 3, 1944
No maid. Have answered advertisements . . . — all the help I can get
is day-workers — keeps me busy all day to get the calls [for Victor's
office].

Saturday, December 2
Maid came — $30.00 per week.

The armed services began drafting all able-bodied men between the
ages of eighteen and thirty-six. Irma's oldest grandson, young Victor, a recent high-school graduate, was one of them.

Thursday, April 8, 1943
Home. Emily called up to tell us that Victor has a chance to join the
army meteorological training course. . . . Baked angel food cake. Prepared pot roast.

Wednesday, January 12, 1944
On train. Reading Forster's *Passage to India*. Very interesting book.
Finished it after dinner. Moved into another car. Light fall of snow
on desert. Soldiers everywhere — in car. Encampments.

Saturday, April 15
Victor C. left at 6:15 P.M. for Camp Grant. Home all day. . . . For the
evening went out to Emily's. Tried to keep her company because we
both felt bad about Victor going into the Army.

Sunday, May 21 — Party
Victor C. came home on a furlough. Train almost 1½ hours late.
Dinner party at Del Prado Hotel. Emily, Albert, Laurie, Victor F.,
Essie, Rudolph, Meta, Florence H., Ruth, and Louis C. Including Victor C. — Eleven of us. Sat for a while in up stairs lobby of hotel
and visited. Very pleasant evening. Victor C. seems so grown up and
somebody to be reckoned with. I think he is going to be a very fine
man. He is already.

Victor C. came home on leave in time for his grandfather's birthday. A
small black-and-white photograph found among Irma's papers shows a
young man in uniform, identified as Victor C., smiling, surrounded by his
family.

Sunday, November 19, 1944 — Celebration for Victor's 75th birthday
Wonderful day.
Seemed as if on account of separations and illnesses, we all valued
one another's affection and relative influences on each other.

Irma wrote very little about where Victor C. was stationed or his
activities during the war. After the war was over, she mentioned that
he had been in Georgia, as well as in Switzerland, but even then did not
elaborate.
The war continued. By 1943, most of the Jews remaining in Europe
were in concentration camps or toiling under slave labor conditions in
factories. Irma's diary entries reflect both the daily news and the close attention she paid to events.

Wednesday, May 19, 1943
Home. Listened to Churchill's speech to The House of Representatives at 11:30. Wonderful speech. Churchill interrupted me making
a jelly-roll. All the commentators this evening speaking favorably
about the address.

Monday, May 24
Interesting letters from Ferd about Nazi prisoners.

Wednesday, August 11
Very warm. Home. Sewing. Churchill and Roosevelt in conference in
Quebec. War news good. . . . Cooked pot-roast.

Thursday, September 9
Still cold. Still excited about Italy's surrender. Reading Walter Lipp-
man on Foreign Policy of U.S.A. to Victor.

By 1944, confident that the Allies would smash the Germans with combined air and ground attacks, General Dwight D. Eisenhower told his pi-
lots on the eve of the D-Day invasion of June 6 that "[i]f you see fighting
aircraft over you, they will be ours."[1] The news of the successful invasion
was quickly transmitted back home.

Tuesday, June 6, 1944
Very busy — dashed over to market. Bought lamb for roasting —
cooking lamb. . . . Invasion day. President on radio [talking about]
War's Aftermath.

American tank forces began to roll across Europe. Back home, on
Monday, June 12, 1944, Irma castigated herself.

While the fate of civilization hangs in the balance with the invasion of Europe at Cherbourg, I am running around, cleaning closets,
cooking meals, trying to keep this house going. Haven't had a maid
since December. My recordings seem so trivial, yet I'd hardly do for
a paratrooper or even an aeroplane pilot. I could put down the events
of the war — maybe I should have, all this time — but then, I'm not
writing a history. I go around in a squirrel cage of cooking meals,
washing up, answering the phone, dashing down town. But I don't
mind it.

Wednesday, August 16
Sewing, putting closets in order — wash away. Invasion of South
France yesterday. Wrote to Alfred. One can't help listening to the ra-
dio — reading the papers. I always sew while listening.

Friday, August 25
Paris liberated by French and American forces. Roumania joined
the allies. War news exciting — very good. Anxious about terrible
battles going on —

Tuesday, November 7
Election Day. Went to polls in A.M. with Victor. Attending to mail,
sewing, etc. Listening to returns in evening. Couldn't sleep. Nervous
over election 'til we were certain F.D.R. won.

Monday, November 20
Too tired to clear up. Went to bank at noon. Then to Kroch's and to
see Dr. Baer. Brought Dr. B.—$100.00 Victory Bond. Met Victor at
Ronsley's — Drove home with him. Supper. Bed.

None of Irma's diaries for 1945 survive, nor is it known whether she kept
any during the immediate postwar period. Her journals begin again on
Mother's Day, Sunday, May 9, 1948.

After the war, when the soldiers returned home, many of those who
had been drafted out of high school enrolled in colleges and universities,
their tuition covered under the G. I. Bill. Irma's oldest grandson, Victor C.,
took advantage of the veteran benefits to enroll in the University of Chicago. At that time, Irma attended philosophy lectures with her other
grandson, Laurie, who was also a student at the university.

Sunday, May 9, 1948, Mother's Day
Both [of Emily's sons] are students in the University of Chicago —
running over to see us when they are not too busy or otherwise
occupied. . . .

After the philosophy lecture last week, I met my oldest grandson.
We had lunch together and then walked along the Midway to Harper
Library. "I'll get you a book on Hume," said he.

As we walked along, he told me that *The Daily Maroon*, the Chicago
paper at the University of Chicago came out the other day in an edition celebrating its 55th anniversary. He told me about the funny
things that happened way back when it was founded, how the *Maroon* said that whenever a celebrated visitor came to [the] University
of Chicago in its earliest days President Harper and his associates entertained the visitor by laying another corner-stone. What is history
to him is memory to me. . . .

It had been raining a good deal, and the Midway on this May day
was a brilliant green in the clear sun light. This oldest grandson, a
veteran of WWII, necessarily sees life from a different vantage point
from mine. He is a born philosopher, and yet I think that the artist in
him is forever struggling with the philosopher. He pointed out shadows and lines to me that I might not have noticed and our walk was
like a stroll through a picture gallery.

Between that Mother's Day and Thursday, March 16, 1950, there is
almost a complete blank in Irma's written record. There are no diaries,

and 1949 is represented in a single letter addressed to her grandson Victor C. The next reference to him occurs on Friday, December 27, 1957.

As I wrote the date I wondered. Could this be the anniversary of Victor C's death? Nobody knows. The tragedy of his suicide!!! After seven years, I still feel the grief of it. I thought I could never feel light-hearted again. Grief is something to be conquered and looking at the stark tragedies that accompany life, make an effort to rise above them, even though our eyes are blurred by tears.

I am reading two books about the Loeb, Leopold kidnapping of little Bobby Franks. In one of them there are pictures. I cannot forget the picture of the mother of Bobby Franks at the funeral of her son. I am sure *she* could never rise above that tragedy.

I did not know the story of [Victor C.'s] suicide until Victor and I returned from the trip to California, where we were at the time. The last time I saw [him] he had slept at our house. It was the night before we left. He asked if he could come for supper and bring a friend. I never said "No" to him. It was very inconvenient but I said, "Yes." When he arrived [he and Victor] went out and bought lamb chops for dinner, for we had planned to have no set dinner. While they were out the friend telephoned to say he couldn't come. When [they] returned I prepared the dinner. My heart sank at the way [my grandson] ate — like a starved animal. It was not usual for him to eat without reference to what any one else might have. He ate three chops hurriedly without finding out if there were any for Victor and me.

After dinner a girl he was to take out telephoned to cancel the date she had with him. He had been erratic for some weeks and looked disturbed and untidy.

I gave him breakfast the next morning. Prepared it the way I know he liked it — toast that was not too hard and breakfast food made crisp on the stove. He said he had an urgent engagement, that he was going to see his psychiatrist and then go about his business. A short time before he had asked Victor to lend him a dollar to give to his psychiatrist for he said he owed him money. Victor wanted to give him more, but he wouldn't take it.

That morning Victor asked him if he needed any money. He said he didn't and wouldn't take any.

He kissed me good-bye at the front door and I watched him as he walked west on 45th Street toward Drexel Boulevard, where he said he would take a bus to go down town. I watched him going down the street and my heart was heavy. I resolved to write to him as soon as I would get to California — *but I didn't* — I was absorbed by the activities and the worries around me and post[poned] writing. I have never forgiven myself.

At first, his death affected me physically. It seemed as if the pain in my head would never disappear and the tears with which I fell asleep at night would never cease — only to wake up in that room in California which I still visualize and which was filled with pain. Then, after three weeks Victor and I went to Los Angeles. We went to movies; I read as much as I could — the story of the struggle of Semmelweiss to introduce sanitation and sterilization into the hospitals in Vienna — and [his] death from an infection and his gradual loss of his mental faculties.[2] It held my interest. It was a time when [my] mind was capable of being diverted but always returned to an awareness of a heavy heart.

After our return home, in a pile of accumulated papers which had arrived during our absence I came upon a copy of the [newspaper] which featured on its front page, a detailed account of [Victor C.'s] manner of committing suicide. It was like opening a wound that showed some slight beginnings of a healing process. Again and again I wondered what [his] state of mind could have been. Even to this day I dare not let myself dwell upon the visual side of it all. I didn't talk about the nervous reaction that it gave me — a sudden jerk that woke me up at night and its counterpart during the day. I knew I *had* to get away from the thoughts of [him]. Even now they have crowded out a brighter picture of living that I might have recorded if I had not remembered. As I put down the date, that this might be the anniversary of [his] death. "Poor little guy — you couldn't make it" — Alfred said as he stood at his grave the day Alfred and I went to [the cemetery] a few days after big Victor's death. How sad can life get!

Some day I must write the story about [my grandson] — his desperate struggle to remain sane. He realized his condition. It might be too sorrowful, too hard to write, for I loved that sweet child completely and he loved me entirely.

I have wanted to erect my monument to him — in words — a monument that would stand for all the young life sacrificed in the flames of war — and the hatred of a monster named Hitler.

An addendum to this entry, written sideways on the page, reads "Grief tore at my heart. There was a heavy darkness in my spirit."[3]

Victor Frankenstein, around 1910.

Irma's daughter Ruth, around 1910.

Irma's daughter Emily, around 1912.

Irma's son Alfred, around 1908.

Victor C., Irma's grandson, on April 15, 1944.

Lawrence (Laurie), Irma's grandson, on January 21, 1944.

Victor Frankenstein's 75th birthday party, November 19, 1944.
Left to right, back row: family friend, granddaughter Irma Betty, grandson Victor C.
Middle row: Emily's husband Albert, Irma, Irma's sister Meta, daughter Emily.
Front row: Victor, family friend.

Changes, 1950–1966

After the war, America and the returning troops appeared to adjust quickly to peacetime. Men rejoined their families, took up the jobs they had left to serve their country, or enrolled in school under the GI Bill. Many women relinquished their wartime jobs in favor of marriage and work at home. Civic projects, postponed during the war, began again. Tract houses sprang up in suburbia to meet the returning veterans' demands for housing. The revved-up economy made people feel prosperous once again. Everyone looked toward the future, but no one who had lived through it could ever forget the war.

In an undated entry from 1953, Irma remembered.

One time when I had a family party and we had put little Emily to bed, she came pattering down the stairs and complained that she couldn't sleep because

"The Germans were making too much noise."

The aunts and Grossmutter talked German and, although I tried to teach each of our own children German, everybody around them spoke English and I was not too successful at it. When we were children we were taught German before we learnt English. Our maids (Mamma had two) were instructed never to give us anything unless we said *Please* and *Thank you* afterward. We had to say these things in German. I thought that was good. I did not succeed in the German part but I did stress the importance of good manners especially toward persons who worked for one.

Later, years after my party Emily's complaint turned into a family proverb.

The Germans, were indeed, making too much noise. And in two world wars they almost succeeded in wrecking civilization. If they have learnt their lesson, they will never again be making too much noise.

Irma packed many activities into the postwar years. She traveled east a number of times to be with her son, granddaughter, and great-grandchildren, took her first airplane ride, attended concerts and art exhibitions, and saw both Ruth and Alfred listed in *Who's Who*. She said that "I have been clearly conscious that life has a beginning, a middle period and an end like every good story has. . . . I had never imagined that age would have its thrill just as childhood, romance and motherhood had."[1]

During those years, Irma also began her autobiography "for the hundredth time." On Sunday, January 21, 1951, she revealed how "[m]y writing would have lost its charm for me unless kept as a relaxation."

Writing, for me, is not work. I love it. If professional it would have become a chore. I have kept it — held it one of the things I love to do and live by. For me, it is as if I were a piano player who would sit down now and then to the piano, run my fingers over the keys and listen to the music.

In addition to her diary entries, Irma began to organize the cookbook she had started when she first married, and to which she had added recipes throughout the years. On Friday, September 28, 1951, she composed a rough-draft introduction.

Cooking . . . is an art. There is much more to it than the fire. [It is the] converting of raw materials into enjoyable edible and "healthful food." Like any other art, it means first selection, transposing, or transposing-converting separate entities (look up entities) into an inspiring, pleasing or challenging whole. And it is more than art. It is a health measure (Better diction).

As happy as these activities made Irma, other events during this era were tinged with sadness: the sale of her beloved house in 1952, which meant the loss of her garden, and, especially, Victor's illness and death, coupled with the gradual weakening of her own strength.

Thursday, September 27, 1951
This slowing up of business is not at all to my taste. I hate it when some one says "Be your age." Yet, being old is not as old as it used to be. It makes me so mad when I stop in the midst of doing things to lie down.

I'm not the man I used to be.
I hate it when everybody yells at me, "Don't Overdo! Don't over-do!" Often I feel guilty when I know I've "over-do-ed." I hate it when Essie rubs it in and says, "You're not sixteen." As though she were.

Although Irma had mentioned selling the house once before in 1930, discussions about what to do with the house apparently began in earnest during 1950.[2]

Friday, March 31, 1950
Victor, Alfred and I held [a] conference in [the] kitchen about our future while I rolled the matzo glacé — exciting, irregular day. Emily came early P.M. Busy all day. Laurie and Victor here for dinner with Alfred. Matzo glacé, soup, chicken and salad, potatoes, etc. matzo cake with wine sauce. Essie, Meta, Rudolph, [other family members], George [nephew] here in evening. Lovely evening. George took Alfred, Meta, Vic and me to air port at 1 A.M. Alfred's plane left at 2. Had coffee after Alfred left. Home at 3:30 A.M.

Once the decision to sell had been made, Irma turned to the question of what she could fit into smaller quarters. In undated papers she wrote that

I was thinking about my books. "You aren't going to take all those books with you?"
My library is alive. Every book in it has spoken to me at one time: Emerson, William James, Thornton Wilder, Shakespeare, more remotely, the Abbé Dimnet intimately — books on method, informative books that have made me see plants and buildings in a discriminating, knowing way, autobiographies which have taken me into their confidence and told me about other lives — worthwhile lives, of persons who have accomplished good things — hardly ever what they set out to do, often better things than they could have dreamed of.[3]

The year following their move to a small apartment-hotel, Irma dryly noted, on Wednesday, August 19, 1953, "My husband I look at each other — two old persons, still finding life good and still finding it sweet, and he says to me, 'Fifty-five years is a long time to live with one woman.' And I answer him, 'It's a longer time to live with one man.' I think being a woman isn't that I want the last word, I like to get even."

Within a few months of that entry, Victor became ill. He spent some weeks at the Mayo Clinic in Rochester, Minnesota. Irma sat by his side day and night. To keep herself occupied, she wrote — diaries and letters.

Hotel Kahler
Sunday, January 10, 1954
Dear Lucile,

They come to us all, these difficult times and bring their own revelations. Victor's illness seems like a terrific storm that is now subsiding. At the height of our fears, Ruth and Alfred were with us, and once more I realized the richness of my life; we spent grim, anxious hours together, precious hours I shall not forget. Always in the major crises of my life, I have found great kindness and sympathy. And right here may I thank you for your expression of concern, which I appreciate indeed. No one can imagine, who has not seen it, this marvellous Mayo phenomenon. It could have happened only, I think in America. I am not exaggerating when I say, that trying to grasp it in all its implications, is one of the greatest experiences I have ever had.

You asked about my work. I have *loved* writing the book which I have felt I must do. I shall finish it before we leave here, and I'll tell you about it, and what fun it has been to write it the next time I see you. Parts of it are good. It will need revision and unification. Whether or no, it will ever be published, I do not know.

I shall not ask you what you have [been] doing for I know it is your nature always to be busy. I have enjoyed so much reading what you have written, and too, knowing about your work that I'm expecting a rewarding experience from your written accomplishment. . . .

When you get a close-up of human suffering, courage and devotion you wonder why more of it doesn't get into current literature — But that's another story. I feel that I have grown immeassureably from this profound experience. You were sweet to write to me. Remember me to Harold and thank him too for your message. Affectionately, Irma R. F.

This letter was pinned to another dated the following day:

Dear Lucile,

The tide has turned, I think. Victor sat up yesterday three times yesterday. Still in the hospital. — Still has special nurses and the road ahead may still be rough. This has been a profound and terrific experience in this Mayo setting which is a place of miracles and dedication.

A new life awaits us. We were planning it yesterday P.M.

I thank you and H. for your messages of love and sympathy.

Among the materials from Irma's time in Rochester was a letter she addressed to Victor, her husband. Although it was dated Thursday, January 7, 1954, there is no indication she ever sent it.

Dear Old Pal,

Since I write better than I talk I want to recall to you the first 15 years of our marriage, as beautiful a marriage as two, hopeful young persons ever embarked upon. These were the years in which our three children were born and we acquired the finest, real home in our particular group.

I want to see all this, and I want you to see it with me in the perspective of the almost tragic events of these last few weeks. *There were 3 crises*:

The first one came when the doctors stood at the foot of your bed and pronounced their dread verdict. I rushed to the telephone. I knew that Ruth and Alfred would be with us to give us strength and hope.

The second crisis, when you had literally passed through the biblical "valley of the shadow of death" and were still hovering in it. You asked me

"Have I been operated?"

I said, "Yes."

And you answered *"Then I'm still alive."* Ruth said she had seen the fear in your eyes when they took you up stairs. I did not want to see it.

And there came a crisis in my life yesterday afternoon when you told me to write to Mr. Lindenthal that you are out of danger. Until you said it yourself I could not accept it.

Then, all of a sudden I became light-hearted once more. For life has been very good to me, owing to you and the richness of reaching our age in the midst of remarkable children, and the blessing of their children and still another generation.

Although it may be short for one or the other, or possibly for both of us, I think we are standing at a cross-roads and a new life together opens before us.

Don't worry too much Victor, dear. The cost of this illness is expensive but you have paid for it. Make an effort to get well not so much by fighting, but by your own knowledge of the healing powers that exist where surgery has been skillful and clean. If you anticipate all the dreadful things that could happen, it will delay your recovery.

And you must recover: We shall have a new life together. Don't be cross. Don't be too critical. Again I have known or experienced [illegible] warmth and the wonder of human sympathy. Not one person among those we call friends, is missing.

We can make the end of our marriage as beautiful as was the beginning — When either one of us goes, I doubt if the other one will wander too long in a world too sad to live in without one's pal.

I love you, Victor dear — Your Irma

Following Victor's death on June 15, 1955, Irma composed a tribute to him:

And every thought of you is
A regret tinged with sadness with its golden edge of Memory
As the Jahrzeit light casts its glow
Over the days that are no more
And every thought of you is a golden edged regret
As the Jahrzeit light casts its glow over the days that are no more
The little lamp we both have loved is lighted
But only I can see it
It is my Jahrzeit light for you
In rememberance of the love that
Lighted my days when you were among us
The Kaddish says
May the memory of the departed be a blessing to those that
    revere it
And so we build monuments out of our memories turning them
    into reverence
I have built your monument out of the hopeful days of our
    courtship
Out of the happy days of our companionship
Out of the sad days that drew us closer together
When the light of your life flickered and went out

Dark were the days that followed
'Til grief faded slowly into sorrow
And each memory has a
Golden edge of sadness and regret
And the Jahrzeit light casts its glow over the days that are no
    more.

Irma repeatedly mentioned her losses — of her brother Kurt, of Victor, her house, and her garden — and her thoughts about growing old. Although Kurt had died in 1957, she did not mention his passing until Tuesday, January 14, 1958, when she began to write down her family history.

We don't know that life is lovely 'til the loveliness is gone and sadness takes its place. I had not known how dearly I loved Kurt [until he died]. In the months I went to see him frequently the spirit of our childhood when we played together seemed to return. This was a grim sort of play. I knew he couldn't recover and Meta and I did all we could to call back memories — memories of the hopeful days when we were young — and it was heart-breaking to know his defeat — while the old *spirit* was not defeated.[4]

Monday, March 3, 1958
Trouble used to irritate me. Sorrow is another thing. It quiets you. You know you must accept the inevitable. Sorrow should vitalize you to do better. Its insights go deep and in the effort you make to overcome its effects, new vision should illuminate your love of your fellow man. Sorrow enters where hope has died, and all men experience it.

Growing old isn't bad: you get used to it. The discoveries in science to prolong life and the art of medicine have made life easier and more wonderful for older people. Then, too, my children are a source of joy to me. Of course there is always a touch of sadness when the comrade of your best years is no longer with you. That's what made them your best years.

Saturday, March 29
I wish I could see the garden again, stand next to big Victor while he bends down and with a finger brushes aside a tiny clump of earth and shows me the little green spear of some early plant with enough live power in it to push up a few grains of earth, probably heavier

than itself, but without that spark of vitality and power which, Victor called the "great miracle of creation." Those were great moments, we accept them casually and go on to the next activity of our own. Are all moments great moments? And how casually Victor and I accepted a fine companionship, a sympathetic companionship for the most part.

Victor, as a doctor, was much interested in the *Élan Vitale*. He told me one time when I was recovering from a somewhat protracted illness, and my hands were trembly, that the "elan vitale" would reassert itself and I'd be all right one day, and it would have come about so gradually that I shouldn't have been aware of it. It did. Victor had said that doctors depend on it.[5]

When it doesn't return? A few days before Victor died, to be exact the Sunday before and he died on Wednesday — or maybe it was the Sunday before that — feeble and almost unable to totter into the front room from his own room in the back of the apartment he asked, "I wonder how I got into this impasse?"

Why does every thought and every rememberance of those who are gone, make us feel so sad?

I *did* often realize that there were precious people and events in my life.

Why can't we accept death and in our spirit wave to the departed as if we were saying, "Coming, Victor. Coming. Not yet, but surely coming. How long no one knows." And then — there will be sorrow, sorrow because there is love.

I must remember "the elan vitale"—I think I still have work to do — a responsibility — I have it now — the "elan vitale" that should *push* one into the work I may still have to do — I'll not call it *work*. Having had a rich and unusual life I am trying to recapture in memory the best parts of it — the richest experiences.

I wish I could say "Thank you" to Victor.

During 1957 and 1958, Irma filled three large books with daily happenings, reflections, poems, stories, and other materials she wished to incorporate into her autobiography.[6] She also mentioned money worries once again.

Tuesday, June 10, 1958
I am *determined* to keep on sending out manuscripts because I'm a disappointment to myself and to everybody who knows me, and be-

cause I need some money if I am not to cash some of my stock in the
A.T. & T. which, once you have it, is too valuable to sell.

Friday, January 17
I stopped writing and began to think of how I would do that book.
Yesterday I put all my diaries into one box, and shall glance through
them, put them in chronological order, and see what hint is in
them that my memory does not recall, although my memory is vivid
enough.

Wednesday, January 22
I could do a book review of "By Love Possessed."[7] Good to analyze it
for my purpose, although the extended work I want to do should be
autobiographical.

Friday, March 28
I want to get them (the memories) down, all the fine things that have
happened in my life of almost ninety years, and then go quietly to
sleep beside the companion of my most-important years.

Saturday, May 31
Diaries are for people who like to write. I love to write. It is like holding a conversation — a one way conversation, it is true. I think further that persons who keep diaries find life so precious that they do
not want it to escape entirely and be lost in the past. It lives a while
longer before forgetfulness overtakes it. There are some things I
would not like to forget.

Sunday, June 29
[A] few minutes ago I was writing in my diary and I got a clear idea
of what so often torments me. Writing is a joy to me—just writing—
like breathing. What bothers me, I think, is that I do not put my writing into some sort of shape and try to *sell* it — Selling isn't altogether
bad. It is that I do not put it into such form that it might have value
to any one else.

Sunday, August 17
If a life has been worth living, it might be worth recording. To my living has been added a gift for expression. No one would put down the
incidents emotions and thoughts of his life, if it had not been so rich
that one does not want to forget or lose it. . . .

Who am I that I should spend time and effort in writing an autobiography[?]

Wm. James asks the question "What Makes a Life Significant?" Perhaps it is not the time in which one has lived, as the worth-whileness we found in the way we lived it. I have never known or heard, or read about any woman whose life has been richer and fuller, or more worthwhile to herself than mine has been, for I have had the rare, good fortune of experiencing life at every point where it is significant to a woman and now, nearing the end of it I hope I can recapture some of its beauty and worth. My book should echo the love of a child for an heroic mother, an inspiring grandfather, the loves of brothers and sisters, friends, husband and children and grandchildren and even great grandchildren.

Love, turned I hope into some kind of beauty. A life I could not have lived without the *husband who inspired me with confidence in myself* and who wrote home one day to my sister

"Irma has written you much of Paris, of course. I count it one of my blessings that she and I were there together."

I like to think that it might have been one of his and my own blessings that he and I were together in the journey of living.

But why, why have I waited, with pages upon pages of writing to put it together when he can no longer see it, and in retrospect share it with me [?]

Thornton Wilder had advised Irma, years before, to write her life story as a series of letters. Finally, during the late 1950s, she tried that literary device.[8] In a series of letters ostensibly addressed to her little great-granddaughter Betsey, Irma reiterated her feelings about love, the importance of family, memories, and the pain of loss.

Dear Little Betsey,

You are the youngest member of our family and I am the oldest. In July you will be 2 years old and I shall be 87 — Almost a century stretches between us. For you the days are an awakening to new perception and to new skills. Shall I tell you a secret about old age? The days for me too, continue to be an awakening and a progress toward new realizations. Let us, together explore them. . . .

Just for the record, little Betsey, I've always wanted to write a book. Everybody expects [. . .] me to write a book, first, because I love to write. In writing you can draw pictures, create music, erect monuments of grand persons and to those we have loved dearly, make poems out of what seem ordinary things, in fact, as Abraham Lincoln put it, where thistles might grow, make roses blossom. And so I'm going to write my book to you. This is enough for our first letter.

Friday, March 28, 1958
So far, I haven't told you much about how love binds people together.

In our family there has always been what is called "a strong family feeling" — and that means we felt that tie which binds people together. Everybody wanted to be helpful to everybody else in the family and what affected one member affected them all.

Sunday, April 13
When I was a young girl, a student in our West Division High School, one of our companions while we ate our lunch, was a charming, capable, intelligent Danish girl. Her father was the Danish consul in Chicago. They lived in a strange rather tumble-down home in a not too attractive part of the city. One day our companion at lunch told us of a visitor that they had had the day before from England. Some one had apologized for the house and the Englishman replied,

"It isn't the 'ouse, but the h'inmates that counts."

This passed into a proverb among us.

In a subtle way, however, I think a house takes on the personality of the inmates. We tried to make it a hospitable house and, as we grew older, and the house grew older, it began to lose all pretense and was stylish only in being old-fashioned. . . .

Now I live high in a hotel — near the top. Your great-grandfather, after an unusually busy life, rests where I shall one day rest beside him. At first I missed him so much that my days were full of sorrow. But, as the years slip by, I know they cannot be many now, before I too, with all my memories, will be but a memory. To be sad and sorrowful and make others sad and sorrowful would not be to heal the wounds that parting inflicts. Your great-grandfather's life was devoted to healing and to make a flower blossom where none had bloomed before. The passing of time applies a balm to our aching hearts if we will but let it. Now I live where outside of my windows there is a beautiful view which I do not own in any sense the way we owned the garden.

Saturday, April 26

Dear Little B,

Yesterday I had some interesting thoughts. The boulevard along which the buses go which I take often is being repaired. I had to walk a block out of my way to take my usual bus to go to Aunt Essie's for Friday night dinner. The bus man was nice. He drove right up to the curb to let me on, didn't growl because I didn't have my fare in my hand, and when I gave him a fare that required change, he put the right amount into his coin box and handed me back my change. I told him how far I wanted to go. A block before we arrived there he turned around, began to slow up his bus and motioned to me.

Standing next to him while the bus glided onto the new roadway which has been completed I asked him, "How do you like the new pavement?"

"How do I like it?" he answered. "It's swell. They ought to have done this twenty-five years ago."

I answered, "Some people say it wasn't necessary even now. That is[,] putting down a new roadway is political graft and all of that."

"Lady," he said, "those people haven't been driving buses along this street. The bus doesn't jiggle and bump. If they'd have put this down a long time ago I wouldn't have had so many backaches."

Now, . . . did you ever think a bus man would have a backache?

I always thought a bus man was something in a uniform, that saw to it that you put your fare into his coin box, handed out transfers if you were entitled to one, got grumpy if you took too long to get onto the bus and stopped if you'd let him know in time.

But why should a bus man have a backache? My word! Is he entitled to a backache? He runs the bus only eight hours at a stretch; sits all the time in a seat that he joggles to fix to his height sometimes — he doesn't really have to work because he can sit on one spot most of the time, sees the same sights every day and some of the same people. Would that give him a backache, or a stomach ache or a weary ache? He doesn't really do anything like brick laying or digging. Just sits eight hours at a stretch in one spot.

I once knew a bus man who sang as he drove his bus. One day I asked him what makes him so happy. I thought maybe he was an Italian opera singer and preferred driving a lumbering bus to singing at the Metropolitan Opera Company where they squabble. He didn't look Italian. He looked Irish. Still he *could* have been Italian.

"Well," he said, "I'm a Mason. And as I drive along I'm learning my Masonic ritual." Maybe singing is a good cure for backaches. But I've met some backaches that nothing but rest would cure.

I couldn't exactly say to bus man No. 1, "Get out of your seat and go and lie down and I'll drive your bus for you." I don't belong to the union and anyway I don't know how to drive.

What can we do about it?

I think maybe we should be more patient with all the people who wait on us, when they get grumpy. Maybe waiters in restaurants and maids in hotels and maids in houses and street sweepers and clerks in stores and everybody gets a backache sometimes. Maybe the world is full of backaches in and out of uniforms and maybe it's full of streets that aren't newly paved, and maybe you and I are lucky that we don't belong to the bus man's union. You're too young and I'm too old. But nobody is too young or too old to try to understand why a bus man shudders when the pavement is bumpy.

Friday, May 30
My dear little Betsey,

Why shouldn't every day be a sort of decoration day? Instead of decorating our graves, why shouldn't we decorate our lives. You need no decoration, but I, who am old and to-day, as my mind seems to be nourishing itself on memories [am] thankful that I can still be gentle still and see so much of the beauty of life. Perhaps when old people are crabby and ugly, they have no beautiful memories, or were not able to see beauty when they were surrounded by it. Am I? . . .

[T]here was something in me that always made the day a special kind of a day, full of flowers, and the scent of flowers, and the feeling of well being in the late spring and the near approach of early summer.

I remember one decoration day when your grandmother who was little Ruthie, and her big sister Emily and her little brother Alfred were all excited. One of our neighbors organized a parade for the children around us of the neighborhood, gave each child a flag, and the children's parade marched down Berkeley Avenue to the sound of a fife and drum, and everybody felt very patriotic. Even I who was in the kitchen baking a cake. They marched by my kitchen window so I could see them — Emily proud as a peacock for she was always very patriotic and had not lived long enough to feel any sadness about Decoration Day; Ruthie, of course, with her intensity of living was bright-eyed and filled with the marching spirit; and little Alfred tagging along, tagging along as he always did, perhaps not understanding it all, happy to be where there was any kind of music and throwing me a shy kind of satisfied smile as the parade passed by my kitchen window. The outside all around them and me in the kitchen where I belonged, baking a cake which I should have been doing . . .

(How proud each one was to be carrying a flag! being in the parade — me in a gingham work dress wearing a kitchen apron, and not having the charm of the children.)

On the porch, between (waiting on) service to patients, your great-grandfather was busy at his annual task of filling the flower boxes. By Decoration Day he always said it was safe to plant the flowers out of doors in the oblong green flower boxes on the flat top of the enclosure railing of the part of the porch resting on the ledge of the porch railing that looked out onto the street. The day before decoration day, always after the porch had been scrubbed with a broom and washed down with the hose by whoever it was who was helping him to take care of the lawn and the garden, always when I [was] proud of how clean the porch was, along would come Victor, the surgeon, your great-grandfather [who also] happened to be my husband, carrying arms full of plants which he had gathered from some near by florist, brought home in his auto mobile, and dumped onto the freshly scrubbed porch — The next day, on Decoration Day, he planted them in the flower boxes, which he had made and painted himself. Those skilled surgeon's hands, I can still see, all covered with dirt, putting the geraniums, lantana, nasturtiums, little white flowers, alyssum, petsineas [?], gaudy petunias, and begonia, into the oblong dirt filled boxes, patting them down into the earth — of course dropping pansies [along with] a lot of the dirt onto the floor — When I would come out onto the porch and remonstrate about the dirt he would hold up his hands to me — and say, as if it were my fault: "Look at these surgeon's hands — should a surgeon have hands like that?"

And if I'd say, "What do you do it for?"

He'd answer, again as if it were my fault, "You want the flowers, don't you?"

"Of course I want them, but you want them worse than I do." Your

great-grandfather had a passion for flowers, and ferns, and all growing things.

Often he would reply rather sheepishly, "Well, I really like them
and they're an ad for my office. Like heck they are. You know, I like
to dig in the dirt. I like the feel of it."

But almost more than he liked the feel of it — he liked the understanding of it. I can see him now (and a lump rises in my throat) ex-
amining every little rootlet and worm and apparently dead beetle he
would find in the earth. It was that inquiring mind and the urge to
be doing that made him the excellent doctor he was — an outstanding diagnostician and a fine surgeon.

The flower boxes were all filled with color, and it is amazing how
colors in the other media will throw each other off balance, and yet
out of doors *in flowers*, will blend into a harmony of beauty. . . .

It was spring time — and we were young.

Victor's death did not stop Irma from entertaining family and friends,
although the effort was becoming somewhat difficult. She was, after all,
nearly eighty-seven years old.

Thursday, May 29, 1958
Dear little Betsey,

To-day I had a luncheon for Essie and my friend Rosalia K. Rosalia thinks one can serve the best of foods by making use of the
canned and frozen, and otherwise prepared foods one can buy to-
day and so I tried an experiment — chicken with mushrooms on
toasted English muffins, A & P orange sponge cake, canned raspber-
ries — coffee, salad, tomato juice to start with — etc. It was good —
I used canned mushroom soup, with some Half & Half added for my
cream sauce. I thought it was too rich — and why use *canned* rasp-
berries when fresh strawberries are in the market — and canned
chicken when one so easily gets fresh chicken, well cleaned? . . .

At any rate I took pains to have the apartment look its best,
[and] washed all the little ornaments. Of the little cup collection
I formerly had, I have three little cups and saucers left. My favorite one, a little fluted cup and saucer with gold edges and roses
on them, I hope to give to you, and my very unique Fünfkirchenware plates which your great-grandfather bought and loved — and
everybody admires, these also I intend you to have.[9] If your Mam-

mee wants them, she may have them, but eventually they are to go to you.

The apartment looks lovely — a real couch-cover on my bed (I usually have a plain spread) my assortment of colorful pillows, flowers around — but, all these things take precious time — and even now I am almost too tired, hours after we had our lunch, to tackle the raft of dishes in my little kitchen — I was up at 7. *No* writing. And the day is gone. . . .

It's lovely to have nice surroundings. I tire more easily than I used to and I cannot do too much.

Monday, June 30

It is not yet 6 A.M. I could not go to sleep again after waking up a few minutes after 5. Busy day ahead. I am expecting Essie and Jennifer S. for lunch. Menu: Tomato juice with crackers and celery; chicken salad, canned pears and hot biscuits — lady finger dessert with strawberries and whipped cream — ice tea. I shall enjoy serving it, but must not do it again for it takes too much time. What kind of life would I lead if I weren't trying futilely to make an author of myself?

Now that I have filled all the blank pages in this book, how much *literature* is there in them? And what *is* literature? Yesterday, going down to Northwestern Station to meet Ruth I was reading Emerson's essay on Plato. Plato was the founder of European literature, as the bible, for us, is the beginning of Asiatic literature, which spread into Europe and influenced European literature tremendously and what *is* it? The recording of thought? Putting some of the thoughts into imaginary personal stories, inventing characters to fit and to illustrate the thoughts. After all, at bottom there are thoughts and literature is, in the last analysis, the expression of the thoughts — a way or a form of expressing them in language or speech. Of course there is description — representing in words, or rather transposing into words, pictures seen by the eye, the impact on the mind of what a person experiences by his senses.

At least the above seems for the moment to represent literature to me. Of course, put into the best language, or speech, of which one is capable.

How much of what I have done to fill these pages that were blank on April 10, can I attempt to make into literature, or, are they literature as they stand? I may try. Literature is, after all, the written word and the Abbé Dimnet stresses the fact that *the idea* is what counts.

Except for the lack of a garden, Irma found that apartment life was not very different from that in a house. She continued her daily walks in her familiar neighborhood, taking public transportation to the more distant stores and cultural events, and writing.

In about 1958, Irma wrote that "[i]n my little world, . . . no one enters except by my own volition (as Emerson puts it). Ah! But that's not true. Many enter it, not by my own volition, because of ties that bind, because of former or future ties."

Sunday, February 16, 1958

. . . [H]ere [in the apartment], the world intrudes because I don't shut it out. It might be within my possibilities to live here by myself and allow only action and persons to intrude who are necessary to my staying alive. Through the years one builds up a personality and suddenly to turn oneself into a hermit while human contacts have ever been a part of one's very existence would be most difficult. In moderation though, as a part, not the whole of every day, retiring for a period as a hostess to one's world, perhaps one could produce that echo of what had been, since I have promised, not only myself, but those dear to me and some persons who are only interested in me, to write that autobiography. Thinking this A.M. of the illness last week, I was thinking that I shouldn't have minded it so much, if I thought my work in the world is done. But it is not done and the years, perhaps even the days, I have left, might be few. Why can't I be *old*? Lean back in my easy chair, take the days as they come (which inevitably I must do) and be satisfied with myself? Perhaps the pattern of my life was set in my earliest days, as the pattern etched traced itself into my most important days, for I have ever wanted to accomplish more than I did. . . .

Am I really old? Is it not a matter of degree rather than an unchangeable fact? I can still do most of the things I did when I thought I was young, but in a lessened degree? But, does one when one is young really feel young? Doesn't the vague feeling of growing older begin when one consciously becomes aware of the passage of time as it spreads over us?

Last night, while I was waiting for the elevator a group of young persons was gathering in our entrance waiting to be taken to a party on the 12th floor one floor above my apartment. Our elevator girl said they were having a roof party. I could visualize the scene. It seemed to me that I had never beheld a handsomer group of young persons. I felt like lingering among them to feel the beauty of young, expectant life. The girls seemed so new and vibrant, so bright eyed and smooth of complexion — one stood out, sparkling challenging eyes, and the rest of her face with a sort of sharp beauty — the young men would be crazy about her — perhaps in former times, in a different social environment, she might have been an historic beauty, the mistress of kings and she might have wrecked empires — she wouldn't have been a gentle Mary, Queen of Scots.

At any rate, in my rapid passing though the gathering group, all the young men seemed tall and all the young persons seemed slender, expectant of fun and life and emotion.

I am sure they never gave me a thought — an old woman, carrying a bunch of papers and books, hurrying though their irregular grouping to reach the elevator and go to her apartment, before it would be crowded with their laughter and gaiety. If I had been in that group in my youth and had even noticed the old lady, I should have felt a fleeting regret for her being an old lady. I doubt if, although seeing me, they were at all aware of me.

I wanted the quiet of my apartment, as much as they wanted the noise of their party. I felt their trembling youth. Mine was not serene old age, for old age is often not serene.

What budding love stories were there in that group? What heartbreaking frustrations? What heavenly consummations?

I could sense it all. I knew that all of this had once been mine. And the echo of it lingers — Knowing it all better than this young, untried group knew it, trembling there on the threshold of life — And they did not know I [had felt] it all — a reward of knowing.

During March 1957, Irma composed a story for one of the grocery-chain newspapers, although she never mentioned whether or not it was published.

BILLY CHOPS AND BETTY CRACKERS

Time was, then, if your children went to market with you they knew the grocer and his clerks. They always were eager to go with you for maybe the kindly clerk would give them a cracker or a cookie, possibly even a hand full of raisins or a stick of red and white pep-permint candy or a banana or an apple. Mamma's cookies which no doubt were far better than "the store" ones never tasted so good as the ones the grocery clerk passed out for the free. Betty Crackers was a great favorite of my small fry.

Billy Chops was too. Billy Chops sometimes gave you a wienie or a frankfurter whichever name you called it by and you ate it raw and it didn't kill you. It wasn't really raw, but it seemed that way. Mr. Billy Chops was a friendly, optimistic fellow. If you bought a steak, he would cut off several layers of steak and give you the exact cut you wanted. "Some one," he said, "will always come in and take what you have." The steaks Billy Chops cut for our family to-day would be worth their weight in gold. As for chops, first come, first served. Chops were not the exclusive fare of persons rolling in wealth. As for the lovely shoulder chop, it was never a collector's item.

There was a personal bond between you and the market people. You wouldn't have been caught dead carrying your groceries home. The delivery boy's horse knew exactly where to stop at your back door. Possibly [he arrived] after the ice man had been there [to] your back entry or your kitchen, carrying his huge ice cube (on his leather protected shoulder) which he swung into the ice chamber of your ice-box held by a gigantic sugar tongs.

It was not yet the day of carts. In the Piggly-Wiggly age you en-tered the market through a turnstile. Some goods were packaged, a few clerks helped you, and you began to carry bags home. I couldn't. I didn't dare. I was the wife of a professional man and although it was alright for me to carry a small bag of [illegible] or nuts, a large sack might have affected my status.

Gradually the Piggly Wiggly transferred itself into the super mar-kets and the big chain stores and marketing became shopping.

Although the cost of food has risen by leaps and bounds, I confess I love the chain stores.[10]

The subject matter in Irma's poems touched upon the same themes as those in her diaries and in her letters to Betsey.

JUNE, 1958

In a month I'll be 87.
It is the evening of my life

Perhaps approaching midnight . . .
And though old age would like to claim me
I say "Not yet"—"not yet"
I still have more living to do.

TO VICTOR

Perhaps death is not the great mystery
Perhaps life is.
Perhaps sorrow is the great challenge
That the play must go on
To seek worth and beauty in life
With a heartache
Only life itself matters — the hungry
Reaching of the soul toward greater
Growth
Never take from any man his story
The beauty and tragedy and
Immortal wonder of life.

WHAT IS BEAUTY?

I loved him.
I do not know how it happened that when I was with him
I saw all things were beautiful and I wanted the whole universe to
    be always beautiful.
And then one day he came and asked,
"Dear heart, what is Beauty?"
I think he must have felt it in my presence as I did in his.
And then as I went about my tasks from day to day, often I asked,
"Dear heart, what is Beauty?"
But the answer came not.
One day I laid the table daintily with snowy cloth and shining
    silver against his coming.
And I knew I put on all the pretty things and the bright things
    because he was coming.
And when he came he brought me one pink rose, sweet, and fresh,
    and lovely.
And as I placed it on the centre of the snowy cloth, I stood and
    Pondered —

Why had I so carefully laid the table for his coming and why had
　　my lover thought to bring the rose?
It was love — love that in the heart of one reflected the love of the
　　other.
And all the dainty things, and all the bright things, and the rose,
　　gave answer to his question,
"Dear heart, what is Beauty?"
And I thought I knew and I asked,
"Is Beauty then, the outward flowering of some inner loveliness?"
By way of answer he kissed me, and in his
Lover's kiss was born something that is forever beautiful.

WHITE HAIR

I do not like my white hair
Some people do
I wish it would have stayed bluish-black
Or even salt and pepper like
Which says you are not young
Nor yet, are you old
I've longed all my life to be beautiful
Longed for it more than to be good
And now my hair is white
With a face that goes with it
White hair makes others good
And gives them beautiful manners
It's not a crown
It's more like a badge
Young things of whom I am jealous
Step aside and let me enter the elevator first
They halt the revolving doors for me
To pass through
Sometimes a gentleman tips his hat to me
And with grace offers me his seat
In the bus
And sometimes a different gentleman wants
To help me across the street
I hate it
Old people want to be independent

To navigate under their own power
As long as they can
Still, I remember, when white hair,
Called out tenderness in me
And I always helped old people
So I always say three thank you's
One I say out loud so they surely hear,
And try a smile
One more I say with an edge of sarcasm,
Thank you for reminding me that I am old,
I forget it so often
And the third thank you I say to God
Thanking him that courtesy has not died out in our hurried and
    distracted world.
I'll wear my white hair proudly
With my head erect
If it calls out tenderness in my fellow man.

Sometime during 1958, Irma suffered a heart attack. While she was re-cuperating in Woodlawn Hospital, a project was brought to her notice. A bill to designate the remaining unoccupied 3.5 miles of the Indiana Dunes as a national monument had been introduced in the Congress. The Save the Dunes Council needed some way to alert the public about the bill and to bankroll efforts to preserve this threatened ecological area. Charac-teristically, Irma volunteered to help.

The dunes had always been a nearby getaway spot for Irma and her family, a place to picnic and to observe nature. In 1917, she had written a short account of a trip they had taken there one November Sunday. The story became a family favorite. She rewrote the tale as The Chronicle of the Befogged Dune Bugs.[11] Next, she recruited a friend, the noted Chicago artist Earl Reed Sr., to illustrate the text. She and Emily added an ex-planatory foreword, she located a publisher, and then she donated the proceeds of the book's sale to the Save the Dunes Council. When The Chronicle came out, Irma had realized one of her dreams.

If Irma kept any diaries after 1958, they do not survive. The last entry for that year is dated Monday, June 30. Quoting from Emerson's Repre-sentative Men, she wrote, "Treat men and women well. Treat them as if they were real. Perhaps they are. Man is a piece of the universe made alive."

A single line, in an unsteady hand, identifiable as having been written in January 1963, follows. It is the last note Irma ever made in her journals:

Life grows more difficult as one grows really old, which means that one's faculties decline and one grows less independent.

Irma died on January 5, 1966. The following day, the *Chicago Tribune* carried her obituary.

Services for Mrs. Irma R. Frankenstein, 94, of the Mayfair Hotel, 5496 Hyde Park Blvd., widow of Doctor Victor S. Frankenstein, one of the first interns at Michael Reese Hospital before the turn of the century, will be held at 11:30 A.M. at the chapel at 2100 E. 75th St. Mrs. Frankenstein died Wednesday in her apartment. She is survived by two daughters, a son, five grandchildren, and six great-grandchildren.

Notes

INTRODUCTION

1. Saturday, April 26, 1958.
2. Sunday, May 9, 1948, Mother's Day.
3. Thursday, December 17, 1931. This entry was followed by a short poem.

> COOKIES
>
> Cookies are the poetry of baking —
> A big cake is too pretentious
> It comes mostly at the end of a meal
> Cookies are just little extras
> Existing for themselves —
> Festive a little — not necessary —
> You have to be in a mood to bake cookies.
> Thinking of children
> And how life is with children
> If you put frosting on them
> It's like the music of children
> Filled with glee, glad that there are homes
> And comfortable people in them
> Who bake cookies with spices and sugar.

On Saturday, April 12, 1958, Irma wrote, "I like my poetry simple, the way Carl Sandburg, who is a friend of mine and once made me happy by saying that I'm a poet, [wrote]." She most likely was introduced to Sandburg (1878–1967) in 1925 through her son, Alfred, a musician and music critic. How Alfred met Sandburg is recounted in William A. Sutton's *Carl Sandburg Remembered* (New Jersey and London: Scarecrow Press, 1979), 146–149:

> One night Keith Preston, a columnist on the *Chicago Daily News*, met Alfred . . . at a concert and told him, "Carl Sandburg wants to see you. He's given me a message that he wants you to get in touch with him." (This was a typical Sandburg procedure. Instead of using letters or telephone calls, he would depend on an oral message and an accidental meeting.)

Sandburg wanted Alfred to write the music for the American folk songs he had collected with an intent to publish. During most of the winter of 1925, the two met at least once monthly while Alfred struggled to notate the songs as Sandburg sang them. However, because "salesmen had decided the book would sell better with piano accompaniment," the songs were reworked and Alfred's name was left out when *American Songbag* finally appeared. Although Alfred said he had little contact with Sandburg after this fiasco, Irma apparently continued her friendship with him. She commented, "I might try his [Sandburg's] advice to write 2000 poems and maybe I'd have one out of the 2000." That Irma was good friends with Sandburg is without doubt. The family retains a number of inscribed presentation copies of his works that were given to her. Her comment on Saturday, January 27, 1951, that "Carl has a copy of some book of Emerson in every room" suggests she had visited his home on at least one occasion. Also, on January 27, 1951, Irma wrote a letter to a friend stating that "Carl told Alfred [I had written] 'Songs of the Kitchen Sink.'" In his comments to Alfred, Sandburg made reference to his own book *American Songbag*, as well as to Irma's short story called "Chicken Salad for Breakfast."

CHICKEN SALAD FOR BREAKFAST

There was a day that flew by, Alfred had flown in from New York the night before and he was to fly out to San Francisco that same evening. And so there was only one day. The old house had been waiting for that one day for six years — And now it was swiftly running through its hours. There had been baking and cooking and salad making as though Alfred had ten tummys instead of one. Every favorite of his growing days was in the new refridgerator and he had only one digestive apparatus with which to serve his country.

Breakfast, the coffee brewed in the familiar electric percolator in the breakfast end of the dining room under the window looking out into the garden — toast on the funny toaster with dangling ear drops the only one of its kind in existence — for when the man who produced that ugly toaster had finished it, he must have gone to his deserved reward to be toasted forever for producing the ugliest thing in the world — but it made good toast when it worked. Real cream in the hot coffee and butter and honey on the toast. When along came Nelson [a friend] with his illuminable diction, greeting Alfred and the breakfast in words of ten syllables. Some way or other Nelson heard that there was a gallon of chicken salad in the refridgerator and some one offered him some, and he accepted.

"My word! Chicken salad for breakfast! I've heard of heights — the height of luxury and the heights of enjoyment and other heights, but chicken salad for breakfast is something nobody has ever been able to put into words or music!" Nelson said it in superb language and the old house heard it and said to itself, "Perfectly proper! Alfred coming home, flying home is the height of all things happy and good — why not?"

But there came another time — When [my grandchildren] took the old house by storm, coming in from winter on a summer day, bringing with them a mess of fish and in the old kitchen the fish scales flew under [a] knife as the celebrated rabbi scraped — and the fish fillets and there was chicken salad in the refridgerator.

Along came I. B. [granddaughter, Irma Betty] — she who chummed with Alfred in the old days, who came to comfort me when he had left home and wailed through a whole week, "Why did you let him go?"

"Chicken salad! Yummy!!" And there stood I. B. eating chicken salad for breakfast and young Victor [grandson] joining her.

4. Sunday, May 9, 1948, Mother's Day. Irma met the Wisconsin writer and Pulitzer Prize winner Zona Gale (1874–1938) on October 29, 1937, when Gale gave a lecture at Lincoln Center called "Fiction To-day." Following the presentation there was a discussion, during which time Irma may have shown Gale a sample of her own writing.

5. Sunday, June 29, 1958.

6. Sunday, May 9, 1948, Mother's Day.

7. Wednesday, September 9, 1953. Irma first connected art with writing sometime during 1924. In an unaddressed, unsent, undated letter written that year, she commented:

I was thinking that after all, writing to me has not been a passionate sense of the mystery of words so much as a passionate sense of the mystery of living. When I sit down to write I never think about words (unless it is in writing verse when one plays about, as it were, with the words). All my writing seems to have grown out of living and I find myself now comparing what I want to do with what sculptors have done — Michelangelo taking a block of marble and working at it 'til a statue emerges. . . . I told you that I'm not so much interested in art in its specific manifestations as I am in the impulse back of it, and in the impulse toward expression included in it.

8. Wednesday, September 9, 1953.

9. Sunday, August 17, 1958.

10. Sunday, April 26, 1958.

11. Undated entry, ca. 1953. Later in life, on Friday, June 27, 1958, Irma wrote:

I took with me yesterday to read on the bus Sir James Barrie's address to the graduating class of his alma mater University in Scotland. A graduating address, I suppose, must have "advice" in it. This one is about "Courage." I have read it many times, both for its content and charm. He said, "We remember the important things and the important things are *the little things*." He goes to give examples. And then he tells the students of the graduating class a good title for an autobiography would be "My Life and What I Have Done With It." That's good to think about in writing one's autobiography — also, what has life done to us?

12. Wednesday, August 19, 1953. Thornton Wilder (1897–1975) taught at the University of Chicago between 1930 and 1937 (see *The Letters of Gertrude Stein and Thornton Wilder*, edited by E. M. Burns and U. E. Dydo [New Haven and London: Yale University Press, 1996], 287). Irma enrolled in a number of his creative-writing classes during that period and also took his 1941 summer course on Greek drama. She counted Wilder among her good friends, corresponding with "Thor-

ney" throughout the years. However, there are no copies of either her letters to Wilder or his to her among the purchased papers. Further, Wilder's sister, Isabel Wilder, claims that Wilder destroyed all the journals and diaries he wrote while at the University of Chicago (T. Wilder, *The Journals of Thornton Wilder, 1939–1961* [New Haven: Yale University Press, 1985]). Irma's family, however, retains four inscribed presentation copies of Wilder's works, along with his 1936 Christmas card to Irma.

Irma recorded only two conferences with Wilder during 1941 and one of Wilder's visits to her house on Sunday, June 22, 1941: "Company in the A.M.—Thornton Wilder, Kurt, Betty—[and other family members]. Laurie [grandson] stayed here. We made ice-cream, then went to movie of *Toys Town* [?] with Victor [grandson?] and Laurie. Dinner at home. Played with Laurie."

On Saturday, February 1, 1958, Irma commented: "I think I knew Wilder pretty well at one time. He had some regard for me—wonderful mind and character."

13. Monday, January 13, 1958.

14. Tuesday, January 14, 1958.

15. Sunday, May 9, 1948, Mother's Day.

16. Sunday, August 17, 1958. See entry for this date in the chapter "Changes, 1950–1966."

17. Tuesday, August 19, 1953. In an earlier entry dated January 9, 1951, Irma asserted, "Our happiness does not depend upon how much we accumulate, but how we use the accumulation."

18. Sunday, May 9, 1948, Mother's Day.

19. Monday, January 6, 1958.

20. Saturday, April 26, 1958. As early as Saturday, August 24, 1929, Irma noted:

I constantly lay aside my writing in order to take part in the living which goes on about me. It has always seemed the more important thing to do. It might not be—but, if it isn't, I am simply justifying myself, in following weakly, the course of least resistance.

1. REMEMBRANCES OF CHICAGO, 1871

1. E. Dedmon, *Fabulous Chicago* (New York: Random House, 1953), 187. Dedmon credits Rudyard Kipling (*American Notes*, 1891) with being the first to characterize Chicago as the "most American of cities." In her journals, Irma twice mentions that Thomas Mann (1875–1955) had the same opinion of the city.

2. Dedmon, 96.

3. Discussing those early days and where certain ethnic groups lived, Irma wrote that there was no real distinction between Germans and German Jews. German Jews simply considered themselves Germans, although it was possible that the non-Jewish Germans did not consider the German Jews to be German. She also noted sometime during 1953 that "[w]e were never made unhappy by prejudice, were never called ugly names. I think we sometimes felt a trifle inferior

to children whose parents were born in America and spoke English — instead of the German we spoke in our house." Her comments are supported by Irving Cutler ("The Jews of Chicago," 75, in *Ethnic Chicago*, ed. M. G. Holli and P. d'A. Jones [Grand Rapids: William B. Ferdmans Publishing Company, 1981]). Cutler states that

[t]he German Jews were on friendly terms with the non-Jewish Germans of Chicago and identified quite closely with them. German Jews and non-Jews of Chicago spoke the same language, and in many instances they had been forced by common political views to leave Germany after the collapse of the revolutions of 1848. The German Jews read German newspapers, attended German theaters, and belonged to German organizations.

And Cary McWilliams, in *A Mask for Privilege: Anti-Semitism in America* (Boston: Little, Brown and Company, 1948), 19–20, notes that

[i]n the period from 1840 to 1880, when the bulk of German Jews arrived, 10,189,429 immigrants entered the United States. Lost in this avalanche of peoples, the German Jews were numerically insignificant and aroused almost nothing in the way of popular antagonism or hostility. It was only in the upper reaches of society that their remarkable success excited feelings of envy and disdain.

4. For a discussion of the social functions charity fairs played before the turn of the century, see E. A. White's chapter, "Charitable Calculations: Fancywork, Charity, and the Culture of the Sentimental Market, 1830–1880," 73–85, in *The Middling Sorts*, ed. B. J. Bledstein and R. D. Johnston (New York and London: Routledge, 2001). White maintains that "the real reason bachelors came to the fair [was] to find a wife. The links between the marriage market and the charity fair were not coincidental; both markets tried to reconcile sentimental impulses and economic necessities" (79). Although this essay deals primarily with Christian charity work, the hypothesis is equally applicable to Jewish charity fairs during that same period.

5. Irma noted this fact in a family history she sent to a cousin in July 1961.

6. Dedmon, 98.

7. H. M. Mayer and R. C. Wade, *Chicago: Growth of a Metropolis* (Chicago and London: University of Chicago Press, 1970), 106–107.

8. See the Chicago Historical Society's publication *The Great Chicago Fire* by P. M. Angle (Chicago, 1946) for "seven letters by men and woman who experienced its horrors."

9. Undated entry, 1958. Balloon frame construction, an innovative building technique, originated in Chicago during the 1830s. In *Hyde Park Houses: An Informal History, 1856–1910* (Chicago and London: University of Chicago Press, 1978), 13, Jean Block explains that

[b]alloon framing employed very light materials — commonly two-by-fours — which could be handled by one man, in place of massive timbers, and the stud-

ding formed an integral, strength-giving part of the frame. Moreover, the balloon frame was put together with common nails rather than intricate mortise-and-tenon joints, which required woodworking skills of a high order to construct. With this innovation, Chicago became a city of wooden houses, fronted by wooden sidewalks, a true fire hazard.

10. Undated loose paper.

11. Thursday, August 27, 1953.

12. Undated loose paper.

13. Wednesday, January 8, 1958. Field, Leiter and Company later became Marshall Field and Company, one of Chicago's finest department stores.

14. Undated blank book, ca. 1953.

15. Thursday, August 27, 1953. In the aftermath of the fire, anti-Irish, anti-Catholic, and anti-immigrant prejudices emerged. Cartoons conveying "the demonic overtones many contemporaries saw in the origin of the Chicago fire" were published. The Chicago Historical Society addresses these sentiments on its Web site [http://www.chicagohs.org/fire/oleary/essay-4.html]: "[Mrs. Catherine O'Leary] was a familiar and recognizable type who could readily be made to stand for careless building, sloppy conduct, and a shiftless immigrant underclass. . . . As a poor Irishwoman and not a sworn enemy of the social order, she was a disempowered comic stereotype, the damage she caused the result of accident, not conspiracy." Irma never indicated that she was aware of these prejudices. By placing the blame for the fire on Mrs. O'Leary's cow, Irma was simply repeating what she had been told about the origin of the fire.

16. Tuesday, March 25, 1958.

17. Thursday, March 27, 1958.

18. Tuesday, March 25, 1958.

19. Undated loose page.

20. Thursday, August 27, 1953.

21. Dedmon, 103.

22. L. Wendt and H. Kogan, *Give the Lady What She Wants* (Chicago: Rand McNally and Company, 1952), 109.

2. RECOLLECTIONS OF CHILDHOOD, 1871–1888

1. Tuesday, January 7, 1958.

2. Thursday, August 27, 1953.

3. Tuesday, March 25, 1958.

4. Undated entry, ca. 1958. See also Mayer and Wade for details about Chicago's rebuilding. Irma was mistaken when she wrote that Louis Sullivan was the father of the skyscraper. That title rightfully belongs to William LeBaron Jenney, an architect-engineer who designed the Leiter building in 1879, as well as the Manhattan Building (1891), using iron-reinforced concrete (J. Graham, *Chicago: An Ex-*

traordinary Guide [Chicago, New York, San Francisco: Rand McNally and Company, 1968], 99, 105).

5. Tuesday, January 7, 1958.

6. Tuesday, March 25, 1958. On Thursday, June 29, 1950, Irma commented, "Big things can happen when you say 'I will.'"

7. Thursday, August 27, 1953.

8. Sunday, May 9, 1948, Mother's Day. According to her diary, Irma met Thomas Mann, his wife, and his daughter, Erika, at a dinner party given by her daughter Ruth and her son-in-law Ferd, in St. Louis on Sunday, March 19, 1939. Irma recorded the other guests as "Dr. and Mrs. Mittleburg, the President of Missouri State University, Mr. and Mrs. Irving Edeson, the President of Washington University, Bishop Will Scarlett, and Abraham Isserman." As late as Sunday, September 27, 1942, she was corresponding with Dr. Mann.

Bishop Will Scarlett (1883–?), called the Episcopal church's premier advocate of the social gospel, was an ardent proponent of social justice and a reformer who worked to change American society along the lines of Christian imperatives. He outlined his ideas about social reform in *The Christian Demand for Social Justice* (1949) and *Toward a Better World* (1949).

Abraham Isserman was a noted attorney who once addressed five hundred workers at a free speech rally in Passaic, New Jersey, where Albert Weisbord was the keynote speaker (*Class Struggle* 4, no. 4–5, April–May, 1934). Isserman was the attorney for the plaintiffs, all members of the Communist Party, in *Dennis et al. v. United States*, argued before the Supreme Court June 4, 1951.

9. Thursday, August 27, 1953.

10. Sunday, May 9, 1948, Mother's Day. Northwestern University was founded as a Methodist institution in Evanston. See F. Rudolph, *The American College and University* (Athens and London: University of Georgia Press, 1962), 350. Northwestern Medical College opened in 1859, although it was first called the Chicago Medical College. See L. B. Arey, *Northwestern University Medical School, 1859–1959* (Evanston and Chicago: Northwestern University Press, 1959); and M. Fishbein and S. T. DeLee, *Joseph Bolívar DeLee, Crusading Obstetrician* (New York: E. P. Dutton and Co., 1949), 40. Irma's husband, Victor, attended Northwestern Medical College on a State Senator scholarship. He graduated in 1895.

The University of Chicago, which had operated as a Baptist institution in 1856, reopened on October 1, 1892. See W. H. McNeill, *Hutchin's University* (Chicago and London: University of Chicago Press, 1991), 1–3; and M. Beadle, *The Fortnightly of Chicago: The City and Its Women: 1873–1973* (Chicago: Henry Regnery Company, 1973), 5. Dr. Emil G. Hirsch (1851–1923) and E. Bernhard Felsenthal (1822–1908), both rabbis of Sinai Congregation in Hyde Park, along with Berthold Lowenthal, a Jewish banker, and four hundred members of the Standard Club in Chicago, were instrumental in raising monies for the newly reopened university.

See P. P. Bregstone, *Chicago and Its Jews* (N.p., 1933), 199. Rabbi Felsenthal served on the university's board of trustees as documented in *History of Chicago*, ed. J. Moses and J. Kirkland (Chicago and New York: Munsell and Company, 1895), vol. 2, 117.

Irma's husband, Victor, who volunteered his medical skills for the United Hebrew Charities, later served on the Advisory Council of the University of Chicago Extension Lecture Course. See A. N. Marquis, ed., *The Book of Chicagoans: A Biographical Dictionary of Leading Living Men and Women of the City of Chicago* (Chicago: A. N. Marquis Co., 1917), 244. Jane Addams (1860–1935) founded this university extension. See J. Addams, "Social Settlement and the University Extension," *Review of Reviews* 20 (1899), 93.

The University of Illinois, Cook County, the West Side Veteran's, and Rush-Presbyterian–St. Luke's Hospitals currently make up the medical center to which Irma referred.

Irma's son, Alfred, was a clarinetist with the Chicago Symphony Orchestra. He also taught music at the University of Chicago in the department he helped to found with Cecil Smith. Irma frequently entertained the university music faculty and Alfred's friends, such as Gunnar Johansen and Ruth Crawford Seeger, at her house, according to Irma's diary entries dated Thursday, April 28, 1938, and Sunday, May 9, 1948, Mother's Day. See also Matilda Guame's chapter in J. Bowers and J. Tick, eds., *Women Making Music: The Western Art Tradition, 1150–1950* (Urbana and Chicago: University of Illinois Press, 1987), 370–388.

The 1873 Inter-State Industrial Exposition Building was demolished in 1892 to build the Art Institute of Chicago, which moved from its 1883 location at Michigan Avenue and Van Buren Street.

11. Undated entry, ca. 1958.

12. Undated letter, ca. 1958.

13. Wednesday, January 8, 1958. *Turnverein* is the name given to the clubs in Germany and the United States that followed the ideals of Friedrich Ludwig Jahn (1778–1852). Members of these clubs, commonly called Turners, were interested not only in physical education (*Turnen*) but also in liberal political and social issues. In time, the Turners split into two groups over the socioeconomic and political issues underlying the German revolutions of 1830 and 1848. The majority believed that political and civil rights would expand in Germany. The others, the radical Social Democrats, believed this would not happen and agitated for immediate social justice. Many of these radicals, some of whom subscribed to Marxist views, came to the United States after Bismarck's antisocialist laws were adopted in Germany.

Irma's grandfather "belonged to the *Achtundvierziger* [the Forty-Eighters], a group that advocated the reforms fought for in the German Revolution of 1848," according to material Irma wrote and gave to a cousin, dated July, 1961.

14. Friday, March 28, 1958.

15. Friday, January 10, 1919. This entry was part of a composition Irma wrote for her English 5 class at the University of Chicago. The instructor commented: "Excellently put. Distinct." On Monday, June 23, 1958, Irma recollected that "[w]hen I was taking English 3 at the University of Chicago, in Mr. Webster's class, the other students said that I have a distinct 'literary style.' I am never aware of it while I am writing. Mr. [Robert] Herrick in English 5 smoothed it out. I always use too many 'ands' and 'buts' and lately I find myself using the word 'for' too often."

Irma liked Herrick's works. On Sunday, March 28, 1937, she commented:

Last night looked through Robert Herrick's *The Master of the Inn* — one of my favorites — beautifully written. I think the greatest thought in the book is: "The Master believed," as I recall it, "that Disease could not be cured for the most part. No chemistry could ever solve the mystery of pain! But Disease could be ignored, and the best way to forget pain was through labor not labor merely for oneself; but also something for others" [quotation from 1908 edition, 54].

I thought I ought to take that to heart. . . . I love the soothing effect on my mind of *The Master of the Inn*. Knowing Robert Herrick, the sarcastic, embittered man, I believe the portrait of "The Master" must have had deep significance for him as he painted it in beautiful prose. Poor Herrick! I'm afraid he never achieved such serenity himself.

16. Undated entry, ca. 1958.

17. Undated letter, ca. 1958.

18. Undated book, ca. 1953.

19. Wednesday, January 8, 1958. Discussing the diphtheria epidemic of 1874, C. B. Johnson, in *Sixty Years in Medical Harness, or the Story of a Long Medical Life, 1865–1925* (New York: Medical Life Press, 1926), 159, wrote that the summer of that year in Illinois and the Midwest had been a season of drought so severe that most wells dried up. People were reduced to drinking "swamp water," a factor later blamed for the outbreak of the diphtheria epidemic.

In the treatment of diphtheria in that day it was the custom to rely on iron, quinine and alcoholic stimulants given internally and chlorate of potash locally. For internal use chlorate of potash was also dissolved in tincture of iron to the point of saturation and to this glycerine or simple syrup was added to make a palatable solution. . . . As it was before the days of quarantine and efforts at disease-prevention, no systematized attempt was made to separate the sick from the well.

20. Thursday, January 9, 1958.

21. Undated entry, ca. 1953.

22. Undated letter, ca. 1958.

23. Friday, August 29, 1958. The term "half-orphan" that Irma found so offensive and hurtful had official usage in the Chicago Nursery and Half-Orphan Society founded in 1860. See *A Home of Another Kind: One Chicago Orphanage and the*

Tangle of Child Welfare, by Kenneth Cmiel (Chicago: University of Chicago Press, 1995).

24. Undated entry, ca. 1953.

25. Wednesday, August 19, 1953.

26. This quotation was taken from Irma's July 1961 family history material sent to a cousin.

27. Sunday, January 12, 1958.

28. Wednesday, April 24, 1957. On Friday, May 31, 1957, Irma wrote:

Two of my sisters, one older and one younger, and my younger brother are now past 70 — Three of us, including myself, well past 80. We have held together throughout our lives. When we are together there is nothing we like better than our rememberance of things past, particularly our rememberance of our childhood days — queer, odd things we did, which made us laugh a good deal mostly. Of course we remember too frustrations and sorrows. We no longer weep over our sorrows and it is better, no doubt, to laugh at our earliest remembrances, than to weep because of our later sorrows from which no life is exempt.

29. Thursday, May 2, 1946.

30. Wednesday, April 24, 1957. During the post–Civil War era, the craze for "culture" swept America. Middle-class families bought pianos and large numbers of children began to take piano lessons, according to Ian Frazier, *Family* (New York: Farrar Straus Giroux, 1994), 166.

31. Undated letter, ca. 1958.

32. Thursday, September 3, 1953.

33. Undated entry, ca. 1953.

34. Undated entry, 1953.

35. Saturday, August 29, 1953.

36. Thursday, January 9, 1958. An 1873 map of the city of Chicago in Mayer and Wade, 71, places the reform school near the lake, south of the Oakland but north of the Hyde Park–Kenwood neighborhoods. Irma's recollection of her brother's "gang" was that it was a loosely organized, somewhat informal group of young boys drawn together more by the happenstance of residence, a desire to play together, and age similarities than for any specific purpose. Frederic M. Thrasher's early study of gangs, *The Gang: A Study of 1,313 Gangs in Chicago* (Chicago and London: University of Chicago Press, 1927) points out that no two gangs were alike, and that gang composition and behavior depended on the personalities of the members, their physical and social environments. Further, Thrasher stressed that not all gangs had formalized memberships or leaders, nor were all gang members delinquents. According to Howard M. Sachar, *A History of Jews in America* (New York: Alfred A. Knopf, 1992), 168, it was not until the 1890s that a more organized underworld that included juvenile delinquents, pickpockets, and street gang members working for Jewish fences developed in the larger U.S. cities.

37. Thursday, May 2, 1946.

38. Friday, September 4, 1953.

39. Undated entry, ca. 1953.

40. Tuesday, September 1, 1953.

41. Sunday, May 9, 1948, Mother's Day.

42. Thursday, August 27, 1953. Mrs. William Vaughn Moody (Harriet Converse Tilden Brainard) was born in 1857 and died in 1932. According to Olivia Howard Dunbar (*A House in Chicago* [Chicago and London: University of Chicago Press, 1947]), she was central to the Chicago Literary Renaissance. Before her marriage to William Vaughn Moody, Harriet taught English literature at the West Division High School (1889). It is possible that she taught Irma's sister Meta there or at Hyde Park High School after Irma's family moved to Forty-fifth Street in the 1890s.

Harriet Moody hosted a salon at her house on Twenty-ninth and Ellis where Carl Sandburg, Loredo Taft and his wife, Robert Frost, Vachel Lindsay, Harriet Monroe, Alice Corbin, and William Henderson, among others, were frequent guests. She also ran the Home Delicacies Association, a catering company, published student papers on her home printing press under the imprint of the Windtryst Press, and wrote a "literary" cookbook. Harriet also joined the Fortnightly discussion group before her divorce from Brainard (Beadle, 1973), 43. See also E. Chamberlin, *Chicago and Its Suburbs* (New York: Arno Press, 1975), 431–435.

Susan Wilbur, whose review of Mrs. William Vaughn Moody's cookbook appeared in the *Chicagoan*, May 1931 (Moody Papers, University of Chicago), suggested, "To have poetry you must first have cookery. Put it the other way around, however. . . . To have cookery you must first have poetry."

43. Friday, September 4, 1953.

44. Wendt and Kogan, 113; Moses and Kirkland, eds., vol. 2, 49.

45. Monday, August 24, 1953.

46. H. David, *The History of the Haymarket Affair* (New York: Russell and Russell, 1958), 15.

47. E. L. Hirsch, *Urban Revolt* (Berkeley, Los Angeles, Oxford: University of California Press, 1990), 6.

48. E. Darby, *The Fortune Builders* (New York: Doubleday and Company, 1986), 243.

49. David, 171. On an Alaskan tour in the summer of 1915, Irma spoke at length with an unemployed miner who had been sitting in front of her hotel. Her comments on Monday, August 2, 1915, indicate that she was quite interested in social and labor issues. She wrote that the man "interested [her] immediately" and criticized the men on her tour who made fun of the miner's forced diet of beans. She recorded a long "political-sociological" discussion that she, another woman, and a judge had with the miner, wherein she became "furious" with the judge for not taking the man's plight seriously.

The Judge told him to go down to Juneau and talk to other laboring men and become a labor leader and then get a political job. The miner had a good mind; he tried to reason things out and he was well informed about the country and working conditions. Why didn't the Judge put himself in his place, and talk manliness and self-respect and hope into him, instead of suggesting preposterous things?

Irma clearly sympathized with the miner, who seemed to her to be trying to overcome his situation, and felt that the judge's opinions were based on privilege rather than logic.

The miner thought that there isn't much justice in the courts and that governments are too often corrupt. The Judge said that we would have no law and order without government, we would revert back to savage times, when physical supremacy reigned, whereas in civilization as we know it, it is intellectual supremacy that counts.

No doubt, our miner's point of view was colored by his diet of beans, by his work for weeks underground in a poorly ventilated shaft, often filled with distressing gases. He said that the owner of the mine was never satisfied; if they worked 7 feet, he wanted 9; if they had accomplished 9, he was impatient because it hadn't been 11. . . . Told us of how he once worked in a copper mine near Ketchikan. Not a bit of copper in sight and everybody knew there never would be — yet there was $150,000.00 worth of machinery, men at work, stock-holders being fleeced and the promoter making his pile.

Irma later had a second conversation with the miner during which they established, in her words, "a bond of sympathy."

Then he told me that he never had an education — worked as a miner in a coal mine on some Duke's estate in England from the time he was a boy. Father died early. Left his mother with three children, two girls and himself. Had to pay part of his earnings (1/3) to Duke (no wonder he's a socialist). After mother died came to British Columbia — worked as a miner. Sisters went out to service and he sent home spare money 'til both were married. Has never had a chance to marry or never had an education except what he got in a night school. Told me he had read Upton Sinclair's *Jungle* — said it wasn't a very good book, but interesting because it presented the side of the poor. Almost apologized for having read it. I told him that I knew about it. He spoke of labor conditions all over the world and I finally made him accede to my statement, that the world *is* growing better, that we have no human slavery, that we treat our criminals and insane better than we used to, but that improving the world is a slow process.

. . . At last the miner wound up by saying, Well, he wasn't so badly off—he had saved a little sum, with which he must be very careful and he has his blankets and so if he can't sleep in a hotel, he can always curl himself up in his

blankets—and be warm at least. I told him that is more freedom and inde-
pendence than we have.

50. Hirsch, 69.

51. Ibid., 80. See also G. N. McLean, *The Rise and Fall of Anarchy in America* (Chicago and Philadelphia: R. G. Badoux and Co., 1886). Anarchists debated the proper role of violence as a revolutionary tool to place the power back into the hands of the workers. According to Hirsch, 37, by early 1879 Chicago was the undisputed center of the U.S. socialist movement. Few belonged to the official party, but it had many supporters among the German trade union movement.

David Lasswell ("The Old New Left: Emma Goldman in Chicago," *Chicago History* I, no. 3, 1971, 170) quotes Emma Goldman's diary entry of May 1901: "Chicago, city of our Black Friday [Haymarket Riot day, 1886], cause of my rebirth!"

3. REFLECTIONS ON EDUCATION, 1875–1891

1. S. A. Rippa, *Education in a Free Society: An American History* (New York: Longman, 1992), 141–212.

2. W. H. Schubert, *Curriculum: Perspective, Paradigm, and Possibility* (New York: Macmillan Publishing Company, 1986), 67.

3. Ibid., 66.

4. Schubert, 68.

5. H. L. Horowitz, *Culture and the City: Cultural Philanthropy in Chicago from the 1880's to 1917* (Lexington: University Press of Kentucky, 1976), 194.

6. Wednesday, January 8, 1958.

7. Tuesday, September 1, 1953.

8. Thursday, September 3, 1953.

9. Sunday, May 9, 1948, Mother's Day. Irma's mother came to the United States in 1866. Irma never mentioned the exact date at which her father immigrated, although she commented, in the July 1961 material, that her father's family had been in Chicago longer.

10. Saturday, August 29, 1953.

11. Irma was mistaken when she said "there was no psychology of learning." However, her error is understandable, because during the 1940s she took a psychology class at the University of Chicago that traced the rise of psychology back only to Germany in the early 1900s.

12. Wednesday, January 8, 1958.

13. Tuesday, September 1, 1953.

14. Wednesday, January 8, 1958.

15. Thursday, September 3, 1953. Ella Flagg Young lived on Chicago's West Side. She began teaching in 1862 following her graduation from the Normal Department of Chicago High School. At the end of 1879 she moved to Skinner School, where she served as principal and taught eighth-grade grammar. Joan

Smith, in *Ella Flagg Young: Portrait of a Leader* (Ames, IA: Educational Studies Press, 1979), 30–31, says that Skinner School "served the upper class of the west side" and was known for employing the "best techniques in educational procedure." Young was more interested in using literature to teach rather than textbooks, telling the 1896 National Education Association meeting, "Literature reveals the possibility of the human soul" (J. T. McManus, *Ella Flagg Young and a Half-Century of Chicago Public Schools* [Chicago: A. C. McClurg and Co., 1916], 84–89). She "attempted to follow up the children and keep in touch with them and their homes in order to hold them in school until they were old enough to meet the demands of society upon them" (McManus, 61). In 1887, Young became the assistant superintendent of the Chicago public schools, the first woman superintendent of the system in 1909, and president of the National Educational Association.

Young was a good friend of John Dewey, and became his graduate student at the University of Chicago when she was fifty years old. Dewey credited Young with influencing his *School and Society* (Smith, xi). Jane Addams wrote a tribute to Young following the educator's death ("Ella F. Young Dies," *Chicago Tribune*, 27 October 1918), saying, "She had more general intelligence and character than any other woman I knew."

16. Tuesday, September 1, 1953. It is probable that the Snell mansion to which Irma referred belonged to William O. Snell, a shipsmith on South Water Street, and the Near West Side's First Ward alderman in 1841. Snell is mentioned in both Robert Fergus's *Chicago Directory* (Chicago: Fergus Printing Company, 1839) and Moses and Kirkland, vol. 2, 115. No references were found about a murder, however.

17. Sunday, May 9, 1948, Mother's Day. After Abraham Lincoln's assassination, Mary Todd Lincoln and her son, Robert, rented at least two houses on the Near West Side of Chicago. The last one bordered Union Park, and most likely it is to this rented house that Irma referred. Robert became a lawyer and eventually the president of the Pullman Company. One of Irma's cousins designed the Pullman couch-bed.

18. Tuesday, September 1, 1953.

19. Friday, September 4, 1953. Regular physical education was not introduced into the Chicago public schools' curriculum until 1886. The decision to include "physiculture" was largely due to the efforts of Henry Suder (1866–1936), a Turner from Germany who had graduated from the North American Gymnastics Union in Minneapolis. Suder arrived in Chicago with his teaching certificate, and quickly started lobbying for the inclusion of a physical education program in the schools. In 1885, the Chicago Board of Education agreed to a trial program of physical education (marching and calisthenics) at Lincoln, Douglas, Brown, and King schools on the city's West Side, in the heart of the German and German Jewish neighborhoods. The experiment proved successful, so in 1886 the board voted to include physical education programs in all forty-six of its elementary

schools. Suder's program was started in three high schools in 1889, and by 1896 all the city's schools incorporated physical education into their curriculum. In 1896, Suder was appointed director of physical education for Chicago schools (Susan Fry, "Henry Suder," *Chicago Tribune*, 24 February 1966).

20. Thursday, September 3, 1953. In 1910, Ruth, Irma's second daughter, wrote in Emily's diary: "I am in second grade in school. I am going to study with Miss Peck." Whether this woman was the same as Irma's Miss Peck cannot be determined.

21. Undated entry, 1953.

22. Saturday, August 29, 1953.

23. Thursday, September 3, 1953.

24. Saturday, August 29, 1953.

25. Friday, September 4, 1953.

26. Undated entry, 1953.

27. Tuesday, September 1, 1953.

28. Friday, September 4, 1953.

29. Sunday, May 9, 1948, Mother's Day.

30. Friday, September 4, 1953.

31. Sunday, May 9, 1948, Mother's Day.

32. Friday, September 4, 1953.

33. Sunday, May 9, 1948, Mother's Day.

34. Friday, September 4, 1953.

35. Thursday, September 3, 1953.

36. Since the Lusitania was a Cunard ship, it was registered as the RMS *Lusitania*. Herbert Stone lost his life on May 7, 1915, when that ship sank after being torpedoed by a German submarine.

37. Friday, September 4, 1953. In an undated paper from 1953, Irma wrote: "Hist[ory] opened up like a picture book And there were trends and answers to whys and wherefores and sequences. But Mr. Fish and math were a nuisance, geometry and q.e.d.'s and who cared whether figures and the letters in algebra and the drawings in geometry balance or came out true."

38. Sunday, May 9, 1948, Mother's Day. In *A History of Reading* (New York: Penguin Books, 1997), Alberto Manguel states (121) that the "novelist Harriet Martineau lamented in her *Autobiographical Memoir*, published after her death in 1876, that 'when she was young it was not thought proper for a young lady to study very conspicuously; she was expected to sit down in the parlour with her sewing, listen to a book read aloud, and hold herself ready for callers.'"

39. Undated entry, ca. 1953. *Thorns and Orange Blossoms* (1886) was written by Charlotte Mary Brame (1836–1884), also known as Bertha M. Clay. *Little Women* came out in 1868. It was one of the few books that could be classified as juvenile literature, although subsequently it has been criticized as appealing only to female, white, middle-class adolescents. According to Barbara Sicherman, "Reading *Little*

Women: The Many Lives of a Text," in *U.S. History as Women's History* (L. Kerber, A. Kessler-Harris, and K. Kish Sklar, eds, [Chapel Hill and London: University of North Carolina Press, 1995], 245–247), the book also provided a model for assimilation to young Jewish working-class immigrant women in the early part of the twentieth century. In 1907, *Little Women* was published in English with a German introduction and notes by Professor G. Opitz, for use in German schools in English instruction. It would have been useful in the Chicago public schools, where German was the primary language for many of the students, and literature was used to teach English.

Sicherman also states that in 1925 the Federal Bureau of Education recommended reading *Little Women* before children turned sixteen (249). Two years later, surveyed high school students ranked it the most influential book they had ever read, ahead of the Bible and Bunyon's *Pilgrim's Progress*. In keeping with this sentiment, Jane Addams wrote to a friend on March 16, 1876, "I have read and re-read 'Little Women' and it never seems to grow old" (Sicherman, 245).

40. Sunday, May 9, 1948, Mother's Day. Irma frequently quoted the writings of Ralph Waldo Emerson. In 1910, when she was outlining a book called "Nursery Ethics," she quoted a number of writers — Emerson, his aunt, Mary, and Maria Elliott of Simmons College, Boston, among them. Irma recorded Elliott as having said, "Education is not knowledge alone. It is the development of the individual, and this development should make every person a force in the world."

41. Undated entry, 1958. It appears that although Irma herself did not receive any formal training in pedagogy when she became a cadet teacher, her own teachers were aware of the prevailing educational theorists and had employed their philosophies in their classrooms. More than likely, they learned their educational philosophies and techniques at normal schools, the early teacher-training institutions. Irma's interest in educational theory and practice did not stop when she married. As late as Thursday, February 5, 1942, she wrote that she "[a]ttended two meetings at the [Chicago Jewish Woman's] Aid. Heard Mandel Sherman [the psychologist] in the A.M. Discussion on High School curriculum in P.M."

42. When the University of Chicago reopened, the American Hebraic scholar William Rainey Harper (1856–1906) took over as president. He vowed that "women would have equal opportunities and treatment" at his university (Beadle, 66). Apparently he succeeded; Moses and Kirkland (vol. 2, 118) found "that the Chicago University is organized on the most liberal lines as to the admission of women to the advantages of its course of instruction on equal terms with men."

43. Sunday, May 9, 1948, Mother's Day. Literary groups in Chicago, such as the Fortnightly, the Friday Club, and the Scribblers, grew out of "salons" or "bluestocking" parties, according to Beadle, 8. They essentially provided women's adult education courses in the form of lectures with literary and cultural themes. The term "bluestocking" was derogatory when applied to women who had literary or educational aspirations. The term's origins most likely lie in the mid eighteenth

century. The Bluestocking Club was a group of British women who met informally to discuss literary and intellectual topics. They invited men of letters and members of the aristocracy to participate. Supposedly, at one time Benjamin Stillingfleet turned down an invitation because he was not appropriately dressed. The hostess, Mrs. Vesey, told him to come in his "blue stockings," the inexpensive, plain worsted wool stockings people wore at home, as opposed to the black silk stockings worn on dress occasions or when visiting (American Heritage Dictionary, *Word Mysteries and Histories: From Quiche to Humble Pie* [Boston: Houghton Mifflin, 1986], 22).

44. Thursday, August 27, 1953.

45. Sunday, May 9, 1948, Mother's Day.

46. Undated entry, 1958. Irma actually was the president of two women's clubs: the Temple Isaiah Woman's Club and the Chicago Woman's Aid, both of which were established before 1900 for the purposes of social reform and philanthropy. Temple Isaiah Woman's Club was affiliated with the second-oldest Jewish congregation in Chicago, founded in 1852. Its first home, built in 1899, was located at Forty-fifth Street and Vincennes. Its new building, designed by Alfred S. Alschuler, was erected on Hyde Park Boulevard in 1924. The complete name for the Chicago Woman's Aid was the Chicago Jewish Woman's Aid (Bregstone, 278). It had a large membership dedicated to carrying out philanthropic works much like those undertaken by the Chicago Woman's Club, a gentile charity organization, and also to sponsoring lectures by both Jewish and non-Jewish speakers. Irma also belonged to a literary club, the Scribblers, along with a number of her friends who were members of the Chicago Woman's Aid. The Scribblers met in the Chicago Woman's Aid rooms in downtown Chicago.

47. Saturday, August 29, 1953.

48. Saturday, August 24, 1929.

49. Tuesday, September 1, 1953.

50. Sunday, May 9, 1948, Mother's Day.

4. GRANDPA AND EMERSON, 1876–1898

1. Sunday, August 23, 1953.

2. Wednesday, August 19, 1953.

3. Undated entry, ca. 1953.

4. Undated entry, ca. 1953.

5. Sunday, August 23, 1953.

6. July 1961 material sent to a cousin.

7. Sunday, August 23, 1953.

8. Undated letter, ca. 1958.

9. Zion Temple was established in 1864, and B'nai Abraham in 1870. These congregations merged into the Washington Boulevard Temple following a move to the Garfield Park area of Chicago. When some of the members migrated to

the suburbs, the congregation moved to Oak Park, where it is now called Oak Park Temple B'nai Abraham Zion (Cutler, 74).

10. Saturday, June 29, 1891 (evening).

11. Sunday, August 23, 1953. Irma wrote to a cousin in July 1961 that her grandfather had taught her that "God *was* around and you served Him, not so much that you expected Him to serve *you!*" When she became a parent, Irma in turn taught her older daughter, Emily, to help those less fortunate than herself. One of Emily's diary entries, dated Saturday, December 2, 1911, reads: "A little girl like myself surely ought to do everything she can for those who are unlucky, and I really truly am trying to. This morning I went to a meeting of our mission band. We made little stockings to fill with candy so as to hang on a Christmas tree for the poor in the Ghetto. At eleven thirty I came home and dressed for dancing class."

12. Among those immigrating to America during this period were a large number of penniless, unskilled Russian Jews, fleeing pogroms in their native land. The arrival of thousands of these refugees in U.S. cities caused consternation among the already assimilated German American Jews. Rabbi Isaac Mayer Wise (1819–1900) commented: "We are Americans and they are not. We are Israelites of the Nineteenth century in a free country, and they gnaw the bones of past centuries. . . . The good reputation of Judaism must naturally suffer materially, which must without fail lower our social status" (Sachar, 125).

As late as 1910, in an undated diary entry, Irma noted that "General Booth, the founder of the Salvation Army considers that the first vital step in saving outcasts consists in making them feel that some decent human being cares enough for them to take an interest in the question whether they are to rise or sink."

Around 1944, in what may have been a reference to Jane Addams's 1920 book *Peace and Bread in Time of War,* in which Addams linked the images of bread with women as the breadgivers to symbols for international peace and salvation, Irma wrote:

Louisa May Alcott in her book "Rose In Bloom" made Rose say that she wanted to be a philanthropist. I had looked up the word when I read the book. . . . [A]t the time I wanted to be a philanthropist too — To-day the work I had done would be called "Social Service" in a haphazard way. . . . Mostly it was relief work, but we had begun to do some fairly intelligent research. . . . [The] girls in our crowd, who did charity were neither trained nor paid workers. We were ladies — the original naming of the term lady was "loaf-giver." I interpreted that rather broadly as meaning [a lady was required] to embroider, play the piano, not use slang. I interpreted Ruskin [in his lectures titled "Sesame and Lilies"] as meaning ladies must be useful. Later I learned to cook, although this is beside the point. Later, after I was married, I learned to cook, because I felt that a loaf-giver should know how to be a loaf-maker.

(The Old English word for "lady" was *hlafdige*. *Hlaf* meant "loaf"; *dige* meant "a kneader of bread" or "a maid." In Middle English, the term for a lady was *lavedi*, and later *lafdi*).

13. The United Hebrew Charities (UHC) founded a relief office and Michael Reese Hospital to help poor Jews. In 1880, Irma's uncle, who had supported the building of *Kehilath Anshe Maarive* (KAM Temple), contributed to building Michael Reese Hospital where Victor interned in 1895. See Bregstone, 7, and I. Cutler, *The Jews of Chicago: From Shtetl to Suburb* (Urbana and Chicago: University of Illinois Press, 1996), 19, 30–31, 156.

14. Addams 1899, 93.

15. R. L. Sherrick, "Private Visions, Public Lives: The Hull House Women in the Progressive Era," Ph.D. diss., Northwestern University, 1980, 2.

16. J. Addams, *Newer Ideals of Peace* (New York: Macmillan, 1907), 182.

17. Wednesday, August 19, 1953. A diary entry for Friday, February 18, 1938, reads: "Up at 7. Busy in the A.M. Down town at 11 to hear Rabbi Berman speak on 'The Jewish Child in the Modern World.'—the cultural aspect impressed while there but in thinking it over, I doubt if I should care to subscribe to all the 'Jewishness' he advocates." This Jewishness, or *Yiddishkeit*, was something which the early German Jewish immigrants to America worked to lose (C. E. Silberman, *A Certain People* [New York: Summit Books, 1985], 173, 181). Silberman also mentions that many assimilated Jews went so far as to celebrate Christmas, as Irma herself did in her own home. However, from what she wrote the few times she mentioned this holiday, her celebrations lacked religious overtones:

Saturday, December 25, 1937—Christmas-day

Arose at nine. Great excitement with [grandchildren] I.B. and Juny about stockings—Had turkey in oven at 9:30. . . . Set table, children frosted the cookies—finished packages—cooked the dinner. . . .

After dinner Juny put on Santa suit and distributed presents up in the library. Jolly time. Listened to broadcast of Dickens' *Christmas Carol* on the radio—Lionel Barrymore as Scrooge.

18. Saturday, June 7, 1958.

19. Undated entry, 1910. According to Cutler, 72, there were great similarities among Reform Judaism, Unitarianism or Universalism, and the writings and teachings of Emerson, a one-time Unitarian minister.

20. Sunday, June 29, 1958. William James, the philosopher and psychologist, "was said to be as important to the twentieth century in America as Emerson was to the nineteenth" (Frazier, 385). James's approach to religion was personal, experiential, and pragmatic.

21. Undated entry, 1957.

22. Sunday, May 4, 1924. Gerson B. Levi wrote *Gnomic Literature in the Bible and Apocrypha, with Gnomic Fragments and their Bearings on the Proverb Collec-*

tions. He also became the rabbi of the combined Temple Isaiah-Israel on the South Side.

23. Tuesday, January 23, 1934. The prayer is *Shema* [Listen]. The full text reads: "Shema Yisrael: Adonai Eloheinu, Adonai Echad! Baruch shem kevod malchuto, le'olam va'ed." [Listen, Israel: Adonai is our God, Adonai is One! Blessed is the name of God's glorious rule for ever and ever.]

Irma's mother had been raised in an Orthodox Jewish family, so when Irma and her family recited the traditional prayer, they were acknowledging this fact, as well as giving their mother comfort by reciting the prayer in Hebrew. The final words of Irma's account were never written.

Years later, on Monday, June 23, 1958, Irma noted that

[o]nce before, on my mother's birthday I wrote, to please myself, a tribute to her. I then wrote it in the form of "The Most Unforgettable Character" and sent it to *The Literary Digest*. They returned it with the comment that they (The Editors) enjoyed reading this *tender* tribute to my mother. I liked the letter — somehow the tenderness that I felt must have been manifest in my writing.

24. Irma frequently spoke about Jewish holidays, beliefs, and rituals to her children and grandchildren, who had been raised Reform and who, apparently, were unfamiliar with Orthodox traditions. When she explained the holidays and their traditions, Irma always added what amounted to a commentary, as in this Thursday, October 2, 1930, entry:

Yom Kippur. Woke up at 6 [A. M.] but didn't get up. Alfred up at 7:30. Came into my room and shaved and we exchanged ideas about sin, recalling old customs and the psychology of fear back of the notion of sin. Told Bud [Irma's son, Alfred] about the Orthodox custom of casting your sins into the water and about the *Sündenbock* [scapegoat]— can't think of the English name for it. We marveled at how humanity can blame a God of Wrath for its own wars and blood-lettings.

5. YOUNG LOVE, 1891

1. Tuberculosis (*Mycobacterium tuberculosis*) often strikes children and can be fatal. Tubercular lesions can occur on the spine, as well as many other sites. The disease, called the Great White Plague, or consumption, was "in the old days . . . almost never curable, and yet in that period there were some notable recoveries" (Johnson, 242). Most of these recoveries were believed to involve good food and fresh air. When Irma wrote about Emil, she frequently mentioned that he had injured his spine. However, Irma's daughter Ruth said she believed that Emil suffered from tuberculosis. In any case, Emil was taken to Philadelphia to be fitted with a back brace in the summer of 1891.

2. During the late nineteenth century, a certain social prejudice arose against the Jews among the wealthier classes in the East. German Jews had assimilated well, and many had begun to make enough money to join the ranks of the middle

and upper-middle classes. They could hardly be excluded from the social and po-litical life of the communities in which they lived, nor could they be excluded from spending their money on pleasures, or at resorts and spas. Whether subtle or overt ("Gentiles only"), this anti-Semitism led to the establishment of hotels and resorts that catered to a Jewish clientele (McWilliams, 21, 115). The Atlantic City hotel at which Irma stayed was most likely one of these.

3. Friday, September 4, 1953.

4. Monday, June 29, 1891. On Sunday, October 17, 1943, Irma identified the Darwin work she had read in 1891: "On radio Darwin's *Origin of Species*—very il-luminating. Read it when I was nineteen."

5. Rabbi Isaac M. Wise, the Reform rabbi who founded the Hebrew Union Col-lege, edited the periodical *American Israelite* to which Irma referred. Irma helped to translate the Einhorn prayer book into English at the request of Rabbi [I. S.] Moses of KAM [*Kehilath Anshe Maariv*] Temple. Rabbi Moses failed to credit Irma's work when the book was published. David Einhorn (1809–1879), a Reform rabbi affiliated with Baltimore's Har Sinai Temple, published a German-language prayer book that dispensed with large numbers of Hebrew prayers, the second days of several holidays, all references to Zion, and anthropomorphic allusions to God (Sachar 1992, 110). It was originally used in American Jewish Reform congrega-tions, where many congregants were first-generation German Jews whose pri-mary language was German, and who felt that German was the "language of cul-ture." Later, the prayer book was translated into English (Bregstone 1933, 7).

6. Undated entry, 1958.

7. Undated entry, 1953.

6. MARRIAGE AND CHILDREN, 1898–1906

1. Sunday, April 13, 1958. Victor's father, Simon, was a tailor. He died in 1905. His mother, Rachel, died in 1920. Although Irma mentioned being paid for her writing, she never clarified this statement. See n. 8 below.

2. Sunday, May 9, 1948, Mother's Day. Irma's sister Esther married Victor's brother, Rudolph.

3. Undated entry, ca. 1953. Irma and Victor married November 28, 1898.

4. Sunday, May 9, 1948, Mother's Day. Victor's office was in the Reliance Build-ing at State and Hubbard Streets in downtown Chicago.

5. In a 1958 entry, Irma records the amount as seven dollars.

6. Undated entry, ca. 1953.

7. Sunday, May 9, 1948, Mother's Day.

8. Undated entry, ca. 1953. According to the records Irma sent to a cousin in July 1961, she continued teaching in religious and public schools, seven days a week, until the year after she was married. As a girl, Irma was the Chicago cor-respondent of a Saint Louis newspaper, the *Jewish Voice*, for which she wrote a weekly column covering news and subjects of interest to the Jewish communities.

She also wrote for the *Sabbath Visitor*, which was apparently Zion Temple's weekly newsletter. It could not be determined whether Irma was paid for any of her religious teaching. Although she stated she had been paid for her writing, she never specified whether it was for the *Jewish Voice* and/or the *Sabbath Visitor* or something else. Copies of her columns could not be located.

9. Undated entry, ca. 1953.

10. Sunday, May 9, 1948, Mother's Day.

11. Undated entry, ca. 1953.

12. Undated entry, ca. 1953.

13. July 25, ca. 1951, titled "Our Gang."

14. Undated entry, ca. 1953.

15. Mrs. Felsenthal was the wife of E. Bernhard Felsenthal, the first rabbi at Sinai Congregation in Chicago, founded in 1861 to serve the more liberal Jews living on the South Side of Chicago.

16. Undated entry, ca. 1953.

17. Sunday, May 9, 1948, Mother's Day. In a booklet written for her sister Meta, Irma's entry for Thursday, May 8, 1924 reads:

Remember how I stopped on Michigan and looked in on a cooking demonstration? You kept tugging at my sleeve. You wanted to go on where they were holding a hat for me until I should come back — then you went on alone and I met you — but I saw the demonstrator decorate a cake. It is very important to know how to decorate a cake. The decorative instinct. Contributes much to, and detracts greatly from, civilization. Mere decoration, stuck on decoration, is inexcusable everywhere except on a cake. Nothing seems to express festivity to such a degree, not even flowers, as an ornamental cake. We know it is done for sheer joy, or the love of doing it, for nothing is more useless and absurd than a cake all done up in furbelows.

18. Sunday, December 20, 1953.

19. For a discussion about taste in interior decoration and silver plate, see Marina Moskowitz, "Public Exposure: Middle-Class Material Culture at the Turn of the Twentieth Century," in B. J. Bledstein and R. D. Johnston, eds., *The Middling Sorts: Explorations in the History of the American Middle Class* (New York and London: Routledge, 2001), 170–184.

20. Irma spelled *vernis* Martin phonetically but not correctly. During the reign of Louis XV, the Martin brothers invented this decorative technique (a varnish) in imitation of Chinese lacquer. Well into the Victorian era, furniture, clocks, and decorative objects were often adorned with this finish.

21. Victorian middle-class decorum enveloped pregnancy in silence, and once women were noticeably pregnant, they were expected to stay at home.

22. Undated entry, ca. 1953.

23. Sunday, May 9, 1948, Mother's Day.

24. Undated entry, ca. 1953. The prevailing obstetrical rule at this time

was "Save both if you can, but preserve the wife," according to Fishbein and DeLee, 67.

25. Childbed fever, or puerperal sepsis, a blood infection, was often fatal in the absence of antibiotics.

26. Sunday, May 9, 1948, Mother's Day. Irma nursed all of her children until they were at least three months old. Commercially prepared infant formula became widely available only after World War II, and by 1956, only 20 percent of newborns in the United States were breastfed (La Leche League International publicity release statistics, August 1999).

27. July 25, ca. 1951, paper titled "Our Gang." Irma reported that her mother said she did not believe doctors should have the last word regarding babies, either how or what to feed them or how fat to allow them to become. The implication was that experienced mothers, i.e., grandmothers and other women who had raised babies, knew better than doctors, who at that time were typically male.

28. Anesthesia had been discovered in 1846, but was considered risky even fifty years later. Patients who needed surgery and could afford the services of a private doctor were most often operated on at home, frequently in the kitchen (Fishbein and DeLee, 42).

29. Undated entry, ca. 1953. Until the 1940s, blue was the typical color for girls' clothes. After World War II, however, blue became associated with boys, and pink with girls.

30. Irma did not identify the Rosenwald about whom she spoke. It may have been either Morris or Julius Rosenwald, both of whom lived in Hyde Park. Julius Rosenwald (1862–1932) was the president and later chairman of Sears, Roebuck and Company. He and a number of other Chicago business leaders spearheaded efforts to restore and convert the Palace of Fine Arts, the last remaining 1893 World's Columbian Exposition building, into a science museum. The Palace of Fine Arts had housed the Field Columbian Museum from the time of the fair's closing until 1920. During the 1920s, the exterior was stripped, then rebuilt using stone. The Rosenwald Museum of Science and Industry in Hyde Park opened in 1933, just in time for Chicago's Century of Progress Exposition. Morris Rosenwald, Julius's brother, was a clothing manufacturer and retail merchant. His business, Becker-Ryan, was the South Side's leading department store. It was purchased by Sears in 1929.

31. Sunday, December 20, 1953.

32. Undated entry, ca. 1953. Emily was born September 2, 1899, Ruth was born May 24, 1903, and Alfred on October 5, 1906.

33. Block, 19, 76.

34. Ibid., 72.

35. Fishbein and DeLee, 43.

36. Letter to grandson dated Sunday, September 23, 1949.

37. Fishbein and DeLee, 42.

38. Block, 75.

39. Lowe, xxi–xxii. See E. Wharton and O. Codman Jr., *The Decoration of Houses* (New York: Charles Scribner's Sons, 1897).

40. Block, 74.

41. Saturday, April 12, 1958.

42. Thursday, April 3, 1958.

7. CHILDREN AND LEARNING, 1910–1912

1. In 1910, Irma quoted a "J. Lloyd Jones" who wrote: "Poverty takes on the color of its surroundings," and "Human nature is the same everywhere." Irma's references to "J. L. Jones" and "J. Lloyd Jones" might well be to Jenkin Lloyd Jones (1843–1918), who wrote *Love and Loyalty* (1907); *Nancy Hanks Lincoln . . .* (1903); *Prophets of Modern Literature* (1895); *The Agricultural Social Gospel in America: The Gospel of the Farm* (T. E. Graham, ed., 1986), among others.

2. Isaiah Temple and Sinai Temple hosted lecture courses. Outstanding lecturers from all over the city and the world were invited to talk about current problems, literary subjects, or topics of general interest. Irma attended many of these lectures throughout her life. Perhaps what excited Irma so much about Professor McClintock's comment was that she knew that Ralph Waldo Emerson had once written something quite similar, i.e., "Men are what their mothers made them."

When she wrote about fairy tales in 1948, Irma mistakenly credited Jakob (1785–1863) and Wilhelm (1786–1859) Grimm with writing "The Ugly Duckling." Hans Christian Andersen (1805–1875) was the author of that tale. However, in an undated note in 1953, she correctly attributed "The Ugly Duckling" to Andersen.

3. The quotation immediately following Mary Emerson's name was actually from Ralph Waldo Emerson's oration titled "Literary Ethics," delivered at Dartmouth College, July 24, 1838. Mary Moody Emerson (1774–1863), Ralph Waldo Emerson's aunt, raised him following his mother's death. She taught him to "scorn trifles . . . ," a lesson which he quoted in this essay, composed as a tribute to her.

4. Herbert Spencer (1820–1903) was a pre-Darwinian evolutionist. His major work is the nine-volume *System of Synthetic Philosophy* (1862–93), which merged biology, psychology, sociology, and ethics.

5. Jean-Jacques Rousseau (1712–1778) was a French deist philosopher whose gospel of "back to nature" set the stage for the later Romantics. His ideas also influenced educational theory. He de-emphasized the importance of book learning, placing special emphasis on learning by experience, and recommended that a child's emotions should be educated before his reason.

6. Horace Fletcher (1849–1919) is commonly noted as the nutrition expert who advised chewing food until it is reduced to a finely divided, liquefied mass, a practice called "Fletcherizing."

7. Christian Daa Larson (1874–?) was the founder of the New Thought movement (1901). He published *Eternal Progress*, a New Thought journal, and wrote what amounts to mystical, philosophical self-help books, such as *The Great Within* (1907); *Hidden Secret* (1907); *On the Heights* (1908); *How Great Men Succeed* (1909); and *Poise and Power* (1908), among others. His philosophy was to "present practical methods through which anyone, the beginner in particular, may realize his ideals, cause his cherished dreams to come true, and cause the visions of the soul to become tangible realities in everyday life," outlined in *The Ideal Made Real, or Applied Metaphysics for Beginners* (Chicago: Progress Company, 1909). His famous *Optimist's Creed*, the gist of which appears in the works Irma quoted, was not published until 1912.

8. In 1910, encouraging herself, and perhaps Emily, Irma wrote that "Emerson preached his gospel in the present — God speaks now. The measure of a great man is in bringing other men to agree with his opinion. Wrote his thoughts in his diary. . . . 'Form the habit of writing your thoughts. Pen in hand you will be able to keep closer to a subject than by merely thinking it over in your easy chair. The mechanical element in writing assists in the power of concentration.'" The fact that Irma kept Emily's childhood diaries, and the fact that they stayed associated with Irma's for thirty years following Irma's death, is remarkable. Additionally, three of Victor's diaries, as well as the ledger of an unnamed bookseller, were also included in the lot.

9. According to a family member, Emily's diary concerning the 1919 race riot in Chicago was donated to the Chicago Historical Society. This riot began on Saturday, July 27, when an African American youth, Eugene Williams, drowned at the Twenty-ninth Street beach. By the time the riot ended, 23 African Americans and 15 Caucasians lay dead, with 291 people wounded.

Like her mother, Emily enjoyed cooking. She noted in her 1909–12 diary that she learned baking in school, then tried out a bread recipe at home. Like Irma, Emily took more cooking classes when she was in her thirties. She opened a catering service around 1939; it never became very successful.

10. These lines are from "A Farewell," by Charles Kinsley (1819–1875). Kinsley also wrote "The Water Babies: A Fairy Tale for a Land Baby" (1863). Perhaps Emily learned this verse from Irma. On Tuesday, January 14, 1958, Irma wrote:

I remembered, the other day, some lines that influenced me profoundly when I was a teen-ager:

> "Be good, sweet maid
> And let who will be clever
> Do noble things, not dream them all day long
> And so make life, love, and that long forever
> One grand sweet song."

11. Ralph Waldo Emerson, not Kinsley, was the author of these lines.

12. The nature-study movement was prevalent in the schools early in the twen-

tieth century. At the height of John Burroughs's popularity, special editions of his essays were published specifically for classroom use. At least forty-six schools nationwide were named after him; in fact, according to Irma's February 7, 1939, diary entry, Ruth's children attended the John Burroughs School in Saint Louis. See also E. Kanze, *The World of John Burroughs* (New York: Harry N. Abrams, 1993). On Tuesday, May 13, 1924, Irma again mentioned Burroughs:

John Burroughs says that the earth floats in perpetual light — night and darkness are only shadows thrown upon the surface of the earth of objects that obtrude between it and the sun. I noticed this noon just before I came into the house that what held the sky, lifting it was illumination, and I was hoping that sadness, and sorrow, and suffering and regrets are only the things that get between me and the sun, and that our souls roll on and come into the light again.

13. The German Building, a remnant of the 1893 Columbian Exposition, burned down in 1925. The Chicago Park Commission had planned to string "a necklace of islands along the water's edge," starting in Jackson Park, but only the Wooded Island was ever built (Mayer and Wade, 298). The Wooded Island is located directly behind the Museum of Science and Industry in Hyde Park. It is a favorite spot for birding. Irma often took the children to the Japanese garden on the Wooded Island. The Japanese government had donated funds for a replica of the Phoenix Hall in Uji to be built for the 1893 World's Columbian Exposition. The replica, called Ho-o-Den Pavilion, was destroyed by fire in 1944. After the Century of Progress Fair closed, the Japanese teahouse was moved to the island. Irma occasionally held Japanese-style picnics in the teahouse with her family.

14. Irma attributed the following line to Charles Augustus Keeler: "Birds are God's animated flowers." Charles Augustus Keeler (1871–1937), a Milwaukee-born poet and close friend of John Burroughs, lived in Berkeley. His verses were compiled in several volumes, including *The Siege of the Golden City* (1896) and *Sequoia Sonnets* (1919). In addition to poetry, he also wrote ornithological studies of American birds.

Fourteen years later, on Monday, May 5, 1924, Irma was still reveling in nature: "Coming across Lincoln Park just now on my way to Parker [School] to attend a meeting of 12th grade mothers I came upon gorgeous tulips — huge oblongs of solid white and red contrasting with the formless green of the grass. Immediately all the hackneyed phrases came into my mind 'riot of color'— carpet of flowers."

15. For example, on Wednesday, March 22, 1911, Emily wrote that

I know this is no time to make an entry in my diary (10:30 P.M.) But I must write. I have just finished reading *New Chronicles of Rebecca* by K. D. [Wiggin].

Oh what beautiful thoughts I have. It seems as though every time I read anything and finish it and it is good literature I get thoughts which are nice, thoughts of deeds to be done in the near and also the far future. . . .

So good night dear Thought Book as Rebecca called her diary.

On Sunday, July 15, 1951, Irma actually brought up the idea of a "thought book." The reference is in terms of including this book in her autobiography.

THOUGHT BOOK

Choose the best time

Stir reader's emotion

An emotional stimulus

Narrative with an emotional purpose

    (punch line hook short story)

series of events effect of the opening on the reader scene, problem, characters, dialogue. Is this the way the person will behave in the situation?

16. Richard Henry Stoddard (1825–1903) edited *Anecdote Biographies of Thackeray and Dickens* (1874) and *The Late English Poets* (1849). He wrote *Foot-prints* (1849) and *Songs of Summer* (1857), among other works.

17. Arbor Day was founded by J. Sterling Morton in Nebraska in 1872. It is celebrated on the last Friday of April every year.

18. Included in this 1910 notebook is a quotation from the preface to volume 2 of *Memorien einer Großmutter* (*Bilder aus der Kulturgeschichte der Juden Russlands im 19. Jahrhundert*) by Pauline Wengeroff (1833–1916).

Treu und ungekünstelt die Vergangenheit zu schildern,

Wie sie noch heute in meinem Herzen und meiner Erinnerung lebt,

Will ich hier den Faden meiner Erzählung "weiberspinnen"

Und Bilder entschwundener zudem vorbeiziehen lassen.

Ich will nicht daran denken daß es ein Buch werden soll.

Ich setze mich wieder an den alten gemütlichen Platz

Und erzähle.

[To paint the picture of the past as truly and faithfully,

As it still lives today in my heart and in my memories,

I here want to weave the threads of my narration

And hold the disappearing pictures as they pass through my mind.

I do not wish to think that this should be a book.

I sit in the comfortable, old place once more

And tell the story.]

19. On Wednesday, October 18, 1911, Emily commented that "I fear I have tried to write things I shouldn't here but I could not express my feelings any other way. I hope if any one should read this scratch they will forget it in a hurry."

20. Pesach is the holiday of Passover, during which time the Jews remember how they were saved while in captivity in Egypt. The *Ark* was a magazine for young Jewish children.

21. Emily had considered writing a story called "Great Heroes" before, on Friday, October 20, 1911.

It is almost impossible for me to believe that Dr. Alexander Hugh Ferguson is dead. That he died yesterday morning after being sick a whole month and I not knowing anything about it until to-day. But then there are many many things in this world that I do not know, and some day as I grow older will. But that is not what I am thinking about. Dr. Ferguson died yesterday morning of heart trouble at his home on 46th St. and Grand Bl. He has been sick for a month. It certainly is a shame. It was he who helped papa save [cousin] Arthur's arm, it was he who was head of the Chicago hospital for so many years, and it was he who did many other things too. When I am older I will write a story about doctors and call it "Great Heroes," and I will have Dr. Ferguson in it.

Like Emily, Irma also referred to books and writing in terms of music and symphonies. This is clearly evident in other diary entries, such as the ones from Monday, January 20, and Thursday, January 30, 1958, in which she talked about James Gould Cozzens's 1957 National Book Award winner, By Love Possessed.

By Love Possessed has a strange effect on me. I know the story, but the book seems to go on, as if it actually were a symphony and you hear the music after it has ceased to sound. That's the kind of book I'd like to write. But How?

The way the Cozzen's book is written — I mean the movement of it, seems in a way, like a symphony — recurring themes, always modified by additional instruments coming in, different shadings as it were. I get the feeling of incompleteness at the end.

8. POLITICS, NATURE, AND TRAVEL, THE 1920S

1. From an undated letter: "I said to Dr. L. in conversation yesterday [Ruth] once told me that I spent too much time on my children but it seemed to me that was my job."

Monday, June 17, 1929

It is many years since I have kept a diary, but I have at last decided to become a writer, if possible. Alfred won the Fiske poetry prize at the University of Chicago the other day, due in some measure to courses in English composition which I have taken. Both Alfred and I can write but we do not take our writing seriously.

Alfred graduated from Francis Parker School in 1924. Emily married in 1920; Ruth married three years later. Both Emily's and Ruth's first children were born in 1924. Ruth's second child, a son, was born in 1928. Irma kept quite busy helping with the new babies, and visiting Ruth when she lived in both Philadelphia and Toronto.

2. The debate between the rationalist Percy Ward (1876–?) and the outspoken journalist and playwright Frank Harris (1855–1931) was republished in Debates on the Meaning of Life, Evolution and Spiritualism, ed. Frank Harris (New York: Prometheus Press, 1993). Anna Marcet (Haldeman) Haldeman-Julius (1887–1941) was Jane Addams's niece. She and her husband Emanuel Haldeman-Julius

(1889–1951) published the *Appeal to Reason* People's Pocket Series. Irma's connection with Addams may have led her to submit her poem to the Haldeman-Julius weekly, or it may simply have been because the *Appeal to Reason* published the debate to which Irma's poem was a response.

3. More information on Illinois women's clubs can be found in Maureen A. Flanagan, "The Predicament of New Rights: Suffrage and Women's Political Power from a Local Perspective," *Social Politics* 2 (1995): 305–330.

4. It would be idle speculation to suggest that when Irma wrote about a "dun-colored" politician, she was casting aspersions particularly on the Irish politicos in Chicago during "Big Bill" Thompson's administration (1915–27). There is no indication in her essay on voting that she meant anything other than that the politician to whom she referred, and whose face she never saw, was bland and colorless.

Irma's diaries show that she continued to exercise her right to vote. She apparently switched parties in time for the April 9, 1940, Democratic primary, in which she voted. Many German American Jews allied themselves firmly with the Republican Party, the party of business, until Roosevelt's New Deal came in during the 1930s. Roosevelt relied heavily on two Jewish advisors, Louis Brandeis and Felix Frankfurter, and his policies apparently spoke to Jewish concerns about social welfare (Sachar, 446–447).

5. Kroch's was one of a number of small, independent bookstores in Chicago. It later merged with Brentano's, then closed during the 1990s.

6. Irma, like most women of her era, graduated from corsets to girdles. During the 1920s, the boyish figure was in vogue, and, since Irma was not built like that, she complained about her weight. Irma, however, always liked wearing stylish hats and flowers in her hair.

Irma frequently mentioned that her mother did not approve of her attending college or working with women's clubs, but apparently felt that Irma should stay at home, raising her children and tending to her husband and household duties.

7. H. Higdon, *The Crime of the Century: The Leopold and Loeb Case* (New York: G. P. Putnam's Sons, 1975), 20–21.

8. Bobby Franks's father had made his money as a pawnbroker. Although originally Jewish, he had converted to Christian Science. Richard Loeb's father, Albert Loeb, was the vice president in charge of Sears, Roebuck and Company's mail-order business. Nathan Leopold Sr. was a successful shipping and manufacturing executive. Meyer Levin commented that "there was one gruesome note of relief in this affair. One heard it uttered only amongst ourselves — a relief that the victim too had been Jewish."

9. Judge Caverly announced his decision on September 19, 1924. The boys were to be sent to Joliet State Prison, each sentenced to ninety-nine years for the crime of kidnapping, and to life for the crime of murder. Richard Loeb never saw the outside world again. He was stabbed to death by his cellmate on January 28, 1936. Nathan Leopold was finally released on parole in March 1958. He moved to

Puerto Rico, married, wrote a book titled *The Birds of Puerto Rico*, and earned a master's degree at the University of Puerto Rico. He died in 1971.

10. Higdon, 124.

11. Most likely this book was Darrow's *Crime: Its Cause and Treatment* (New York: Thomas Y. Crowell, 1922). Darrow (1857–1938) lived at the Hyde Park Hotel and frequently took walks on the Wooded Island. Until the Leopold and Loeb trial, his most notable case had been his defense of the Communist Labor Party. See Darrow, *Argument of Clarence Darrow in the Case of the Communist Labor Party in the Criminal Court, Chicago* (Chicago: C. H. Kerr, [c1920]).

12. Irma never mentioned Lindbergh's anti-Semitism, which became public knowledge during the 1930s.

Travel apparently agreed with Irma; she made a second trip to Europe in 1926, and reflected in an undated letter to Meta:

I was up early this A.M. and I am feeling particularly wonderful. I have often heard persons say that you get the real benefit of your vacation when you are home again, but I never could quite understand it. My mind feels rested. I think it is because the sights we saw, and the experiences we had were so compelling that our minds got out of their old dusty grooves and the revelations have given me, at least, fresh inspiration and strength. I return to old tasks with a new point of view. I am sleeping better than I have slept in ten years and so I wake up every A.M. refreshed and eager to expend my energy.

While we were travelling events that had happened maybe a week or two previously seemed to have happened ages ago. New impressions were continually impressions that had been new but a short time before, and it seems almost, as if time had been longer. I do not mean to imply by this that we ever were bored even for a minute. Everything was different. And so we have returned tremendously refreshed with a new outlook on the present and the future. History somehow becomes alive in Europe and life itself seems less trivial and tragic in a new sense of continuity which was one of my revelations. I use the word "revelations" advisedly. It sounds almost as if I had lost restraint. But when you stand in the presence of something great and a new understanding of its greatness comes to you — or, you understand finally why it is great, I think you may permit yourself to use the word *revelation*.

There are no real things except those intangible spiritual verities which are forever eluding us. Yet by these all our conduct is actuated. If our human relationships change —

The thoughts that come (good title for story or novel) in the silence of the night are as much fact, as the realities through which we live in the bustle of the day. . . .

The things we saw are in the guide books, but guide books I find are not much alive until one has been over the ground. But one's experiences in these remarkable places, how they affect one etc, I think are valuable. I have never in my life been so eager to work. Except for Switzerland which is no surprise when you have traveled in America for Switzerland is exactly like its picture, most of the things of beauty we saw were the flowering into beauty of some human soul. I wish I had time to tell you about Michelangelo's "Moses," Titian's "Assumption" and Tintoretto's "Paradise." Tintoretto, the art book says, loved a difficulty and we all chafe at our difficulties —

I told you that I'm not so much interested in art in its specific manifestations as I am in the impulse back of it, and in the impulse toward expression included in it.

9. STAYING AFLOAT DURING THE 1930S

1. Miss Vivette Gorman demonstrated cooking and baking with natural gas at the People's Gas, Light and Coke Building. "On the main floor, in a specially designed kitchen, continuous baking demonstrations [were] held. . . . In April, special auditorium cooking demonstrations two afternoons and two evenings each week [were held]. Tickets [were] free" (Graham, 392).

The Tip Top Inn, later called the Tip Top Tap, was located in the Allerton Hotel, now the Allerton Crowne Plaza.

2. Ravinia in Highland Park, Illinois, opened its gates on Monday, August 15, 1904. It was a park where an electric fountain, a baseball field complete with grandstand, a carousel, a theater with a pipe organ, a casino, a dining and dancing hall, and a concert pavilion entertained patrons from all around the world. The enterprise was built by the A. C. Frost Company to encourage business for its railroad, which ran along the west side of the park's edge. When the railroad failed in 1910, a group of North Shore residents purchased the park. It reopened in 1911, quickly becoming known for hosting world-class operas and classical music events, the "summer capital of music" (Bregstone, 376–377). The Great Depression forced the park to close following the 1931 season. It was not to reopen for four years.

3. Mayer and Wade, 362–365.

4. The Frigidaire Company had a building at the 1933 Century of Progress fair. Irma mentioned in a July 18, 1939, diary entry that she had attended the fair, where she undoubtedly saw electric refrigerators.

5. Green kern soup, made from sweet corn that was boiled for three hours, was one of Irma's favorite recipes. The Great Atlantic and Pacific Tea Company was founded in 1859. By the 1930s, the company had opened A & P grocery stores all around the United States.

6. The only mention Irma ever made of cocktails with alcohol was on Monday, January 17, 1938, when she wrote that "[w]e had cocktails of crème de cocoa, gin and cream which Albert mixed for me." Otherwise, her references were — as here — to tomato juice, fruit, or shrimp cocktails.

7. Membership in clubs and temples were some of the first extra expenses to be eliminated when the depression hit the middle and upper-middle classes. Club

memberships could be rather easily dropped, since membership rolls were not public in the way that, for example, losing a house to foreclosure would be. See Beadle, 213.

8. Irma included the Jewish People's Institute, Temple Sinai's Sisterhood, the National Council of Jewish Women, and B'nai B'rith among those organizations she felt she could drop. All of these organizations performed important functions in the Jewish community through philanthropy and antidefamation efforts, but dropping memberships in them would carry no public stigma that might have an impact upon Victor's medical practice.

The Jewish People's Institute, located in a synagogue at 3500 W. Douglas Boulevard on the city's west side, had been established to meet the needs of mostly Russian and Eastern European Jewish immigrants. The building, constructed in 1927 by Grunsfeld and Klaber, is now the landmark home of the Julius Hess school.

In the mid 1800s, a group of Jewish German immigrants sought to find fraternity and fellowship with other, mostly Reform Jews, to help one another assimilate into American society, and to dispense sick benefits and life insurance (Bregstone, 19). Toward this end, in 1843, German and Austrian Jews in the United States founded the fraternal order of B'nai B'rith. The first Chicago lodge was formed in 1857. Part of B'nai B'rith's work later involved the Anti-Defamation League, especially active right before and during World War II (Sachar, 674–675).

The National Council of Jewish Women was founded by Hannah Greenebaum Solomon (1858–1942). The NCJW mission was both philanthropic and educational. Irma was friends with Mrs. Solomon, attending her 80th birthday celebration on Monday, January 10, 1938.

9. Marshall Field and Company's store policy was to "sell for cash" (J. Tebbel, *The Marshall Fields: A Study in Wealth* [New York: E. P. Dutton & Co., 1947], 127). Ironically, credit was extended only to those who least needed charge accounts.

10. Tickets for the High Holy Days services were an added expense.

11. Irma's secret bank account was something many women of her social status and era opened and maintained. They used their "mad money" accounts to buy gifts for their husbands and family, for personal purchases, and as a source of cash distinctly separate from money or allowances their husbands gave them to run the house and pay expenses. Farm women, too, had such accounts into which they put their "butter and egg" money. These funds could be deposited in a bank or simply kept somewhere private in the woman's house. There is no suggestion in any of Irma's papers that she considered having such an account daring or unusual. This entry was the only one in which she mentioned her secret account.

Victor's office was still attached to the back of the house. The maids Irma hired did double duty answering Victor's telephone, scheduling patients, and taking messages. The laundry woman washed the family's clothes as well as the linens from the office. When Irma's maids quit, as they frequently did, she tried to do both the house and office work herself, or to hire a maid to work part-time, thereby saving money. Irma always cooked for her family, however.

12. Gifts, trades, and loans made among family members were another way in which economic hardships were alleviated. During the depression years in which Irma kept diaries, the number of times she invited her family for meals increased to the point where she was cooking for some set of relatives almost every day. That she was better able than others to afford the cost of meals is only suggested in her entries. The extra expense associated with entertaining, however, placed a real strain on Irma's budget, so that by the end of the summer of 1937 she was in debt.

13. John Steinbeck's *Grapes of Wrath* (New York: Viking Press, 1939), although a fictional work, vividly captured the horrors and injustices of the depression. The year after it was published, it was made into a movie starring Henry Fonda, Jane Darwell, and John Carradine.

14. At the height of the depression, some patients paid their doctor bills in produce or other goods rather than in cash. While this reduced food costs for the doctor, it did not pay the fixed expenses. Irma noted a number of times that Victor brought home ducks, smelt, oranges, and berries that patients had given him. At one point, after processing a large amount of berries, she vowed that she would never again put up jellies and jams, since commercially prepared ones were available at a reasonable price.

10. WAR AND ITS VICTIMS, 1933–1957

1. S. W. Sears, *Air War against Germany* (New York: American Heritage Publishing Co., 1964), 117.

2. It is possible that Irma was reading *The Cry and the Covenant* by Morton Thompson (Cutchogue, NY: Buccaneer Books, 1949), a fictionalized account of Ignaz Semmelweis's discovery of the relationship between medical hygiene and infectious illness.

3. Irma wrote about this tragedy many times during the following years. One such commentary is in a fragmentary, undated letter included with material from 1958. The intended recipient of the letter was not indicated.

As for myself there is a phrase in the Kaddish prayer, "May their memory be a blessing to those who treasure it" where there is so much of good and sweetness in the memory of Victor — that good and sweetness should not remain an inactive memory. . . . although I may have failed with Victor, I did sometimes succeed in making him happier. I read a prayer the other day that had in it this plea: "Forgive us, Oh Lord, our failures, our thoughtlessness, and our *unintentional mistakes.*"

Then again on Monday, January 13, 1958, she reflected,

In looking for a date yesterday in a former diary, I came across a 5 year diary sent to me by Victor C. when he was in Georgia, in service. There are few recordings in it; Vic's death and tragic story come within the period the diary would cover. I was too disturbed emotionally and too grief stricken to write much in those years. It is a beautiful, little red book and, instead of a 5 year diary, I shall turn it into a one year diary, I have a feeling that it is sacred in a personal sort of way, I put down a little of Vic's tragic story in its first eleven pages, which were blank — beginning the real diary yesterday the 12th, an important date in the family annals for Alfred left the U.S. yesterday P.M., for Germany, the guest of the West German government.

To-morrow I shall continue my memoirs. To-day I have some errands down town and have not much time in this early A.M. if I want to accomplish my errands.

I wrote a part of this story in the diary he had given me. It brought back tears of sorrow — This should be a new time. Memory is a storage garden in which our most precious blossoms should cast their beauty over the present, emitting the music and the fragrance of other days into our present journey 'til it reaches into another past and ever the future beckons before us.

The diary to which Irma refers above was not included in the box of purchased journals.

11. CHANGES, 1950–1966

1. Sunday, May 9, 1948, Mother's Day.

2. See "Staying Afloat during the 1930s," entry for Thursday, October 2, 1930.

3. Abbé Ernest Dimnet (1866–1954) was a French clergyman and writer. His book *The Art of Thinking* (New York: Simon and Schuster, 1928), became a best-seller in 1929, the year Irma mentioned reading it. At one point, during the 1930s, Irma thought to incorporate Dimnet's ideas into a book she intended to call "The Art of Living."

4. If Irma wrote about Essie's death, in 1964, her comments were not found in the purchased materials.

5. Henri Bergson (1859–1941), the French philosopher and Nobel laureate, was the first to write about *élan vitale* in terms of energy and forces (see *Creative Evolution*, trans. Arthur Mitchell [New York: Henry Holt, 1911]). Irma mentions reading Bergson's *Creative Evolution* on Sunday, March 7, 1937.

6. Much of the material contained in these three volumes appears in the first chapters of this book.

7. Following her reading of James Gould Cozzens's book, Irma toyed with the idea of writing her own book, called "By Love Inspired." See n. 21 in "Children and Learning, 1910–1912."

8. On Saturday, February 1, 1958, Irma wrote that "Wilder once suggested to me that I write a book in the form of letters and I *love* to write letters. Letters to whom? To Wilder himself? By what name? Or letters to different persons might be better, including one to Wilder — under an assumed name? Why not try it?"

9. Fünfkirchenware, literally "five churches' ware," was a type of ceramics from Pécs, Hungary (in German, the town's name is *Fünfkirchen*). The town has long been famous for its churches and for its elegant synagogue modeled after a temple in Budapest. Pécs is also known as a center of coal mining, champagne production, and leather-goods manufacture.

10. On Friday, March 1, 1957, Irma noted that she wanted to write an article for the A & P grocery-store newspaper. The only story found among Irma's papers that remotely concerns grocery stores is "Billy Chops and Betty Crackers." In it she mentions Piggly-Wiggly, A & P's chain-store rival and the first true self-service food stores in the United States. The Tennessee-based chain was founded in 1916 by Clarence Saunders.

11. *The Chronicle of the Befogged Dune Bugs* was published by Tri-State Litho Printing Company. Each copy sold for one dollar. In the foreword, Irma noted that the tale was originally read at one of the literary "Monday evenings" that Dr. George Burman Foster, head of the Department of Comparative Literature at the University of Chicago, hosted.

Bibliography

Addams, J. 1899. "Social Settlement and the University Extension." *Review of Reviews* 20:93.

———. 1902. *Democracy and Social Ethics*. New York: Macmillan.

———. 1907. *Newer Ideals of Peace*. New York: Macmillan.

———. 1918. "Ella F. Young Dies." *Chicago Tribune*, 27 October 1918.

Andreas, A. T. 1975. *History of Chicago*. Vol. 3. New York: Arno Press.

Angle, P. M. 1946. *The Great Chicago Fire*. Chicago: Chicago Historical Society.

Arey, L. B. 1959. *Northwestern University Medical School, 1859–1959*. Evanston and Chicago: Northwestern University Press.

Beadle, M. 1973. *The Fortnightly of Chicago*. Chicago: Henry Regnery Company.

Block, J. 1978. *Hyde Park Houses: An Informal History, 1856–1910*. Chicago and London: University of Chicago Press.

Bregstone, P. P. 1933. *Chicago and Its Jews*. Np.

Burns, E. M., and U. E. Dydo, eds., with W. Rice. 1996. *The Letters of Gertrude Stein and Thornton Wilder*. New Haven and London: Yale University Press.

Byron, B., and F. Coudert. 1928. *America Speaks*. New York: Modern Eloquence Corporation.

Chamberlin, E. 1975. *Chicago and Its Suburbs*. New York: Arno Press.

Cutler, I. 1981. "The Jews of Chicago." In *Ethnic Chicago*, ed. M. G. Holli and P. d'A. Jones, 69–108. Grand Rapids, MI: William B. Eerdmans Publishing Company.

———. 1996. *The Jews of Chicago: From Shtetl to Suburb*. Urbana and Chicago: University of Illinois Press.

Darby, E. 1986. *The Fortune Builders*. New York: Doubleday and Company.

David, H. 1958. *The History of the Haymarket Affair*. New York: Russell and Russell.

Dedmon, E. 1953. *Fabulous Chicago*. New York: Random House.

Deegan, M. J. 1988. *Jane Addams and the Men of the Chicago School, 1892–1918*. New Brunswick, NJ: Transaction.

Dunbar, O. H. 1947. *A House in Chicago*. Chicago and London: University of Chicago Press.

Fergus, R. 1839. *Chicago Directory*. Chicago: Fergus Printing Company.

Fishbein, M., and S. T. DeLee. 1949. *Joseph Bolivar DeLee, Crusading Obstetrician*. New York: E. P. Dutton and Co.

Flanagan, Maureen A. 1995. "The Predicament of New Rights: Suffrage and

Women's Political Power from a Local Perspective." *Social Politics: International Studies in Gender, State and Society* 2: 305–330.

Frankenstein, I. R. 1921. "The Meaning of the Moon." *Appeal to Reason*. People's Pocket Series, "Has Life Any Meaning: A Debate," ed. E. Haldeman-Julius. Girard, KS: Appeal to Reason.

———. 1958. *The Chronicle of the Befogged Dune Bugs*. Np: Tri-State Litho Printing Co.

Frazier, I. 1994. *Family*. New York: Farrar Straus Giroux.

Fry, S. 1966. "Henry Suder." *Chicago Tribune*, 24 February 1966.

Graham, J. 1967. *Chicago: An Extraordinary Guide*. Chicago, New York, San Francisco: Rand McNally and Company.

Guame, M. 1987. "Ruth Crawford Seeger." In *Women Making Music: The Western Art Tradition, 1150–1950*, ed. J. Bowers and J. Tick, 370–388. Urbana and Chicago: University of Illinois Press.

Higdon, H. 1975. *The Crime of the Century: The Leopold and Loeb Case*. New York: G. P. Putnam's Sons.

Hirsch, E. L. 1990. *Urban Revolt*. Berkeley, Los Angeles, Oxford: University of California Press.

Hitchens, H. L., ed. 1941. *America Goes to War*. Chicago: Columbia Educational Books.

Horowitz, H. L. 1974. "Varieties of Cultural Experience in Jane Addams' Chicago." *History of Education Quarterly* 14:77.

———. 1976. *Culture and the City: Cultural Philanthropy in Chicago from the 1880s–1917*. Lexington: University of Kentucky Press.

Johnson, C. B. 1926. *Sixty Years in Medical Harness, or the Story of a Long Medical Life, 1865–1925*. New York: Medical Life Press.

Kanze, E. 1993. *The World of John Burroughs*. New York: Harry N. Abrams.

Klemperer, V. 1999. *I Will Bear Witness: A Diary of the Nazi Years, 1942–1945*. New York: Random House.

Laqueur, W. 1998. *The Terrible Secret*. New York: Henry Holt and Company.

Lasswell, D. 1971. "The Old New Left: Emma Goldman in Chicago." *Chicago History* 1, 3:170.

Lowe, D. G. 1979. *Chicago Interiors*. New York: Wings Books.

Manguel, A. 1997. *A History of Reading*. New York: Penguin Books.

Marquis, A. N., ed. 1917. *The Book of Chicagoans: A Biographical Dictionary of Leading Living Men and Women of the City of Chicago*. Chicago: A. N. Marquis.

Mayer, H. M., and R. C. Wade. 1970. *Chicago: Growth of a Metropolis*. Chicago and London: University of Chicago Press.

McClelland, A. E. 1992. *The Education of Women in the United States: A Guide to Theory, Teaching, and Research*. New York: Garland Publishing.

McLean, G. N. 1886. *The Rise and Fall of Anarchy in America*. Chicago and Philadelphia: R. G. Badoux and Co.

McManus, J. T. 1916. *Ella Flagg Young and a Half-Century of Chicago Public Schools*. Chicago: A. C. McClurg and Co.

McNeill, W. H. 1991. *Hutchin's University*. Chicago and London: University of Chicago Press.

McWilliams, C. 1948. *A Mask for Privilege: Anti-Semitism in America*. Boston: Little, Brown and Company.

Meynell, A. C. T. 1900. *John Ruskin*. New York: Dodd, Mead and Company.

Moses, J., and J. Kirkland, eds. 1895. *History of Chicago*. Vol. 2. Chicago and New York: Munsell and Company.

Moskowitz, M. 2001. "Public Exposure: Middle-Class Material Culture at the Turn of the Twentieth Century." In *The Middling Sorts: Explorations in the History of the American Middle Class*, ed. B. J. Bledstein, and R. D. Johnston, 170–184. New York and London: Routledge.

Rippa, A. S. 1992. *Education in a Free Society: An American History*. New York: Longman.

Rudolph, F. 1962. *The American College and University*. Athens and London: University of Georgia Press.

Sachar, H. M. 1992. *A History of Jews in America*. New York: Alfred A. Knopf.

Schubert, W. H. 1986. *Curriculum: Perspective, Paradigm, and Possibility*. New York: Macmillan Publishing Company.

Sears, S. W. 1964. *Air War against Germany*. New York: American Heritage Publishing Co.

Sherrick, R. L. 1980. "Private Visions, Public Lives: The Hull House Women in the Progressive Era," Ph.D. diss., Northwestern University.

Sicherman, B. 1995. "Reading *Little Women*: The Many Lives of a Text." In *U.S. History as Women's History*, ed. L. Kerber, A. Kessler-Harris, and K. Kish Sklar, 245–247. Chapel Hill and London: University of North Carolina Press.

Silberman, C. E. 1985. *A Certain People*. New York: Summit Books.

Smith, J. 1979. *Ella Flagg Young: Portrait of a Leader*. Ames, IA: Educational Studies Press.

Sutton, W. A. 1979. *Carl Sandburg Remembered*. London: Scarecrow Press.

Tebbel, J. 1947. *The Marshall Fields: A Study in Wealth*. New York: E. P. Dutton and Co.

Thrasher, F. M. 1927. *The Gang: A Study of 1,313 Gangs in Chicago*. Chicago and London: University of Chicago Press.

Watson, L. C., and Maria-Barbara Watson-Franke. 1985. *Interpreting Life Histories: An Anthropological Inquiry*. New Jersey: Rutgers University Press.

Wendt, L., and H. Kogan. 1952. *Give the Lady What She Wants*. Chicago: Rand McNally and Company.

Wharton, E., and O. Codman Jr. 1897. *The Decoration of Houses*. New York: Charles Scribner's Sons.

White, E. A. 2001. "Charitable Calculations: Fancywork, Charity, and the Culture of the Sentimental Market, 1830–1880." In *The Middling Sorts: Explorations in the History of the American Middle Class*, ed. Burton J. Bledstein and Robert D. Johnston, 73–85. New York and London: Routledge.

Wilbur, S. 1931. "Review of Mrs. William Vaughn Moody's Cookbook." *Chicagoan*, May 1931. Moody Papers, University of Chicago.

Wilder, T. 1985. *The Journals of Thornton Wilder, 1939–1961*. New Haven: Yale University Press.

Willis, G., W. H. Schubert, R. V. Bullough Jr., C. Kridel, and J. T. Holton, eds. 1993. *The American Curriculum*. Westport, CT and London: Greenwood Press.

Wish, H. 1952. *Society and Thought in Modern America*. New York: Longmans, Green and Co.

———. "The Chicago Fire." Chicago Historical Society [online]. Available at http://www.chicagohs.org/fire/oleary/essay-4.html.

Index

The Daily Maroon, 151
Darrow, Clarence, 110, 119–120,
    210n10
Dearborn Independent, 109
deaths in family: Emil, 52, 75; Irma,
    179; Mamma, 51; maternal grand-
    mother, 14; Pappa, 13–14; Victor,
    162; Victor C., 152–154,
    213–214n3
Decoration Day, 169–170
The Decoration of Houses (Wharton
    and Codman), 85
Defense Meeting, 146
Depression of 1893, 48
Dewey, John, 27, 32, 194n15
diaries, 105–106, 125–126, 165,
    205n8; excerpts, dating of, xii
Dimnet, Ernest, 159, 173, 214n3
dinner parties, 70–71
diphtheria epidemic, 13, 189n19
diseases and illnesses: anaemia (ane-
    mia), 37; blood poisoning, 14; diph-
    theria, 13, 189n19; fever, 3, 72;
    measles, 13; pneumonia, 72; quinsy
    sore throat, 13; tuberculosis, 53
Dolly (horse), 83
domestic help, 5–6, 12, 72, 82–84,
    99, 122, 124, 131, 135–137,
    140–141, 148, 212n11

economy: c. 1871–1888, 21–23; of
    the 1920s, 124; in depression
    years, 127
education: Clinton, Iowa, country
    school, 28–29; college, 39–40;
    curricula, 30, 33; early school ex-
    periences, 28; Elizabeth Street
    School, 29–30; English language
    studies, 33–34; environment and,
    27–28; first-grade reader, 29;
    foolscap paper, 31; as habit, 28;
    homework, 31–32; Latin studies,

36–37; letter and composition
    writing, 34–36; living as, 42; math-
    ematics, 37; nature curriculum,
    97; penmanship, 33; philosophy
    for, 40–41, 196n41; physical edu-
    cation, 30, 194–195n19; public
    schools, 28; school books, 31;
    school store, 31; science primers,
    39–40; Skinner School, 29, 32–36,
    193–194n15; slates, 30–31; uni-
    versality of, 85; West Division
    High School, 36; of women, 41
educational theories: c. 1875–1891,
    26; Progressivism, 27
Eighteenth Amendment, 109
Einhorn, David, 201n5
Einhorn prayer book, 59, 201n5
Eisenhower, Dwight D., 150
"elan vitale," 164
electricity, 66
Elliott, Maria, 196n40
Elsa, 106
Emerson, Mary, 89–91, 204n3
Emerson, Ralph Waldo, x, xix, 26, 39,
    46, 49–50, 89, 92, 103, 130, 178,
    196n40, 204n3
Emil (brother), 13–14, 17, 31, 39,
    52–53, 57–63, 75, 200n1
Emily (daughter), 51, 74–78, 81–82,
    84, 98–100, 106, 122, 126, 135,
    137, 147–149, 155, 169–170,
    205n9, 208n1; Arbor Day nature
    essay, 103–105; diary of, xi, 95–
    97, 198n11, 206n15, 207–208n21,
    207n19; first love, death of, 110;
    nature notes of, 100–102; nature
    poems, 103; nature verse analysis,
    103; published essays, 106; stories
    of, 106–108; Sunday School prize,
    106–107
Emma, 72
Engel, George, 24–25

Hegel, Georg Wilhelm, 26
Herbart, Johann Friedrich, 26
Herrick, Robert, 189n15
High Holy Days, 51
hired help, 5–6. See also domestic
  help
Hitler, Adolf, 139, 144, 154
Holmes, Oliver Wendell, 79
home decor, 85
Home Owner's Loan Corporation
  (HOLC), 127, 129, 134
Hoover, Herbert, 124, 143
horse-drawn vehicles, 19–20
horses, 19–20, 83, 85
hospitals, 84–85
hot water, 66
House Beautiful magazine, 36
housekeeping, 67, 81, 122–123,
  126–127; germs and, 85
housing, 84
How the Other Half Lives (Riis), 48
"How We Spent Our Summer," 64
Hull, Cordell, 145
Hull House, 48–49
Hyde Park, 84; kidnapping and mur-
  der in, 119–120

"I will" insignia, 9
Illinois Central Rail Road, 4
Illinois Federation of Women's Clubs,
  111
immigration, 1–2, 23, 87; of Russian
  Jews, 109, 198n12
Indiana Dunes, 178
International Suffrage Alliance, 119
International Summer School, 117
*Interpreting Life Histories: An Anthro-
  pological Inquiry* (Watson and
  Watson-Franke), xiii
Inter-State Industrial Exposition
  Building, 188n10
Irish immigrants to Chicago, 1

Irma: Alfred's birth, 84; Anti-Defamation League membership, 145; on
  apartment life, 173–174; apartment on 45th Street, 66, 70; on
  appearance, 54, 116; on art and
  writing, 183n4; Atlantic City excur-
  sion, 53–62; attitude toward life,
  xx; autobiographical letters, 166–
  175, 214n8; on autobiography, ix,
  164–166; birth of, 2; on books,
  159; budgeting money, 67; childhood, 9–25; children, supplemen-
  tal education of, 97–98; Christmas
  celebrations, 199n17; Clinton,
  Iowa, country house, 12–13; on
  clothes, 128; club activities, 116,
  120–121, 132–133, 144–147,
  197n46, 211n7, 212n8; conscience
  of, 46; conversation with bookseller, 114–116; on cooking, 66,
  68–69, 158; creative writing
  classes, 183–184n12; on criminals
  and criminality, 120–121; cut-glass
  collection, 70; death of, 179; on
  decoration, 202n17; diaries and
  journals of, ix, 105–106, 125–126,
  165, 205n8; on dinner parties,
  70–71; diphtheria bout, 13; educational experiences, 27–42; Ellis
  Avenue home, 71, 85–86; Emerson, inspiration drawn from, 46,
  49–50, 196n40; Emily's birth, 73–
  74; on empathizing with others,
  168–169; on entertaining, 67–68,
  171–172; expenses, accounting of,
  128–138; first pregnancy, 72–73;
  first romance, 37–38; first year of
  marriage, 67; on furnishings, 70–
  72; on Germans, 157–158; on
  grandmother's death, 14; Great
  Depression years, 124–138; grey
  stone house on 45th, 81; grocery

Irma (continued)

story, 174–175; on growing old, 158–159, 163, 173–174, 190n28; on growing up, 21; Hebrew education of 45; high school, 36–37; honeymoon, 66; horoscope, 138; house on 24th Street, 10–11; on housework, 67, 81, 122–123, 126–127; on justice, 47; on life as education, 42; literary style of, 189n15; on literature, 172; on loss, 64, 167; on marriage, 65–73; on May mood, 115; on memories, 16–17, 105–106, 190n28; on money and allowances, 18; money worries, 164–165; monthly expenses (1938), 134–135; moral obligation of, 49; on motherhood, 74–84; nonreligiosity, 47–49; on philanthropy, 198n12; philosophy lectures, 151; piano lessons, 63; playing jacks, 15; playing lotto, 16; playing outdoors, 18; poems of, 110–111, 175–178, 181n3; on postwar years, 158; on reading, 38–39; on regret, 123; relief agency involvement, 46–48; on religion, 43–44, 200n24; religious newspaper contributions, 45, 201–202n8; romance with Mr. Levi, 54–59; Ruth's birth, 81–82; Sabbath school teaching, 45; secret bank account, 135, 212n11; on selling house, 159; social values of, 47–49; on sorrow, 163; swinging in rope swings, 17; teaching positions, 40–41, 201n8; on technological progress, 121; thought book, 207n15; on "training by example," 46; travels and traveling, 62, 109–110, 116–118, 122, 124–125, 210–211n11; on truth,

beauty, and God, 50–51; University of Chicago studies, 41–42, 109, 183n12; on Victor (husband), 162–163; on Victor C.'s suicide, 152–154, 213–214n3; voting experiences, 112–113, 209n3; on war, 117–118, 141–144; wartime efforts, 144–147; wedding engagement, 65–66; West Randolph Street basement house, 14–16; on writing, xix, 158, 165; writing aspirations, 110, 114–116, 118, 123; writing template, 105; on writing versus living, 184n20; on youth, 173–174

Irma Betty (granddaughter), 126, 156, 182–183n3

Isaiah Woman's Club, 88

Isserman, Abraham, 187n8

Jackson Park, 98

Jahn, Friedrich Ludwig, 188n13

James, William, 26, 50, 166

Jenney, William LeBaron, 186n4

Jewish dietary laws, 44

Jewish holidays, 44–45, 51–52, 106, 133, 137, 207n20

Jewish People's Institute, 133, 212n8

Jewish relief agencies, 141; Jewish People's Institute, 133; Kopperl relief agency, 47; United Hebrew Charities, 188n10; United Hebrew Relief Association, 48

Jewish traditions, 51

Jewish Voice, 45, 201–202n8

Jews: homeless, 142–143; Palestinian homeland for, 109. *See also* German Jews

Jones, Jenkin Lloyd, 99, 204n1

joy, 118

"June, 1958," 175–176

Women's Trade Union League, 112

Wooded Island, 99

world patriotism, 117

World War I, 109–110

World War II: Battle of Britain, 144; beginning of, 144; D-Day invasion, 150; draft, 148; food and fuel shortages, 147; health care during, 144; Italy's surrender, 150; labor shortage, 148; Pearl Harbor, 145; rationing, 147; war bonds and volunteerism, 146; women workers, 148

World's Fair of 1893, 84

World's Fair of 1933, 127, 137

Wright, Frank Lloyd, 9

Yom Kippur, 52, 133, 137

Young, Ella Flagg, x, 27, 29, 32, 34, 40, 193–194n15

Young Joseph (Mann), 144

Zion Temple Sabbath school, 45